POWERFUL
REFORMS
WITH
SHALLOW
ROOTS

Improving America's Urban Schools

POWERFUL
REFORMS
WITH
SHALLOW
ROOTS

Improving America's Urban Schools

Larry Cuban and Michael Usdan

EDITORS

Foreword by Elizabeth L. Hale

TEACHERS
COLLEGE
PRESS

Teachers College, Columbia University
New York and London

Published by Teachers College Press, 1234 Amsterdam Avenue, New York, NY 10027

Library of Congress Cataloging-in-Publication Data
Powerful reforms with shallow roots : improving America's urban schools / Larry Cuban and Michael Usdan, editors ; foreword by Elizabeth L. Hale.
      p. cm.
   Includes bibliographical references and index.
   ISBN 0-8077-4292-9 (pbk.) — ISBN 0-8077-4293-7 (cloth)
      1. Education, Urban—United States—Case studies.   2. Educational change—United States—Case studies.   I. Cuban, Larry.   II. Usdan, Michael D.
   LC5131 .P69 2002
   370'.9173'2—dc21   2002027128

ISBN 0-8077-4292-9 (paper)
ISBN 0-8077-4293-7 (cloth)

Printed on acid-free paper

Manufactured in the United States of America

10   09   08   07   06   05   04   03   8   7   6   5   4   3   2   1

CONTENTS

FOREWORD

Powerful Reforms with Shallow Roots provides an "up-close and personal" review of governance and leadership changes in six of America's large cities' school systems. The governance and leadership reforms being implemented in city school systems from Baltimore to Seattle are reviewed and reported through six case studies.

Lessons learned and their implications for action are identified. Reformers beware: The current model of urban school reform—politically active and organizationally focused—shows promise but is not a panacea.

A number of issues presented themselves in each of the cities studied and seemed to transcend place-based circumstances. The case studies identify and describe these issues: the heart of the matter—student achievement; teacher quality and staff development; the seesaw question of centralization or decentralization; the importance of mayors; the business of business in education; the decline of school board influence; teacher unions; new models of school leadership roles and positions; the K–12 connection to higher education; standards, assessment, and accountability; and high school reform. The six stories are important and unique, and inform reformers of the potential stumbling blocks they might encounter.

The Institute for Educational Leadership (IEL) is honored. This important Teachers College Press publication stems from a School Leadership for the Twenty-first Century Initiative that previously developed the report series, *Leadership for Student Learning*. To date, the IEL-published series includes the following reports: *Redefining the Teacher as Leader, Reinventing the Principalship, Restructuring School District Leadership, Recognizing the State's Role in Public Education,* and *Urban School Leaders—Different in Kind and Degree.*

This volume's insightful on-the-ground analyses of governance and leadership issues in six major U.S. city school districts buttress an inescapable conclusion: The urban school reform agenda must become "standards plus." If we are to increase student achievement, the larger community must be connected. This book reaffirms much of IEL's work, namely our efforts to span the boundaries that all too often separate the schools from their larger community.

Elizabeth L. Hale
President, IEL
January 2002

ACKNOWLEDGMENTS

We acknowledge with thanks not only the funding from the Carnegie Corporation and Broad Foundation, which made this particular volume possible, but also the generous support of the Ford Foundation, the U.S. Department of Education, the UPS Foundation, and the MetLife Foundation for the IEL's School Leadership for the Twenty-first Century Initiative from which this volume directly evolved. Special thanks are due to Mary Podmostko and the staff at IEL for their support.

We thank Mike Kirst at Stanford University for his wise counsel and our coauthors for their patience with our E-mail and phone requests for timely submissions. We also appreciate very much Carole Saltz and Brian Ellerbeck at Teachers College Press who saw in this book something worthwhile for policy makers, practitioners, researchers, and informed parents. Finally, we express gratitude to the numerous individuals in the six case study communities who took time from their busy schedules to be interviewed by our team of researchers. In thanking those who helped make this book possible, we need to be clear that we—not they—are responsible for the factual accounts and interpretations.

Larry Cuban
Michael Usdan
January 2002

Introduction

LEARNING FROM THE PAST

Larry Cuban and Michael Usdan

What shall we do with our great cities? The whole country is affected, if indeed its character is not determined, by the conditions of its great cities.[1]

The year was 1891. Progressive reformers of the day had hit upon a solution to make cities great: Improve schools to build strong American citizens by assimilating immigrants, increasing literacy to reduce poverty, and preparing workers eager to enter industry and business. To have schools achieve these purposes, new leadership and major reforms in school governance were needed.

A century later, another generation of reformers hit upon a similar solution of improving urban schools to solve problems in the nation's cities. Concentrated poverty, racial and ethnic isolation in urban ghettos, and high rates of unemployment and crime led mayors, civic leaders, and business executives in the 1990s to harness the future of their cities to improving schools. To make cities livable for young families, schools had to be places where parents, employers, and taxpayers could count on children learning to read, write, compute, and reason like their suburban classmates to gain the skills and credentials that would open doors for them to an information-based economy. And making urban schools perform well, these reformers believed, required major changes in district governance and leadership.

Civic, business, and educational reformers a century apart worked to make both cities and their schools vital places to live, work, and learn. In the century between the Progressives' reform of urban schools and the reformers in the 1990s, other generations of leaders applied the solvent of school reform to national and urban problems. A brief trip through the past establishes the constancy of school reform and the linkages between then and now.[2]

In the years bracketing the turn of the twentieth century, Progressive reformers yanked schools out of urban political machines, downsized large appointed city school boards that dispensed patronage, and ended the bribing of school officials. They recruited civic-minded business and professional gentlemen (with an occasional woman) to serve on boards of education, and urged that these small boards hire professionally trained administrators to manage the schools. For well over a half-century after these reforms, university-educated superintendents and principals served elected (and some appointed) school boards that were insulated from partisan politics. Civil service regulations guided school boards' hiring of school staff, virtually ruling out nepotism and patronage while impartial and public bids reduced considerably the bribing of school officials in buying textbooks, building schools, and transporting children.[3]

After World War II, however, another generation of reformers blasted public schools for inadequately dealing with international and domestic threats to the nation. During the 1950s, critics berated public schools for failing to keep pace with the scientific and military progress of the Soviet Union. The United States needed to produce more engineers and scientists to defend the nation in the Cold War. Suburban and urban educators responded by raising academic standards and increasing the number of math and science courses. Academic excellence became the beacon for educational leaders to follow.

The international threat, however, soon gave way to a serious domestic problem that another group of critics believed school leaders should solve. As the Civil Rights movement spread from the South to the rest of the nation in the wake of the *Brown v. Board of Education* decision (1954), attention shifted from the Soviet threat to the inferior schooling black students received in the South and big cities. Desegregation, rural and urban poverty, and dreadful conditions in so many urban schools housing minority students sparked another generation of reformers who sought equality in education. Civil Rights marches, school boycotts, and the ouster of urban superintendents ricocheted across the nation's cities. Federal wallets opened and a U.S. President declared a War on Poverty. Educational leaders designed urban school programs to lift those at the bottom of society into the middle classes.[4]

Yet by the mid-1970s, critics charged that the War on Poverty, like the one in Vietnam, had been lost. Reformers who wanted schools to reduce social injustice and improve the life chances of poor black and white children had failed, according to faultfinders. To worsen matters, these critics believed schools—especially those in cities—had abandoned their mission of teaching basic knowledge and skills, instilling respect for authority, and maintaining discipline. Incidents of violence in urban schools, illiterate high school graduates, and shabby teaching became front-page news and subjects of Hollywood films.

At about the same time, rising inflation, increased unemployment, and U.S. firms' losing their market share to Japan and Germany seized the policy-making agenda. The workplace was being transformed by computerization and the United States was a step behind its competitors. From manufacturing to processing insurance claims, companies automated operations, trimmed workforces, and increased productivity. As the revolution in the nature of work swept across the private and public sectors, schools seemed stuck in the past. If schools, especially those in cities and low-income suburbs where millions of children attended, could not produce sufficient graduates to enter an information-based workplace, then the nation's global competitiveness was at risk.[5]

Since the *Nation at Risk* report (1983) judged public schools so mediocre as to jeopardize the economic future of the country, blaming educators has become common fare in the media. In the past 2 decades, a broad coalition of corporate executives, public officials, and business groups has pressed educational leaders to copy successful businesses. School leaders should do what corporate leaders have done: trim bureaucracies, focus on measurable goals, manage through incentives and penalties, and hold employees accountable for reaching desired goals. Presidents, mayors, business executives, and parents have said (and say again and again) that public schools must focus on preparing students for jobs.[6]

Responding to scorching and unrelenting criticism, educators in suburbs, rural districts, and big cities, beginning in the early 1990s, have sought organization and educational effectiveness by embracing systemic reform. They have established standards-based curricula, aligned the curricula to tests, monitored test scores closely, and rewarded and punished teachers, principals, schools, and students when scores rose and fell. By aligning efficiently the core components of a school system, district leaders could reach into classrooms and get teachers and students to perform well academically, as measured by standardized tests.[7]

EXPECTING MORE FROM SUPERINTENDENTS

Amid the rush toward accountability-driven school reforms, the refrain has swelled into a loud chorus demanding every superintendent to manage bureaucracies efficiently, lead principals and teachers in instructional matters, and mobilize political coalitions of teachers, parents, and students to move schools from being inadequate and just good enough to ones that are unalloyed good.

These expectations of superintendents implied that leading city schools is the same as leading suburban, small town, and rural schools. That is not the case at all. Crucial differences distinguish urban school leaders from those in other districts.

First, while the early history of suburbs has been one of searching for racial and ethnic homogeneity, larger homes, and better schools, cities have been (and are) cauldrons of diversity that have both enriched and enervated schools. Century-old conflicts over assimilating immigrants, desegregating schools, and reducing poverty have been proxies for dealing with issues of color and class, both mainstays of urban schooling. Leading urban districts—from San Diego to Harrisburg, Pennsylvania—has demanded from superintendents a keener sensitivity to inequalities and a well-developed capacity to deal with racial isolation, ethnic conflict, and economic disparities as they affect academic achievement both in the schools and the city itself. Yet no urban superintendent can afford to ignore the current wisdom, forged by corporate executives and public officials, that high academic standards and improved test scores lead directly to well-paying jobs, even when the concentration on tests produces each year winners and losers in the academic sweepstakes.

As a result of public demands for improved academic achievement among those students who have historically done least well in school, persistent issues of race, ethnicity, and class have required urban superintendents in small and large districts from Compton, California, to Baltimore, Maryland, to expand their customary repertoire of political, managerial, and instructional roles to cope with the abiding conflicts that arise time and again. For many urban superintendents, unequipped or unwilling to deal with these issues, the job is overwhelming. Frequent turnover among school chiefs has created the image of an impossible job and a turnstile superintendency. Those urban superintendents who thrive in the post learn to lead by consciously distributing the political, managerial, and instructional roles throughout the system to cope with the conflicts arising from issues of race and class as they affect test scores and the broader purposes of public schooling.[8]

The second feature that separates urban superintendents from their suburban colleagues is the strong belief, shared with many business and civic leaders, that schools can help restore a city's economic, cultural, and social vitality. The once great American cities that were taken for granted in the early decades of the twentieth century declined dramatically in post–World War II decades as they lost their appeal (and business) to suburbs—particularly when poverty and crime were cast in racial terms during the 1960s. As Cleveland mayor Michael White said, "Big cities [became] a code name for a lot of things: for minorities, for crumbling neighborhoods, for crime, for everything that America moved away from." The mistaken belief that cities were ungovernable took hold.[9]

Not until the early 1990s with major shifts in work and the economy did some cities begin to see a reverse migration from suburbs and employers relocating because of lower land and labor costs. Boston, Chicago, and San Francisco have begun to regain their cachet of greatness, while other cities such as Austin and San Jose have become magnets for technology-based businesses. "Like a mighty engine," former New York City mayor David Dinkins said, "urban America pulls all of America into the future."[10]

For many urban politicians, business leaders, and superintendents, the quality of public schools plays a key part in attracting employers and young families to their neighborhoods and sustaining the vitality of cities. Good schools affect mayors' reputations. Superintendents, unlike their peers elsewhere, have become key players in the revival of urban America and urban politics. Thus President George W. Bush, appointing the Houston, Texas, superintendent as his Secretary of Education in 2001, acknowledges symbolically this current truth.

These sharp distinctions between urban and suburban schools counter the prevailing assumption buried within standards-based reform that school leadership is the same across districts. Leading urban schools, unlike leading other districts, is intimately tied to a unique and complex mission: Improve schooling to reduce the grim consequences of poverty and racial and ethnic isolation on academic achievement while increasing the life chances of families and their children to succeed economically and to contribute to their communities.

CHANGING GOVERNANCE SYSTEMS AND LEADERSHIP

Beginning in the mid-1990s, these differences in leadership requirements slowly and openly became acknowledged. Major changes in urban school governance aimed at improving academic achievement have begun to alter urban school districts. In Baltimore (until 1997), Chicago, Boston, and Cleveland, mayors have appointed school boards and superintendents; in these places schools have become another department of the city's administration. In Philadelphia, Detroit, and New York, mayors exercised substantial influence in picking school board members and exerted increasing control over school matters. In other cities, school boards have lost confidence in the ability of rise-from-the-ranks superintendents or outsider educators to manage big systems and have chosen noneducators to lead their districts. As one of Chicago mayor Richard M. Daley's aides put it, "expecting an educator [to] run a $3 billion operation isn't realistic." In the early to mid-1990s, former U.S. Army generals have led Seattle and District of Columbia schools; an ex–U.S. Attorney was named school chief in San Diego in 1998; a former governor was appointed Los Angeles's superintendent in 2000; and the New York City Board of Education appointed a corporate attorney in 2000.[11]

These reforms in urban school governance and leadership (mostly white, middle- and upper-middle-class suburbs and rural districts have not moved in this direction) are further evidence that cities impose vastly different challenges upon those who seek to lead urban districts. Even though suburban and small town superintendents perform the central managerial, political, and instructional roles, the history, demography, governance structures, and cultures in urban districts make a substantial difference in leading schools. Because of these contexts, leading the Boston Public Schools, for example, imposes upon the superintendent tasks and obligations very different from those of his colleague 20 miles away in Newton.

These unique contextual realities and the growing national interest in new modes of urban school governance and leadership make this book particularly timely in our estimation. A word about how the book began might help bolster our claim that that this study is timely.

The origins of the book date back to a discussion between Michael Usdan and two program officers of the Carnegie Corporation, Michelle Cahill and Michael Levine in early 2000. At the time, Usdan was serving as president of the

Institute for Educational Leadership (IEL) and was seeking foundation support for IEL's School Leadership for the Twenty-First Century Leadership Initiative. The Carnegie program officers, while positive about the overall IEL initiative, were particularly interested in funding a component that would focus on the unique leadership needs of large urban school districts. In the course of the conversation, agreement was reached that Larry Cuban of Stanford University would be asked to join the IEL Initiative as a special consultant working on the urban dimensions of leadership.

From those conversations, we—Cuban and Usdan—decided to investigate in depth a number of national reforms deeply affecting urban districts. As we worked together, it became clear that we shared similar beliefs about these reforms.

First, we believed that national policies crafted by state and national leaders under both Democratic and Republican administrations on such issues as standards-based curriculum, testing, and accountability assumed that American schools—including those in cities—were failing. Further, the policies assumed that all schools needed the same prescription: the application of business principles to school operations, efficient top management, alignment of organizational functions, and harder work from students, teachers, and principals.

We rejected these assumptions as simplistic. All schools were not failing and urban schools, in particular, were substantially different from suburban schools. In their theories of action and policy talk, reformers largely ignored the history of urban schools and the persistent wrestling with issues of poverty, race, ethnicity, and social class. Moreover, reformers' theories overlooked urban districts' current lack of sufficient staffing, money, and other resources.

Second, national and state reformers argued that what urban districts needed was not more money or more staff but what all districts needed: a good dose of better governance and efficient management in order to get those students and teachers to concentrate on raising academic achievement.

For cities, what this meant was that throughout the 1990s, a number of mayors assumed control of appointing school board members and superintendents and proclaimed that they were now responsible for students' academic achievement. In other cities, school boards, viewing the problems of their schools as managerial and bureaucratic, sought corporate officials and noneducators to lead their systems rather than appointing up-from-the-ranks superintendents.

We believed that it would be worthwhile to investigate these governance reforms because they tied changes in leadership to what happened in classrooms. Although we were skeptical of the assumptions that changes in political control and nontraditional leadership of urban districts would produce improved student performance, we wanted to find out why these changes occurred, what happened when the changes were implemented, and whether teachers and students did, indeed, perform better.

We selected cities that included both governance and leadership changes, recruited coauthors who were experienced in researching urban districts, and embarked on describing and analyzing in clear, concise prose the governance and leadership changes in six cities over the past decade. We wanted a short, readable, and pithy book on urban governance and leadership that would challenge readers' beliefs with both data and arguments.

We seek to illuminate the very volatile and dramatically changing landscape of urban districts through case studies of six systems that have recently undergone significant changes in their governance structures designed to raise students' academic achievement.

THE CASE STUDIES

The six cases in this book were written during a time when many cities across the country were in flux. While the governance and leadership changes vary, two common elements are the loss of school boards' influence when mayors have assumed more control over school systems and the increased involvement of business leaders in urban school governance.

The case studies focus heavily upon the emerging new relationships between mayors, business leaders, and their choices of school leaders. Our analysis will concentrate upon cities with active business and civic coalitions that have implemented new governance structures and hired either educators or noneducators as superintendents.

The level and intensity of mayoral involvement varies across a wide spectrum. From mayors who now appoint the school board or superintendent (e.g., Chicago, Boston, and Baltimore before 1997) to mayors who may be allotted by law some appointments to school boards but apply unrelenting budgetary pressure to extract favorable policies (e.g., New York before 2002), the continuum of mayoral involvement captures different governance structures with direct to indirect involvement in city school systems.

Indeed, although each city has its own unique context and political culture, many mayors have initiated action on school issues because of their mounting frustration with the educational status quo in their cities. Most mayors and business leaders now recognize that the economic vitality of their communities is dependent upon the improvement of their schools; the traditional separation of schools from mainstream politics or government—a divorce negotiated by early-twentieth-century Progressive reformers—increasingly appears no longer viable.[12]

Efforts to reform urban governance and improve students' academic achievement in the past decade have focused upon three major strategies in the nation's urban districts: greater mayoral involvement and control, the hiring of noneducators to manage city school systems, and combinations of both. Although there certainly are other strategies being employed, our emphasis will be upon these three.

The case studies of Baltimore, Boston, Chicago, Philadelphia, San Diego, and Seattle address the key questions and assumptions guiding this book.

1. Why did business and political leaders in six cities alter the traditional school governance structures?
2. What can policy makers, business and civic leaders, and informed citizens learn about urban school reform aimed at improving student achievement from these specific governance and leadership changes?

Behind these questions are basic assumptions—a theory of action—driving the reforms that our book examines in detail:

- Linking urban school governance to existing political structures (including the business community) will produce organizational effectiveness, which in turn will lead to improved teaching and learning as measured by standardized test scores and enhanced coordination with city-provided offerings in recreation, the arts, and medical and social services.
- Better managers, whether educators or noneducators, will make urban school systems more efficient and effective by tightly aligning organizational goals, curriculum, rewards and sanctions, professional development of teachers and principals, and classroom instruction to academic achievement.
- When noneducators who lead urban districts are connected openly to existing political structures (including business elites), chances of improving and sustaining students' academic achievement increase.

These assumptions can be summed up crisply in a theory of action about school improvement that drives those reformers committed to these governance and leadership changes: Increased political effectiveness (governance and leadership changes) and enhanced organizational effectiveness (systemic alignment of functions within the district) will produce classroom effectiveness (improved students' academic achievement).

Our research strategy of using six cities for focused comparisons illustrates how the theory was put into practice and the range of issues with which school, business, and civic leaders have coped over the past decade. We examine district leadership using a framework focused on the core political, managerial, and instructional roles performed by superintendents whether they are educators or noneducators. Each person, of course, enacts these roles in different blends, through diverse sets of relationships within school districts, and in varied contexts. However, researchers have found that school leaders perform, at the minimum, these core tasks. Using this framework to study school leaders in selected cities undergoing governance changes enables us to describe how they come to grips with difficult issues of schooling, including the persistent low achievement of low-income racial and ethnic minorities.[13]

Unfortunately, little evidence exists about the impact of earlier urban governance changes upon academic achievement (e.g., decentralization, community control experiments in the 1960s) and evidence is even more scant on the relationship between recent changes (i.e., nontraditional leaders, mayoral involvement) and students' academic performance. Data from several cities appear promising; the academic gauge's needle of achievement is moving in the right direction. In other cities, the needle hardly moves. Whether governance changes in these districts where the needle is moving have established structures and processes that produce these gains in student achievement is still too early to say.[14]

New governance arrangements are being implemented in growing numbers of urban communities as public patience finally has run out with nonperforming systems. Indeed, the core instructional, managerial, and political roles of urban superintendents and school boards are being reconfigured and rethought in many urban centers. In addition to the six case studies that will be presented here, a host of significant governance changes are occurring in smaller as well as the larger urban districts throughout the nation. For example, mayors in districts ranging from Sacramento and Oakland in California to Harrisburg, Detroit, and Cleveland in the East have moved aggressively in making governance changes.[15]

In the mega-cities of New York and Los Angeles—former mayors Rudy Giuliani and Richard Riordan respectively—while failing in their efforts to take direct control of their school systems, certainly increased the use of their existing power to influence the schools. In 2000 Mayor Riordan openly and successfully supported and financed the election of a slate of new school board members while Mayor Giuliani's aggressive involvement since 1993 in school governance, including pressuring a series of chancellors to leave the district and appointing a portion of the board of education, continued unabated for his two terms. Michael Bloomberg, elected mayor of New York in 2001, had campaigned on a platform to exert more control over the public schools, even saying, "If reading and math scores aren't significantly better, I will look in the mirror and say 'I've failed' and I've never failed at anything in my life." In 2002, the New York state legislature authorized the Mayor to appoint the school system's Chancellor and 8 of the 13 members of the city's Board of Education.[16]

Nontraditional superintendents now run a number of the nation's largest school systems. In addition to Chicago, San Diego, Philadelphia, and Seattle (all of which will be discussed in this volume), nontraditional superintendents now reign in Los Angeles and New York City with a former governor (Roy Romer of Colorado) and a former corporate lawyer (Harold Levy) serving respectively in these huge and nationally visible districts.[17]

These examples represent just a sampling of the changes roiling the nation's urban districts as mayors, superintendents, and school boards seek deep changes in practitioners' and students' performance. Our goal in the six case studies is to describe and analyze these new approaches, which, while unlikely to provide instant structural or political solutions for long festering complex school issues, are stimulating important new thinking about the connections between macro changes in governance and micro changes in students' learning in the nation's cities.

In developing our case studies, we interviewed key figures within the school districts and in other related city institutions who had been involved in the school reforms. Interviews were informed by an analysis of key primary sources such as documents and reports, secondary sources about these cities and their schools, and other records synthesized by the case studies' authors. As in similar studies, the case analyses are necessarily limited and represent only snapshots of complex situations at a single point in time. They cannot and do not pretend to capture in any comprehensive and long-range manner very fluid and ever-changing actors and circumstances.

We have no illusions about our data. Most of the governance changes we describe are quite new and their linkage to tangible school improvement outcomes such as standardized test scores are tenuous, at best. We do believe, however, that these comparative cases provide an important early analysis of the strengths and limitations of significant governance changes that may exert substantial influence upon urban education in the years ahead.

SELECTING THE CITIES

We selected six geographically diverse cities that have made substantial governance and leadership changes within the past 5 years consistent with the major questions and assumptions we posed earlier.

Six chapters follow in this order: Chicago, Boston, Seattle, San Diego, Philadelphia, and Baltimore. Our reasoning is that the first two cities represent early cases of direct mayoral involvement and influence; Seattle and San Diego represent instances of noneducators being appointed as superintendents; Philadelphia, after having noneducators as superintendents and indirect mayoral involvement since the early 1990s and showing little improvement in test scores, was taken over by the state in 2001; the final case is Baltimore, which had mayoral control for decades, dropped it, and now is in a mandated partnership with the state of Maryland and has yet to show dramatically improved academic achievement after decades of experimentation under different forms of governance. These cities capture a variation in governance and leadership that goes from Boston where the superintendent sits in the mayor's cabinet to Seattle where a retired general and business executive have led the schools and had little contact with the mayor.

The governance and leadership changes in these cities mirror diverse strategies through which mayors, school boards, and superintendents believed improvements in students' academic performance would occur. Whether a superintendent is an educator or noneducator, whether a school board is elected or appointed, or whether a mayor is hip-deep in school affairs or not, the school district leader's roles of managing a system efficiently, mobilizing and sustaining political support for the reform agenda, and leading practitioners to show gains in students' academic achievement must be discharged effectively if schooling the nation's urban children is to improve.

These core political, managerial, and instructional functions provide the ties that bind together our geographically and politically diverse cities as civic, business, and educational leaders made important governance and leadership changes in their schools. But these major changes may well be insufficient, and that is why we include the phrase "shallow roots" in the title of the book.

WHY ARE THE ROOTS SHALLOW?

The case studies will show powerful reforms being planned and implemented in major urban school systems throughout the country. The emphasis on student achievement and the accompanying standards, testing, and accountability strategies have already shown enormous potential for reshaping teaching and learning in some, but not all, of these cities. Improving academic achievement in long-established large urban systems, however, takes time, stable leadership, and political will. It is too early to tell whether such conditions and gains in student achievement are sustainable in the cities we studied.

We found in a number of cities considerable promise in the increased political stability, greater than these school systems have enjoyed in many years. New coalitions of influential business and political leaders in Boston and Chicago, for example, have provided the necessary political cover for the two school leaders to push their agendas of standards-based alignment of goals, curriculum, incentives and penalties, and professional development for teachers and principals. Yet even in these cities such powerful reforms exist in politically fragile environments. In Boston, for example, the chemistry between a popular mayor and a nationally respected school superintendent has enhanced governance reform. The Boston reforms are "shallow" in the sense that they are heavily dependent on the continuity of these two leaders. If one or both of these individuals were not on the scene, we would question the sustainability of the current reforms. In Chicago, the mayor has provided the schools political stability for 6 years. Few previous superintendents held office that long. But still Mayor Daley replaced Paul Vallas, his first appointed CEO and former budget director, with Arne Duncan, another noneducator, as district CEO, thus dismissing a leader in the midst of an ongoing reform. Daley's new CEO has gone on to revise and even discard policies of his predecessor, and with changes in the teachers' union leadership and approach to reform in 2002, the roots may be shallow here as well.

Historical and contemporary developments in New York City, Philadelphia, and Memphis remind those of an optimistic bent that even major governance and leadership changes are brittle. Replacement of superintendents in those cities quickly altered and even dismantled reform structures and strategies.[18]

In San Diego, the reform-minded administration has maintained the support of the community's business and political leadership, but maintains only a tenuous 3 to 2 majority on the school board. In short, a change in just one seat on the elected board could undo a powerful systemwide strategy for improving student achievement. Moreover, the extremely contentious relationship that has existed between the superintendent and teachers union leadership make San Diego reforms even "shallower."

Without judging their overall worth, the long-term viability of the reform strategies that we describe in our six large city school systems may be compromised fatally by what is perceived by many, if not most, teachers and administrators as a dysfunctional top-down strategy of systemic reform that has characterized the entire approach to school reform taken by influential political, business, and some educational leaders. This strategy, rightly or wrongly, has alienated many teachers and administrators regardless of their unions' formal position on governance reforms. Many practitioners feel that they have not been sufficiently involved in the reform process. They feel that since they are the ones who must put such reforms into practice in their schools and classrooms that they might at least have been more directly involved in designing and implementing the changes.[19]

Finally, concerns about the sustainability of reform are further deepened by the difficulty of maintaining the commitment of business and civic leaders who themselves work in sectors undergoing frequent turnover yet chafe at the slow pace of school change.

All of these issues give us pause about the prospects of institutionalizing such "powerful" reforms and have led us to use the metaphor of "shallow roots." In the case studies that follow we were not able to determine with confidence the extent of practitioner support for the reforms designed by top school and community leaders. We do sense, however, that there has not been time for the reforms to be fully "cooked" and implemented or for patterns of improvement in academic achievement to clearly emerge to give us confidence that teachers and principals have enlisted fully in the campaign to ensure their institutionalization in the system. We assert that the reforms in this volume, however positive they may be, will continue to have "shallow roots" without the essential support and leadership of teachers and principals who do the actual work of improving students' academic achievement. We will return to this fundamental issue in the final chapter.[20]

We believe that this volume, purposely written in jargon-free language, will inform policy makers, business leaders, educators, and civic-minded parents about the abiding complexities of urban school reform and the linkages between the success of schools and the vitality of cities. America is an urban nation. As it was in 1891, so it is over a century later: "The whole country is affected, if indeed, its character is not determined, by the conditions of its great cities." The case studies that follow only remind us again how much we agree with those early-twentieth-century progressive reformers.

NOTES

1. Lyman Abbott quoted in Joseph Cronin, *The Control of Urban Schools* (New York: Free Press, 1973), p. 4. The first section of this chapter is adapted from Larry Cuban, *Urban School Leadership—Different in Kind and Degree* (Washington, DC: Institute for Educational Leadership, 2001).

2. For two different views of the history of school reform in these decades, see David Tyack and Larry Cuban, *Tinkering Toward Utopia* (Cambridge, MA: Harvard University Press, 1995), and Diane Ravitch, *Left Back: The Failure of School (*New York: Basic Books, 2001).

3. David Tyack, *One Best System* (Cambridge, MA: Harvard University Press, 1974).

4. Diane Ravitch, *The Troubled Crusade* (New York: Basic Books, 1983); Richard Kluger, *Simple Justice* (New York: Vintage, 1975); James Patterson, *Brown v. Board of Education* (New York: Oxford University Press, 2001).

5. See Dorothy Shipps, "Echoes of Corporate Influence: Managing Away Urban School Troubles" in *Reconstructing the Common Good in Education: Coping with Intractable American Dilemmas*, eds. Larry Cuban and Dorothy Shipps (Stanford, CA: Stanford University Press, 2000), pp. 82–105; Carol Ray and Roslyn Mickelson, "Business Leaders and the Politics of School Reform," *Politics of Education Association Yearbook, 1989* (1990): 119–135.

6. U.S. Commission on Excellence in Education, *A Nation at Risk* (Washington, DC: U.S. Government Printing Office, 1983). For an example of the literature on applying business principles to public schooling, see David Kearns and Denis Doyle, *Winning the Brain Race: A Bold Plan to Make Our Schools Competitive* (San Francisco: Institute for Contemporary Studies, 1988).

7. Marshall Smith and Jennifer O'Day, "Systemic School Reform" *Politics of Education Association Yearbook, 1990* (1991): 233–267; Susan Fuhrman, ed., *Designing Coherent Educational Policy: Improving the System* (San Francisco: Jossey-Bass, 1993); William Clune, "The Best Path to Systemic Educational Policy: Standard/Centralized or Differentiated/Decentralized?" *Educational Evaluation and Policy Analysis*, 12 (1990): 347–353.

8. Richard Elmore, *Building a New Structure for School Leadership* (Washington, DC: Albert Shanker Institute, 2000); James Spillane, "Distributed Leadership: Toward a Theory of School Leadership" (paper presented at the annual meeting of the American Educational Research Association, Montreal, Can., 1999).

9. Fred Siegel, *The Future Once Happened Here* (San Francisco: Encounter Books, 1997), p. viii; the phrase about cities being ungovernable comes from Douglas Yates, *The Ungovernable City: The Politics of Urban Problems and Policy Making* (Cambridge, MA: MIT Press, 1977).

10. Siegel, *The Future*, p. viii.

11. Paul Hill, "Hero Worship," *Education Next, http://www.educationnext.org/20014/26hill.html* (2001). The quote comes from Dorothy Shipps, Joseph Kahne,

and Mark A. Smiley, "The Politics of Urban School Reform: Legitimacy, City Growth, and School Improvement in Chicago," *Educational Policy* 13(4): 537 (1999).

12. David Tyack, *One Best System*; Charles Mahtesian, "Schools to City Hall," *Governing*, 6 (1996): 37–40; Michael Kirst and Katrina Bulkley, "New Improved Mayors Take over City Schools," *Phi Delta Kappan*, 81 (2000): 538–546; Sol Hurwitz, "The Outsiders," *American School Board Journal*, 188 (2001): 11–15.

13. Larry Cuban, *The Managerial Imperative* (Albany: State University of New York Press, 1988) elaborates the political, managerial, and instructional roles of superintendents; see especially chapter 5.

14. While many assertions were made in the mid- and late 1960s that administrative decentralization and different versions of parental and community control of public schools would produce gains in student achievement, the evidence is weak at best, even from ardent advocates. See Marilyn Gittell, *Participants and Participation* (New York: Praeger, 1967), and Mario Fantini, "Community Control and Quality Education in Urban School Systems" in *Community Control of Education*, ed. Henry Levin (Washington, DC: Brookings Institution, 1970), pp. 40–75. For the movement toward site-based management in the 1970s and 1980s and the lack of linkages to students' improved academic achievement, see Jane David, "Synthesis of Research on School-Based Management," *Educational Leadership* 46(8): 45–53 (1989); Betty Malen, Rodney Ogawa, and J. Krantz, "What Do We Know about School-Based Management? A Case Study of the Literature—A Call for Research," in *Choice and Control in American Education*, Vol. 2, *The Practice of Choice, Decentralization, and School Restructuring*, ed. John Witte and William Clune (New York: Falmer Press, 1990). For efforts to improve urban schools through state and district takeovers, see Kenneth Wong and Francis Shen, "Does School District Takeover Work? Assessing the Effectiveness of City and State Takeover as a School Reform Strategy" (paper presented at the annual meeting of the American Political Science Association, San Francisco, 2001).

15. Kirst and Bulkey, "New Improved Mayors."

16. For Mayor Richard Riordan, see Kerry White, "Candidates Backed by Riordan Win in L.A. Board Races," *Education Week*, 21 April 1999, p. 6; for Mayor Rudy Giuliani, see Robert Johnston, "Settlement Ends Crew's Tenure as N.Y.C. Chief," *Education Week*, 12 January 2000, pp. 1, 14; for New York's Michael Bloomberg, see Catherine Gewertz, "N.Y.C. Mayor-Elect Wants Control over Schools," *Education Week*, 14 November 2001, p. 3. Bloomberg quote comes from "Michael Bloomberg, In His Own Words," *New York Times,* 9 November 2001, p. D9. For the Mayor's taking control of New York schools, see Catherine Gewertz, "N.Y.C. Mayor Gains Control over Schools," 19 June 2002, *Education Week*, 1, 20.

17. For Los Angeles superintendent Roy Romer, see Matthew Miller, "The Super," *Washington Monthly* (June 2001), pp. 34–45; for New York City Chancellor Harold Levy, see George Packer, "The Suit," *New York Times Magazine*, 11 March 2001, pp. 52–58.

18. For Philadelphia, see Mark Stricherz, "Philadelphia to Scrap 'Cluster' Plan

in Bid to Save Money," *Education Week*, 9 May 2001, p. 20; Dale Mezzacappa, "Political Tension Led to School Takeover," *Philadelphia Inquirer,* 23 December 2001, p. 1. For Memphis, see Debra Viadero, "Memphis Scraps Redesign Models in All Its Schools," *Education Week*, 11 July 2001; for New York City schools, see Packer, "The Suit."

19. For the role of unions in urban school reform, see Robert Rothman, "How Teacher Unions Are Working with Districts to Improve Schools," *Challenge Journal* 5(1): 1–8 (2001); Kate Zernike, "A Hard-Nosed Teachers' Union Backs Changes and Schools Gain," *New York Times*, 31 July 2001, pp. A1, A21. The American Federation of Teachers and the National Education Association created a coalition of local unions to link unions and school reforms to advancing student learning; formed in 1995, the Teacher Union Reform Network contains 21 urban local affiliates of the two unions (Rothman, "How Teacher Unions," p. 2).

20. For sources that make claims similar to ours, see Richard Elmore and Milbrey McLaughlin, *Steady Work* (Santa Monica, CA: Rand, 1988); Michael Fullan, *The New Meaning of Educational Change* (New York: Teachers College Press, 1991); Linda Darling-Hammond and Gary Sykes, eds., *Teaching as the Learning Profession: Handbook of Policy and Practice* (San Francisco: Jossey-Bass, 1999); James Spillane, "Challenging Instruction for 'All Students': Policy, Practitioners, and Practice" in *From the Capitol to the Classroom: Standards-Based Reform in the States*, ed. Susan Fuhrman, (Chicago: National Society for the Study of Education, 2001), part 2, pp. 217–241.

Chapter 1

THE BUSINESSMAN'S EDUCATOR: MAYORAL TAKEOVER AND NONTRADITIONAL LEADERSHIP IN CHICAGO

Dorothy Shipps

Six years ago the Chicago Public Schools pioneered a new experiment in school governance that turned on its head the long-standing taboo against mixing mayoral politics and education. Early-twentieth-century reformers believed that "politicians regarded schools as part of the spoils system and awarded jobs and contracts not on the basis of competence or competition, but as political favors."[1] Nearly a century later, one Chicago Public Schools official offered an unqualified endorsement of mayoral control: "The mayor's office has been very forthcoming in getting the city government offices and the business community to be cooperative with the Chicago Public Schools. I don't think the Department of Streets and Sanitation, in the past, paid very much attention to Chicago Public Schools. . . . The media has helped us. Communications has helped us. . . . I could go on and on. City hall has been very, very, very, very helpful."[2]

In the earlier era, nearly every American city severed school governance from city hall, most often relying on nonpartisan school boards and appointed educational leaders instead. Today, reformers and politicians who think that troubled city school systems need the political clout, accountability, and resources of city hall, and the managerial talents of business, often look to Chicago as an example. The Chicago experiment is still young, its long-term consequences are unknown, but some early patterns are emerging. This chapter explores some of the lessons for policy makers that are being drawn from Chicago's 6-year experience. Summarized briefly they are as follows:

- Achieving mayoral control requires the active support of civic leaders, especially from business groups, as well as politicians.
- Mayoral control centralizes authority, challenging policy makers to find ways to insure public school governance is responsive, democratic, and transparent.
- Mayors can provide political support and new resources to jump-start improvements in finances, physical structures, support systems, and public relations.
- Day-to-day operations of big city school systems require the expertise of management professionals, reinforced by legal and fiscal discretion.
- Improving student achievement and instruction is not intuitive; it requires high levels of professional educational expertise that can conflict with mayoral control.

These five emerging themes are explored by drawing on studies of successive governance reforms in Chicago over the past 12 years.[3]

Mayoral control in Chicago is linked to an unusual confluence of political events and business activism, not readily transferred elsewhere. The short-term consequences of decision making in Chicago's new regime may differ sharply from what is found in other experiments with mayoral control. Policy makers should be cautious about adopting Chicago's form of mayoral control as a prototype because of differences in local governing traditions and Chicago's overreliance on managerial techniques to resolve long-standing instructional problems and poor student performance.

HIGHLIGHTS OF THE CHICAGO EXPERIMENT

In the summer of 1995, a Republican legislature and a Republican governor, thoroughly disappointed with both the cost and performance of Chicago's public schools, legislatively put Mayor Richard M. Daley, a Democrat, "totally in charge." A key Republican legislator defined the problem that led to this change as "a total lack of accountability, nobody was responsible for anything." The solution, as she saw it, was to have "one responsible person" about whom everyone could say "if the schools are better it is to your credit; if they are not better, it is you to blame."[4]

Following 6 years of experimentation with a governance law (1988) that radically decentralized the school system, the 1995 law recentralized governance in Chicago's schools. The new law strengthened a long-term centralization trend evident throughout the twentieth century, and, in a break with the past, removed educators from the system's top decision-making posts.[5] The mayor now appoints all of the top school leaders, including the system's chief executive officer (CEO), a small school board, its president, and an inspector general.[6] A corporate-style management team, including a chief financial officer, chief operations officer, chief purchasing officer, and chief education officer, assists the CEO. These leadership positions are no longer subject to civil service requirements or educational qualifications.

The new law gave the CEO the authority to monitor the performance of all Chicago schools and to sanction them with "remediation," "probation," "reconstitution," "intervention," and, if he chooses, to impose these sanctions on an "educational crisis" fast track.[7] Each sanction was left to the CEO and the board to specify, but their authorization has proven nearly unlimited, even to the point of dismissing all employees of any school without a hearing. The CEO also authorizes the course of study and retains all powers delegated to central office subordinates under earlier governance arrangements.[8] Directly below him in this steep hierarchy are about 600 principals, who are charged with carrying out the directives of the CEO and his management team and who, ultimately, retain their positions at the pleasure of the CEO.[9]

The new management team was given unprecedented fiscal flexibility. Separate tax levies are now collapsed into the general fund and 25 state grant categories consolidated into two block grants. All obstacles to outsourcing and privatization are removed. Any employee may be legally dismissed with 14 days notice if privatization or outsourcing makes his or her position redundant, although this has proven difficult to implement in the case of teachers. The law also abrogated 13 parts of the school code—including class size and teacher assignments—that had been won through collective bargaining with the Chicago Teachers Union (CTU), and forbade the union from striking for 18 months.[10]

ORIGINS OF MAYORAL CONTROL

This new governance structure was enacted in the state capital, but substantially written by state and local business groups. An umbrella organization of business associations known as the Illinois Business Education Committee (IBEC), established in 1994, coordinated local and statewide corporate involvement in this legislative process. As soon as the coattails of the "Gingrich Revolution" put Republicans (briefly) in control of the Illinois house as well as its senate and governor's office, IBEC received calls from the Republican legislative leadership asking for an educational reform proposal for Illinois by December 1994.[11] Already drafting legislation, the group responded with a proposal based on their collective experience with reform in Chicago, leavened with a healthy dose of management preferences. The law applied only to Chicago, but contained nearly every element that IBEC sought.

Chicago-based business associations in IBEC were led by the city's most prestigious group, the Commercial Club of Chicago, and its even more elite Civic Committee, but also included two related groups, Chicago United and Leadership for Quality Education, as well as the mass membership, Chicagoland Chamber of Commerce.[12] The Commercial Club has a 125-year history of attempts to restructure school governance, cut costs, enhance vocational studies, and adjust accountability.[13] This group has viewed the local public schools as instrumental to the city's business and civic climate. Their goals in 1995 were to improve the schools as a way of encouraging economic growth in the city, but also of enhancing the image of the city and validating their own management theories.

Some statewide business associations had also staked out their positions 100 years ago, most especially the Illinois Manufacturers Association (IMA). Others were relative newcomers, like the Illinois Business Roundtable (IBR) established in 1991.[14] They were less concerned about the city's relative advantage in attracting business and raising property values, and more concerned with lowering costs and, as a matter of principle, limiting union influence.[15] All agreed with Republican legislators that a single person in charge of the system was ideal. "We wanted ownership here, we wanted somebody to take responsibility. We didn't want to have somebody say, 'Well we could have, if only.'"[16]

Not all of Chicago mayors would fit this bill, but Democrat Richard M. Daley (1989–present), like his father before him, was an ideal candidate.[17] A well-respected local television news anchor described the necessary qualifications: "The Republicans [were] much more inclined to give it to Daley than they would have Harold Washington. Richard J. Daley is a great 'Republican' mayor . . . because his philosophy is that government should be run more like a business."[18]

Daley had been the business candidate for mayor as early as 1982, when Harold Washington bested him in a narrow victory with an unprecedented African American turnout. Washington favored neighborhood development and the empowerment of community-based organizations; Chicago's business community had been wary of Washington's efforts to reverse a century of downtown development concentrated in the commercial center of the city.[19] After Washington's death in November 1987, Daley easily won the special 1989 election called to fill Washington's remaining term, arguing even then for improvements in the school system.

The standard for business support goes back to the first Mayor Daley. "I don't have the sense that Mayor Bilandic or Mayor Byrne or Mayor Washington welcomed our input in the same way," as one business association leader said.[20] An attorney involved with local business groups linked Richard M. Daley's influence to his patrimony, "Richie knows a fair number of the members of the business community because he was his father's son and, therefore, got to know a lot of them as he grew up. And, from what I know about the Chicago business community, they feel very comfortable with Richie."[21]

Local business groups were also predisposed to centralizing control in the mayor's office because they had experienced changes in their own ability to provide civic leadership since Richard J. Daley's death in 1976. In Daley Sr.'s time, a "handful of CEOs" dominated civic affairs. "Leadership [today] is more inclusive, but it is also harder to get things done," explained another business leader.[22]

The same statement could have been made about Chicago's schools before the 1995 law was enacted. Chicago business leaders knew this well, for they had also helped to create the pre-1995 school governance structure.

PENDULUM SWINGS OF
DECENTRALIZATION AND CENTRALIZATION

The 1995 law stands in stark contrast to the 1988 reform law it "amended." The 1988 reform law was written by many of the same local business associations, this time in coalition with community activists. That unlikely coalition sought to decentralize school governance and to curtail city hall and district office authority in the name of antibureaucratic restructuring. They intentionally hamstrung central authorities to give parents, and the school principals they were newly empowered to select, the responsibility for most educational decisions. Activists saw this as "people power" and likened it to community control. Commercial Club business leaders preferred to view decentralization as managerial devolution, likening it to customer-oriented business planning.[23]

Mayoral control of Chicago's schools is partly a political backlash to the decentralization law of 1988. Community groups in the 1988 coalition had been empowered by Mayor Washington and were seeking to institutionalize that power in a newly decentralized public school governance structure. They crafted parent-dominated Local School Councils (LSCs) that were given unprecedented fiscal and personnel authority.[24] To insure that neither city hall nor central office bureaucrats would capture the school board, they also created another representative body, the School Board Nominating Committee (SBNC), to identify candidates and present slates to the mayor from which he was bound to select board members.

Every mayor of Chicago has selected the school board since the 1870s, but the SBNC's screening process diminished this prerogative for Mayor Daley. He greatly resented having to choose school board members from among slates of candidates provided by self-selected community leaders, and often rejected whole slates in protest, leaving the school board incomplete for years at a time, and drawing criticism from around the city. In his mind, "Many people who were nominated are not qualified."[25]

For their part, business association leaders who helped write the 1988 law were thoroughly dissatisfied with the management of the schools by educators and cautious about political control by parents. Business leaders insisted upon reform oversight by an independent group, eventually giving control to the existing business-led School Finance Authority (SFA).[26] Under the 1988 law, the SFA's oversight authority was increased to include managerial as well as fiscal oversight (e.g., mandating district downsizing and devolution plans, investigating the district for fraud and corruption).[27] By 1995, Daley had come to resist oversight by the SFA as much as interference from the SBNC, accusing it of "micromanaging" the schools and becoming its own bureaucracy.[28]

The net effect of 550 LSCs making school-based decisions and the SFA's systemwide oversight was to fragment governance and siphon power from the central school board. The 1988 governance structure was certainly inclusive and democratic, but it was also inefficient. It empowered many decision makers and required powerful interest groups like Chicago's business associations to compete for influence with community activists, parents, and ethnic and racial groups in unaccustomed ways.

Moreover, after the first flush of euphoria faded, long-standing fiscal and labor problems resurfaced. The inability of this mixed-authority governance structure to provide fiscal stability and labor peace combined to feed lingering suspicions of bureaucratic and professional recalcitrance. One business leader explained the disappointment with the 1988 experiment: "We felt like we were running through the schools saying 'you're free! Jailbreak! You can now act differently!' Nobody came out of the cells, because they were very comfortable. I don't think we . . . understood the central forces in a bureaucratic structure and the isolation that has so damaged teaching as a profession."[29]

When the brief Republican takeover of legislative leadership in 1994 opened a window of opportunity, business quickly responded. They drew upon their own corporate structures in drafting the 1995 law. As in 1988, their proposals focused on central management, combining a corporate structure they understood—where decision making is centralized, but functionally divided, and accountability is located in the operating units—and their faith in Mayor Daley. Encouraged by the Republicans and statewide coalition partners, they were stronger in their embrace of financial flexibility, privatization, outsourcing, and antiunionism than they had been 6 years earlier. The SFA was put in abeyance, and the SBNC abolished. Only LSCs remain from the 1988 law, but their formal authority is now subject to CEO oversight. One Democratic legislator described the thinking behind the law as "to run government like a business."[30]

As in the 1988 reform, no new money was provided for implementation. Statewide business groups broke with the Chicago-based business associations in IBEC over this issue, and the statewide groups won. They assumed that any remaining inefficiencies and waste were the primary causes of chronic budget shortfalls since 1979; "don't show me the money," they said, "until you show me some real changes in the way we run the schools."[31] The law passed with only four Democratic votes.[32]

THE MAYOR'S MANAGERIAL COUPS

The law was signed on May 31, 1995. Mayor Daley had appointed a new school board, its president, a CEO, and the first management team by July 1.

From the first, this team was politically and personally loyal to the mayor. Nearly all the top administrators of the system were drawn from the ranks of city hall administrators, while the new five-person Board of Trustees was chosen from among the mayor's business and city hall allies. CEO Paul Vallas clarified: "In order to change the system, you really needed to not only change department heads, but you needed to go three, four deep."[33]

Vallas had been a former Democratic legislative assistant on the committee to investigate the school system's fiscal collapse in 1979, and a budget director in city hall. One statewide business association leader described his credentials primarily in terms of his lack of professional education experience: "Paul never had as part of his career path a superintendency of the third largest school system in the country. It's not an issue to him whether he stays in that office or not; the issue to him is, can I make my mark here?"[34] In mid-second term, Paul Vallas did leave the post of CEO of the Chicago Public Schools (CPS), and quickly began a campaign for governor of Illinois.[35] Daley appointed a younger man, Arne Duncan, to be the system's next CEO. Duncan had been Vallas's chief of staff for one year, and had worked after college in the district office, but otherwise had no formal training or experience in education.[36] Daley's initial choice for president of the board was an equally loyal supporter, his former chief of staff, Gery Chico.[37] Commenting on the mayor's avoidance of professional educators, his education aide said that it "isn't realistic" to ask an educator to "run a $3 billion operation."[38] An experienced education editor was more direct: "This administration doesn't think much of educators!"[39]

In making his initial choices, Daley was signaling that his first priority would be what also troubled businessmen. "It was, to a large extent, a financial problem. It was an efficiency problem certainly."[40]

The first few months brought a spectacular set of managerial achievements, setting a tone for the next 6 years. A combination of Vallas's budgetary know-how and the flexibility given to him by the 1995 law erased previous projections of a $150 million deficit within months of his appointment.[41] The consolidation of tax levies and block grants "really freed up close to $130 million. . . . We basically made about $170 million adjustment on the expenditure side . . . renegotiating health care contracts and cutting expenditures, eliminating nonessential positions."[42] Through budget cuts, attrition, and privatization arrangements, 1,700 nonprofessional staff positions were outsourced or reassigned.

There were other reasons for these successes. The SFA was no longer able to challenge the school system's budgetary claims. Now in control, the mayor was more willing than he had been under the 1988 decentralization law to use the city's taxing authority to support increased expenses in the schools.[43] Strong backing from business groups helped to release additional funds for the schools from a reluctant Illinois legislature.[44]

Bankers also helped finance the building of 26 new schools and renovation of hundreds more by rapidly raising the school system's bond ratings, which increased the system's access to borrowed capital and lowered the price and in-surance costs of debt.[45] The CPS press office attributed 5 successive years of bond rating increases to multiyear budgeting, strengthened relations with the city, two successive 4-year union contracts, undertaking the massive renovation and con-struction program, achieving community support, and increased accountability.[46] "But," according to one business association leader, "it is also true that the rev-enue from bonds comes from the business backing of Vallas."[47]

The other early important achievement was negotiating a 4-year contract with the teachers union, and an early contract renewal in 1998, ensuring labor peace in the midst of reform. Achieving labor peace was especially difficult since "one of the arguments [business] used early on with the Senate was 'This is a great way to stick it to the Chicago Teachers Union.'"[48] Daley, like his father before him, depends on an electoral coalition that includes the unions. The legislature's actions in 1995 put him in danger of losing labor support.

Masterfully turning this challenge to political advantage, he agreed to bar-gain back the lost CTU prerogatives in exchange for the union's agreement not to oppose the law.[49] He kept the bargain, adding 3% annual raises in the first 4-year contract and 2–3% yearly raises in the second.[50] These efforts have im-proved labor relations with union leaders and "largely co-opted them."[51] As early as 1991, one union leader foretold Daley's governance style: "The difference was a mayor who wanted to avoid conflict."[52] CTU president Tom Reese concurred, "our relationship with the employer is better now than a few years ago."[53]

By the summer of 1997, accountability sanctions for schools generated the unavoidable conflict over teacher tenure. Of approximately 700 teachers in seven high schools being "reconstituted," 183 were told to take early retirement or find another position in the system. Dismissed teachers remained on the payroll as "reserve" teachers and were given up to 18 months to find another CPS post. By February 1999 (5 months after a second 4-year contract was signed), 138 teach-ers, (40 among the original 183, the rest from schools with declining enrollments or curricular changes) were "honorably terminated," provoking a suit by the union. When a federal judge upheld the decision, CTU president Reese criti-cized the 1995 law for attempting "to destroy our union and schools," but avoided criticizing the mayor.[54]

The "chummy" relationship between city hall and CTU leadership was even-tually challenged from within the union. Teachers overwhelmingly rejected Reese and his entire cabinet in May 2001, in the third leadership challenge from Deborah Lynch and her "proactive caucus." Lynch was intent on bringing new ideas to the union's negotiations with city hall (e.g., small schools, teacher lead-ers, and an alliance with the progressive urban union collaboration, Teacher Union Reform Network, or TURN).[55]

Close ties to city hall have also increased services to schools from other city agencies. The public libraries have supplemented reading programs, Streets and Sanitation has cleaned around school grounds, the Departments of Human Services and Child and Welfare Services coordinate their work more routinely with the schools, and police have been more responsive to crime and violence in and near schools. One central office administrator observed, "That has been the most beautiful part of this management team. We have had the resources—just almost automatically—that other [Chicago] superintendents did not."[56]

Some of those resources, including funding for the massive school building and renovation program, have come from the special access that the mayor has to the Democrats in Washington, D. C.[57] Mayor Daley gave the Clinton White House a Democrat to point to who had "turned around" a big city school system through "greater accountability."[58]

"Vastly expanded" outsourcing has also helped to encourage support from the mayor's long-term business allies.[59] The management team has been criticized for granting large no-bid contracts and a lack of controls on corporate contracts, although businessmen see such influence as "inevitable."[60] Mayor Daley is a large fan of privatization in city departments, but by 1997 Vallas was forced to admit, "I don't know if we've saved money on privatization."[61] He called the costly, and highly sensitive, information management systems of CPS "over-privatized" when an audit revealed lax financial and contractual safeguards.[62] In other cases, big contractors have simply failed to provide the level of service promised, or passed on additional charges to schools, forcing the system to "debar" companies from doing business with the schools.[63]

Although business groups have easy access to the mayor, community groups and parents have seen their influence on school policy diminish from a high point under the previous governance structure. One business association leader described the difference as a function of scale: "There's been less opportunity for [reform groups] to be as useful because the issues are so much bigger, . . . the state budget and some other things. They just can't advocate with the same efficacy as civic groups can or the business community or the board itself."[64]

African American groups protest school contracts that often exclude them, and complain that repairs and new Advanced Placement courses and other schooling options come to their neighborhoods last. Such disparities are noticed, they assert, only after they complain to the press.[65] There is evidence to support their claims. Nearly every study of the system has shown that African American children and especially those in "predominately" (over 85%) African American and/ or high-poverty schools (more than 90% low-income students) fare the worst. By their own report, LSCs in these schools are the most likely to be troubled with corruption and internal dissent and be unable to perform their duties.[66] Magnet and college prep schools are least likely to be fully funded in predominately black neighborhoods, and 33 of the system's low performing high schools were not able to offer AP classes until 2001–02.[67]

The relationship between the board—once a hotbed of citizen discussion and complaint—and the citizenry is also attenuated. Board meetings are brief, with little debate and almost no disagreement between CEO Vallas and board members. The only disagreements registered in the press between Paul Vallas, Gery Chico, and the mayor have been over who should receive most of the credit for the good things accomplished, or the blame for what's left undone.[68]

Mayor Daley relentlessly promotes the managerial and political achievements of his control through the media and from the bully pulpit afforded him as the chair of the Council of Mayors.[69] This has disarmed critics who initially assumed Republicans gave the Democratic mayor total authority in order to watch him fail. Nearly everyone in Chicago seems to agree that "there is more political support for the school system now . . . than ever."[70]

His bully pulpit is also used to provide political cover and administrative support to the leaders on his school management team. The image of a leader rallying his loyal troops is strong among the city's civic leaders. One characteristically said: "He supported his men. I don't know what he says to Vallas. I wouldn't classify him right up there with John Dewey. But he supported them, and that's the most critical thing."[71]

Vallas also understood the usefulness of the media and was "masterful at feeding them."[72] Public relations was a specialty of the CEO's team who understand that the media "have allowed the system to rebuild its credibility, and that's credibility with the parents, credibility with the legislature, credibility even with our bond holders. The media has been our conduit to the world."[73] Even routine management tasks were exploited for their public relations potential. In the early months of the reform, Vallas and his team both were routinely featured on the nightly television news and on the front pages of newspapers exposing some relatively minor form of "waste" in the system and vowing to fix it.[74] Analysis of the media coverage in their first 2 years determined that they had already achieved a symbiotic relationship with the newspapers.[75] "The local media has given them terrific press," said IBEC's business leader, although adding that he was "not sure that [the press] necessarily are sufficiently critical."[76]

EFFECTS ON SCHOOLING AND ACADEMIC ACHIEVEMENT

Attempts to improve instruction and increase student learning have had mixed results. Even the few remaining skeptics acknowledge that the mayor has used his "dictatorial authority" to focus everyone's attention on improving test scores. "Work to improve the school system has stepped up with the new administration because they've made it very clear that improved achievement citywide, in all schools, even serving the most challenging kids, is expected. And the mayor is behind this."[77] On the other hand, the tests Vallas identified to evaluate school and student performance do not meet basic legal and educational standards, and the results of overlapping accountability sanctions have been mixed.

Chicago uses norm-referenced test scores from the Iowa Test of Basic Skills (ITBS) as the means to evaluate school and student performance, attaching "accountability" consequences for student failure. "No more social promotion" was an attractive political slogan for the mayor, and the ITBS offered what seemed like a good tool. But this is an inappropriate test for these purposes. A recent National Research Council report singles out Chicago for making the mistake of using a test that "has not been validated" for "identifying low-performing schools and students."[78] Like all such tests, the ITBS is, by itself, an insufficient indicator of performance. Printed on the test booklet is the caution "should not be used alone" in making high-stakes decisions for students.[79]

After the U.S. Justice Department began to inquire whether Chicago's sole reliance on these tests was discriminatory toward minority children, Vallas decided to stick with the ITBS, at least through the first few years of the twenty-first century, but to broaden the criteria for advancement in 2000–2001. The new criteria apply to eighth-grade students just below the cut score. They include classroom grades, attendance, completed homework, and good conduct.[80] Any change to a more suitable test "would be viewed with suspicion," as his chief accountability officer put it, and might cause the system to lose credibility with the media and the public.[81]

Experimenting with this test-based accountability system began with the eighth-grade elementary students in spring, 1996. Students who failed to meet the cut score on the reading portion of the test were not permitted to graduate to high school, were remanded to a summer school test-prep program created for the purpose, and were given a second chance in August. If they still failed to meet the score, they were retained in elementary school. In 1997, this policy was extended to students in 3rd, 6th, and 10th grades, the promotion criteria were expanded to include the math ITBS test, and cut scores were raised, as they have been most years since. Each year since, about 10,000–12,000 elementary students (14%) have been retained, while the proportion of students meeting the cut score have inched up, from a low of about 75% to a high of about 85%.[82]

Aggregated test scores have risen every year since Daley took control; but aggregated scores, as most educators are aware, hide many disparities. Careful dissaggregation and longitudinal research by independent researchers is beginning to document that African American and Latino children (the vast majority of the students) fare much worse than white children under these policies. The numbers of students who fail to be promoted to the next grade (or graduated) have not declined, but even worsened in 2000.[83] Even so, one-quarter to one-third of the children who fail to meet the cut score are inexplicably, perhaps capriciously, "waived" through to the next grade.[84] Failing African American students are four and one-half times more likely than failing whites to be retained (Latino bilingual students have been exempted from the promotion policy until recently), and the vast majority of retained students come from low-income elementary schools. Chicago's retained students do no better, and sometimes worse, in subsequent years than those with the same failing scores who were socially promoted.[85]

Constant pressure to raise scores at all costs can also provide perverse incentives to schools and teachers. African American children receive by far the slowest instructional pacing, increasing the chances that they will be retained because they were not given the opportunity to learn the material on which they are being tested.[86] The predicted hidden drop-out rate has also become apparent as drop-out rates began to rise in 1998.[87]

ITBS scores have also been used since October 1996 to determine whether schools will be placed on academic probation or one of the other more severe forms of "intervention." Initially, the threshold was set at 15% of students scoring at or above national norms, but has been raised to 20%. This method of ranking schools netted 109 (of about 550) in 1996–97 and stood at 70 schools in 1999–2000. Each year, one or two dozen schools are eliminated from the probation list while others are added either because they improved, or because they moved to a more serious sanction. CPS measures success by the total number of schools that come off the probation lists each year, although many, especially high schools, simply move from one category of sanction to another and back again.[88] Here too, minority neighborhood schools experience these sanctions most often, and it is not clear what must be done to improve their performance. Schools on probation fall disproportionately in the poorest (and therefore the most likely to be African American) neighborhoods in Chicago.[89] The system's low-performing high schools (about 60% of the system) have been found "no better" than before the mayor's team attempted to improve them through accountability sanctions, including many changes in principals and much teacher turnover in the worst of them.[90]

Managerial techniques perfected to weed out low-performing employees, and noncompetitive companies are being applied to schools, in a "ready, fire, aim" strategy.[91] Many wonder if this can improve student learning. Even generally supportive business leaders have expressed their doubts about the educational expertise at the top of the system, "There's a weak educational team in the central office and clearly Paul [Vallas] doesn't let them operate on free reign," "they have an initiative a day, in an environment of inadequate . . . talent."[92]

This lack of educational expertise at the top of the system has caused political problems as well. In 1997, for instance, CEO Vallas, who determined the passing cut scores each year for the ITBS tests, set a nonexistent grade equivalent score of 7.0 for graduation from elementary to high school. Misunderstanding the meaning of a grade equivalent score, he may have assumed it was intuitive, and that every possible score was always represented in every distribution. That year, nearly 1,000 students were told they had failed and were barred from graduation rehearsals, when they had actually passed the eighth-grade tests. After the information was leaked to the press, Vallas asked the students involved to submit individual requests for waivers in order to graduate.[93]

The polarization between students who continue to do poorly despite the motivation of high-stakes testing, and those who are able to raise their scores, has encouraged Vallas to experiment with dozens of "enrichment" projects and programs, beginning with the mandatory test-prep summer school for students who do not meet the cut score on both the reading and math exams. After-school remedial programs, "transition" schools retained for eighth graders who are 15 or older, the elimination of physical education, expanded pre–K and kindergarten programs, and scripted lesson plans for teachers in sanctioned schools—9,360 programs in total—are among them. Vallas considers the scripted lessons the ultimate in teacher support: "This is not rocket science . . . if you're a new teacher, or a weak teacher, or a teacher that doesn't have skills, or if you have a teacher that's burned out . . . if you stick to that curriculum you'll be able to deliver quality instruction."[94] The unintended consequences of the test-driven accountability scheme also encourage reductions in the breadth and depth of the curriculum and greater focus on test preparation, especially in schools with high percentages of black and Latino students.[95] Because these programs overlap and come and go, it is nearly impossible to determine which are helping to raise the aggregate scores and which might have negligible effect.

DEVELOPING TEACHER AND PRINCIPAL CAPACITIES

Many Chicagoans now agree with Linda Lenz of the *Catalyst: Voices of Chicago School Reform*, the city's preeminent education newsmonthly, that "the main reason for school failure is that principals and teachers have not been supported and trained to meet the needs of low-income children."[96] Yet so far, building teacher and principal capacity has taken a back seat to accountability. Vallas emphasized improving the pool of applicants, with fast-track teacher certification, management training and screening for principal applicants, and the recruitment of nontraditional candidates.[97] Until recently, the system's 28,000 teachers and 600 principals have been left alone unless their school is sanctioned in some way. But changes in emphasis may be forthcoming. The state legislature enacted a law in 1999 requiring all Illinois teachers to take 120 clock hours of class work (about 2–3 college courses) every 5 years to be eligible for recertification, and the district responded last year with a catalog of free courses. And in his 1999 reelection campaign, Daley pledged to open a "Teachers Academy." Since then, his idea has been transformed into an elementary school professional development school for training new teachers expected in fall 2001, and a similar secondary-level professional development school to open in fall 2002.[98]

In perhaps the strongest admission of the new system's failure to support struggling schools and teachers, CEO Duncan responded by eliminating the Office of Intervention responsible for overseeing high schools hit with the strongest sanctions: these schools actually saw test scores decline. He aims to avoid Vallas's overreliance on school sanctions as "sticks" to stimulate their improvement. He also announced plans to hold schools accountable for student growth rather than for meeting national test score norms, and to require 2 hours of reading in every elementary school, while providing schools with reading specialists.[99]

PUBLIC INFORMATION

Another troubling concern has been the lack of transparency in the system, and the difficulty citizens have had uncovering the effects of these educational efforts on students. All the positive aggregate data on rising test scores provided by the district must be disaggregated by race and school and reanalyzed by privately funded, independent organizations, which hire social scientists affiliated with local universities or community-based organizations for this purpose. Their work receives far less publicity than that which the system broadcasts. Often, Vallas admitted, he disagreed with the findings of these independent researchers and challenged them. Recently, he sought to develop an in-house research capability to "counter research from outside groups."[100]

Professionally honest review of the system's performance has been hampered by a lack of routine and open access to data from the system and regular, independent evaluation of its effects, unintended and otherwise. Although only a few months into his term as of this writing, Duncan may be building the capacity to provide more complete performance data; he has reestablished a Research and Program Evaluation office in the district, and hired a formerly independent statistician to run it.

For the past 6 years the system has been characterized by an avowed and consistent effort to extol the "good news." The CPS Communications Office publishes a "whole list of successes" to keep the momentum going. Leaders in the system professed to "welcome critics" but would prefer they "just don't do it publicly."[101] Business supporters worry that "this is very fragile, this whole thing." "Supposing somehow the press became negative, that would put a greater burden on the mayor to resist that negative."[102] Reporters acknowledge their role as well: "Where the mayor is becoming king and controls so many of the city functions, and even the peripheral functions . . . you got to be careful that you don't end up with a lot of 'yes' people running things."[103]

IMPLICATIONS FOR POLICY MAKERS

Chicago's corporate community is unusually well organized and has been engaged in school governance reform for many decades. As a consequence, when corporate leaders found a mayor they were prepared to trust, and when circumstances gave them opportunity, they drafted a law authorizing him to run the schools. They also gave him the managerial flexibility they were accustomed to in their own enterprises.

Chicago is a one-party city—no Republican has occupied the office of mayor since 1931. Local offices have no term limits, and the Daley name is synonymous with governing. For these reasons, business leaders expect stability in this arrangement. Policy makers elsewhere—where the traditions of governance are more contested, or where civic actors are less powerful or less supportive—should anticipate less stability, perhaps hotly contested mayoral elections in which the difficulties of improving schools drive voters from one reform agenda and political party to another in a succession of mayors.

Chicagoans did not lose the right to select their school board representatives when the mayor took control; they never had it. Community activists who had enshrined school-based "parent power" in a previous reform lost influence almost immediately, and the powers once given to LSCs have steadily eroded. Neither the mayor nor his CEO want alternative sources of authority to challenge their decisions. When parents have complaints about how the new governance and accountability mechanisms affect their children, they learn quickly to avoid public exposure and seek instead "back channel" help. This lack of democratic representation and parental responsiveness is compounded in Chicago by a lack of transparency: Unbiased, nonpromotional information about the school system has been difficult to obtain. With these lessons in mind, policy makers who seek to centralize control of the schools in city hall should consider alternative means of insuring citizen participation in decision making, parental responsiveness, and information transparency.[104]

Accountability is a key assumption behind Chicago's mayoral takeover. A local reporter put it best: "When people's feet are held to the fire, they respond a little bit more than they would otherwise."[105] When given accountability for the schools, the Chicago example shows that mayors can respond by acquiring more resources for schools. As local political party leaders, they can promise electoral support in exchange for extra funding from state and federal leaders. Mayor-enforced cooperation between city agencies adds services to schools and reinforces their importance as centers of community life. Mayors can buffer the education system from political critique by backing administrative decisions that might be controversial. And if they seek to leave a physical legacy like Mayor Daley did, improving school facilities is easier for mayors than boards of education because mayors have access to city funds and credit. Each of these efforts sends the symbolic message that public schooling is important to the most powerful people in the city.

Tarnishing Mayor Daley's efforts are recurrent questions about the unfair distribution of these physical, fiscal, and symbolic benefits. Policy makers seeking to learn from the Chicago experience should attend closely to the way Mayor Daley has concentrated resources and energy on the schools, but be careful to avoid undermining that progress by their inequitable distribution across the city.

Big city school systems, like Chicago's, have massive logistical, financial, and coordination problems. Managing them is full-time work and requires the highest professional skills. For too long it has been assumed that an education professional can oversee these functions with little more training than a few introductory management courses. In the context of local government downsizing and outsourcing these assumptions tempt ongoing fiscal and contractual problems. Examples provided here clarify that even highly sophisticated business managers, like the Vallas team, have difficulty monitoring work that is contracted to others. However, Chicago's experience also clarifies that giving school leaders the fiscal flexibility to allocate funding where needed and the legal authority to set priorities free from layers of regulation may be as important as who is in charge.

Policy makers need to focus on the underemphasized problem of finding ways to hold school managers publicly accountable for the choices they make once they are given control. In theory, political accountability means that dissatisfied voters can select another mayor, who can then identify another management team for the schools; but this accountability mechanism gives the mayor and his team every incentive to hide the bad news and highlight the good, to obscure disparities and downplay problems. No one disputes that Chicago political and business leaders are more sophisticated media managers than the professional educators who used to run the system. Because of this, institutionalizing long-term fiscal and educational monitoring mechanisms is more important when mayors take control, rather than less so.

The great blind spot of the Chicago experiment is its lack of educational expertise in top decision-making posts. Chicago demonstrates that what seems intuitive (e.g., grade equivalent scores, teaching to the test) is not. Experienced and well-trained education professionals need to make instructional and curricular decisions to avoid the unnecessary mistakes of well-intentioned, but uninformed, business managers. Teachers and students deserve to receive the benefit of the vast amount of research and empirical evidence available about what works. Educational leadership is also needed to guide effective teacher and principal training programs. And while accountability programs are efficient ways to highlight the achievement gap between middle-class white students and low-income students of color, top-quality educators are needed to design and implement instructional programs that reduce the achievement gap.

Chicago demonstrates that mayoral control does not come easily. And once won, it is only the beginning of a protracted learning process: How to insure democratic responsiveness and transparency, which managerial techniques improve cost-effectiveness, and what measures of student performance best guide teacher and student improvements. A mayor's political savvy and authority can bring new resources and heighten attention on schools. But Chicago highlights an important caution: Keeping high-quality educational expertise at the top of the system remains a top priority.

NOTES

1. David B. Tyack, "City Schools; Centralization and Control at the Turn of the Century," in *Building the Organizational Society*, ed. Jerry Israel (New York: Free Press, 1981), pp. 55–72.

2. Interview, 1 July 1997.

3. Research on which this chapter is based include studies the author conducted or participated in that were funded by the Carnegie Corporation of New York, the Spencer Foundation, the Chicago Annenberg Challenge, and the Annie E. Casey Foundation. All interviews were conducted by the author (or a graduate student), tape-recorded, and transcribed. Anonymity was promised to all interviewees.

4. Interview, 6 June 1997.

5. David B. Tyack and Larry Cuban, *Tinkering Toward Utopia* (Cambridge, MA: Harvard University Press, 1995).

6. The appointed board was as small as five members for the first 4 years after the 1995 law was enacted, then grew to seven members in 1999.

7. In 1999 another sanction, "Re-engineering," was added to the list. It permits a larger role by a school's teachers in determining which changes follow from intervention. See *www.Catalyst-chicago.org* for updated versions of school sanctions and criteria.

8. These central office subordinates include subdistrict superintendents.

9. Amendatory Act to the Illinois School Code and other statutes, 1995 (initially House Bill #206).

10. Dorothy Shipps, Joseph Kahne, and Mark Smylie, "The Politics of Urban School Reform: Legitimacy, City Growth, and School Improvement in Chicago," *Education Policy* 13(4): 518–545 (1999). See this article for greater detail on the specifics of the 1995 law.

11. Senator Newt Gingrich masterminded a strategy for these midterm elections in which Republican candidates signed on to a conservative "Contract with America." In combination with a disappointing first 2 years of the Clinton presidency, the contract helped create a landslide of Republican wins throughout state and federal governments known as the "Gingrich Revolution." Senate President James "Pate" Phillip and House Speaker Lee Daniels contacted IBEC. Governor Jim Edgars had long been in touch with the businessmen.

12. IBEC also included Chicago's century-old Civic Federation (a taxpayer watchdog group), the East/West Corporate Corridor Association, and Anthony S. Bryk, Professor of Education at the University of Chicago, then on leave as the special assistant to the Chicago Public Schools (CPS) Superintendent. Bryk was the only regular nonbusiness participant.

13. Dorothy Shipps, "The Invisible Hand: Big Business and Chicago School Reform," *Teachers College Record* 99 (1): 73–116 (1997).

14. IBEC's statewide members also included the Illinois Retail Merchant's Association and the Illinois State Chamber of Commerce.

15. Interview, 24 July 1997.

16. Interview, 5 September 1997.

17. Of 70 interviews conducted in 1997, the largest number of positive comments made about Richard M. Daley's contribution to school reform dealt with his capacity to bring public and private resources to the schools. Informants gave him especially high marks for collaborating with the business community.

18. Interview, 24 July 1997.

19. Barbara Ferman, *Challenging the Growth Machine: Neighborhood Politics in Chicago and Pittsburgh* (Lawrence: University Press of Kansas, 1996). Wim Wiewel and Pierre Clavel, eds., *Harold Washington and the Neighborhoods: Progressive City Government in Chicago, 1983–1987* (New Brunswick, NJ: Rutgers University Press, 1991).

20. Interview, 7 November 1991.

21. Interview, 5 November 1991.

22. Henry C. Mendoza, cited in Barbara Rose, "Strained Tradition: Refashioning the Civic Leadership Network," *Crain's Chicago Business*, 24 January 1994, p. 1.

23. Shipps, Kahne, and Smylie, "Politics of Urban School Reform."

24. LSCs were authorized to set school goals, hire and fire school principals, and approve the expenditure of about $500,000–$850,000 in discretionary funds. These discretionary funds came from a legislated redirection of state Chapter 1 (antipoverty) supplements. After 1989, Chicago's Chapter 1 funds were to go directly to schools.

25. Mary A. Johnson, "Bid to Cut School Board Ends Up in Committee," *Chicago Sun-Times*, 5 May 1994, p. 19. See also Mark Hornung, "School Summit Faces Critical Questions: Changes Seen for Board Choice System," *Crain's Chicago Business*, 17 June 1991, p. 4; "Opinion: Give Mayor a Voice on School Board Picks," *Crain's Chicago Business*, 21 June 1993, p. 12; "Editorial: Get Moving Mayor—Fill Out School Board," *Chicago Sun-Times*, 26 August 1994, p. 35.

26. The SFA was modeled after the 1975 Finance Authority of New York, and had been won by Chicago bankers in 1979 as part of a bailout package negotiated with Governor Thompson, and passed within days by the state legislature. In exchange for fiscal oversight of the Chicago system by the SFA (including the authority to abrogate contracts that it felt might create an unbalanced budget), bankers agreed to provide short-term loans and to purchase $500 million of below investment grade school bonds to secure the bankrupt system. State aid anticipation certificates secured the loans and special obligation notes from the City of Chicago, the bonds were secured by additional taxes the SFA itself could levy.

27. See Shipps, "Invisible Hand," for details. See also Joint House and Senate Chicago Board of Education Investigation Committee, *The Chicago Board of Education's 1979 Financial Crisis and Its Implications on Other Illinois School Districts, Final Report* (Chicago: Author, 1981).

28. Fran Spielman, "Daley Assails School Finance Authority," *Chicago Sun-Times*, 22 February 1995, p. 19.

29. Interview, 15 December 1997.

30. Interview, 10 October 1997.

31. Interview 12 September 1997.

32. Rick Pearson and John Kass, "GOP Drops Schools in Daley's Lap," *Chicago Tribune*, 25 May 1995, p. 1.

33. Interview, 5 September 1997.

34. Interview, 5 September 1997.

35. Mayor Daley had floated Vallas as a gubernatorial candidate 6 months earlier, but Vallas initially rejected the opportunity. It was widely reported in the press that he and Mayor Daley were in disagreement over how to improve students' still-low reading scores. Then too, the Chicago Teacher's Union had elected an entirely new leadership a few weeks before Vallas's resignation in June 2001, and the president of the School Board, Gery Chico, resigned within days of the CTU election. This led to the speculation that the mayor sought a new management team to respond to the new labor voices in the city. See "The Next CEO: The Kind of Leader the System Needs," *Catalyst* 12 (February 2001): 1.

36. "Chicago Public Schools, Fall 2001: An Organization Chart," *Catalyst* [Online] *www.Catalyst-chicago.org* (2001).

37. For more detail, see Shipps, Kahne, and Smylie, "Politics of Urban School Reform."

38. Interview, 8 August 1997.

39. Interview, 11 August 1997.

40. Interview, 24 July 1997.

41. Lorraine Forte, "New Law Lets Board Shift Money to Balance Budget," *Catalyst* 7 (1995), pp. 7–10.

42. Interview, 3 September 1997.

43. One of the most unusual ways that the mayor has leveraged city finances is to divert a portion of the city's Tax Increment Financing (TIF) deferments to the reconstruction of neighborhood schools, although the original purpose of TIF designation (including nearly all the downtown district) was to give developers a tax break for taking on urban redevelopment projects and, when the deferment expired, let the communities keep the additional tax revenue that is generated from improved property. This is an uncommon bonding strategy in which bonds are floated in anticipation of increases in taxes. Even though 20 of the district's building initiatives are tied to TIF, the funds raised are only a small portion of the budgeted amounts. Brett Schaeffer, "Watchdog Group: CPS Capital Plan a Project Wish List," *Catalyst* 12 (April 2001): 23.

44. Sheila Washington, "Ryan Announces $400 Million in School Grants," *Chicago Defender*, 12 July 1999, p. 5; Rosalind Rossi, "Board OKs $48 Million Tax Levy for Schools," *Chicago Sun-Times*, 18 December 1997, p. 20; Dave McKinney, "153 School Districts Come Out Winners, But Tax Package Not a Boon to All," *Chicago Sun-Times*, 7 December 1997, p. 10.

45. Interview, 15 December 1997.

46. CPS Office of Communications, "CPS Receives 5th Straight Bond Rating Increase," (Press release, 23 May 2000).

47. Interview, 15 December 1997.

48. Interview, 23 June 1997.

49. Interview, 27 October 1997.

50. Gary Wisby, "Rank and File Teachers Approve New Contract," *Chicago Sun-Times*, 11 November 1998, p. 11.

51. Interview, 26 June 1997.

52. Interview, 12 December 1991.

53. G. Heinz, "Teachers, CPS Hit the Books on Long Pact," *Crain's Chicago Business*, 9 March 1998, p. 4.

54. "News in Brief: A National Roundup," *Education Week*, 24 February 1999; Patricia Manson, "Law Revamping City Teachers' Tenure Upheld," *Chicago Daily Law Bulletin*, 19 July 1999, p. 1.

55. "A New CTU Drummer," *Catalyst* 12 (2001): 1.

56. Interview, 25 August 1997.

57. Joe Ruklick, "New $5.7 Million Grant Money to Help Poor-Performing Chicago Schools," *Chicago Defender*, 6 March 2000, p. 3.

58. Scott Fornek, "President Hails Chicago Schools," *Chicago Sun-Times*, 29 October 1997, p. 1; Office of the Press Secretary, President Bill Clinton's "The State of the Union," 30 January 1998.

59. John Ayers, "Business and Civic Leadership for Change: The Houston Experience" (paper presented at "Making the Grade: Assessing the Reform of Houston's Public Schools," 2000).

60. Interview, 15 December 1997.

61. Interview, 6 September 1997.

62. Rosalind Rossi, "School's Chief Information Officer Ousted," *Chicago Sun-Times*, 11 February 2000, p. 20.

63. Greg Heinz, "Surprise! City Deal for ComEd: Before Outages, Schools Enter 8-Year Power Pact," *Crain's Chicago Business*, 23 August 1999, p. 1; Jorge Oclander, "Firm to Charge Schools More for Supplies," *Chicago Sun-Times*, 24 May 1996, p. 1; Chinta Strausberg, "Vallas Denied Claims He Sat on Data about Phony Firm," *Chicago Defender*, 29 April 2000, p. 4.

64. Interview, 30 June 1997.

65. Chinta Strausberg, "Jackson Calls to Replace Educational Profiling, Add Funds" *Chicago Defender*, 30 March 2000, p. 3; Rosalind Rossi, "Northside Prep Called No Threat to Desegregation," *Chicago Sun-Times*, 19 March 1999, p. 20; Dan Weissmann, "Mell, Burke Wards Near Top in School Repair Spending," *Catalyst* 12 (1997): 1.

66. Susan Ryan, Anthony S. Bryk, Gudelia Lopez, Kimberley Williams, Kathleen Hall, and Stuart Luppescu, *Charting Reform: LSCs—Local Leadership at Work* (Chicago: Chicago Consortium on Chicago School Research, 1997).

67. Dan Weissman, "Everyone Wins, Some Win More," *Catalyst* 10 (1998): 1–9; Rosalind Rossi, "AP Classes in All Chicago High Schools," *Chicago Sun-Times*, 20 December 2000, p. 27.

68. Steve Neal, "Chicago Needs a Lesson on Sharing the Spotlight," *Chicago Sun-Times*, 7 May 1999, p. 8; Fran Spielman and Rosalind Rossi, "Daley Demands School Reform: Mayor Says Educators Must Focus on Improving Students' Reading," *Chicago Sun-Times*, 16 February 2001, p. 1.

69. F. James, "Daley Lectures on Schools: If Chicago Can Turn Around, Others Can, Mayor Says," *Chicago Tribune*, 6 June 1997, p. B3.

70. Interview, 11 August 1997.

71. Interview, 18 June 1997.

72. Interview, 26 June 1997.

73. Interview, 26 June 1997.

74. J. Oclander, "Firm to Charge Schools More for Supplies."

75. Kenneth K. Wong and P. Jain, "Newspapers As Policy Actors in Urban School Systems" (paper presented at the annual meeting of the American Political Science Association, Washington, DC, 1997).

76. Interview, 8 July 1997.

77. Interview, 11 August 1997.

78. Jay P. Heubert and Robert M. Hauser, eds., *High Stakes: Testing for Tracking, Promotion, and Graduation* (Washington, DC: National Academy Press, 1999), pp. 30–31.

79. See also Rosalind Rossi, "Public School Test Policy Hit: Too Much Rides on Scores, Critics Say," *Chicago Sun Times*, 28 January 1999, p. 12.

80. Joe Ruklick, "Watchdog Group Hits CPS with Law suit," *Chicago Defender*, 26 October 1999, p. 1; CPS Office of Communications, "Vallas Responds to Allegation of Discrimination in CPS Promotion Policies" (Press release, 21 October 1999); "School Reform Timeline: 2000," *Catalyst* [On-line], *www.Catalyst-chicago.org* (2000); Anna Mendieta, "Schools Aim to Toughen Standards: 8th Grade Bar May Be Raised," *Chicago Sun-Times*, 27 July 2000, p. 12.

81. Heubert and Hauser, *High Stakes*, p. 31.

82. Don Moore, *Chicago's Grade Retention Program Fails to Help Retained Students* (Chicago: Designs for Change, 2000); CPS Office of Communications, "CPS Promotes Retained Students; Promotion Policy Helps Students Catch Up" (Press release, 22 January 1999); Melissa Roderick, Jenny Nagaoka, Jen Bacon, and John Easton, *Update: Ending Social Promotion: Passing, Retention, and Achievement Trends among Promoted and Retained Students, 1995–1999* (Chicago: Consortium on Chicago School Research, 2000).

83. Roderick et al., *Update*; Rosalind Rossi, "One of Three Eighth Graders to Miss Graduation," *Chicago Sun-Times*, 26 May 2000, p. 10.

84. Melissa Roderick, Anthony S. Bryk, Brian A. Jacob, John Q. Easton, Elaine Allensworth, *Ending Social Promotion* (Consortium on Chicago School Research, 1999).

85. Moore, *Chicago's Grade Retention*; Roderick et al., *Ending Social Promotion*.

86. Julia B. Smith, BetsAnn Smith, and Anthony S. Bryk, *Setting the Pace: Opportunities to Learn in Chicago's Elementary Schools* (Chicago: Consortium on Chicago School Research, 1998).

87. Maureen Kelleher, "Dropout Rate Climbs As Schools Dump Truants," *Catalyst* 10 (1998): 1.

88. "Chicago Public Schools Intervention Status (02-P36-C)" (2000); Chicago Public Schools Lists of Schools on Academic Probation (FY1999–2000); and "High School Accountability Strategies, 1996–2000: A Scorecard," *Catalyst* [On-line], *www.Catalyst-chicago.org* (2000).

89. "Board Keeps Test Data under Wraps," *Catalyst* 10 (1998): 25–7.

90. Rosalind Rossi, "AP Classes," p. 27.

91. Interview, 15 December 1997.

92. Interview, 26 June 1997; interview, 8 July 1997.

93. Rosalind Rossi, "Hundreds May Pass Eighth Grade After All," *Chicago Sun-Times,* 7 June 1997, p. 1.

94. Interview, 6 September 1997.

95. Joe Ruklick, "Challenge Iowa Test," *Chicago Defender,* 20 May 2000, p. 1; Caroline Hendrie, "Researchers See Some Progress in Chicago High Schools," *Education Week,* 12 May 1999, p. 12; Smith et al. *Setting the Pace.*

96. Linda Lenz and Veronica Anderson, "Been There, Done That, Mr. President," *Catalyst* 11 (2001): 2.

97. "Staff Development a Low Priority," *Catalyst* [On-line], *www.Catalyst-chicago.org* (1998); Mandy Burrell, "Teachers for Chicago Out, Fast Track Certification In," *Catalyst* 11 (2001); Alexander Russo, "Chicago, NY Welcome a New Breed of Principals," *Catalyst* 11 (2001). The emphasis for principals on management training and recruitment has overshadowed a longer running collaboration between the principal's association and the school system to train new principals and provide some support to others.

98. Deborah Williams, "Teachers Academy Planners Still Juggling Ideas," *Catalyst* 11 (2000).

99. "Duncan Charts a New Path for Chicago Public Schools," *Catalyst* 13 (2001): 24–29.

100. "Ex-Superintendent Becomes Consultant for Chicago Schools," *Telegraph Herald*, 16 January 1999, p. 7.

101. Interview, 26 June 1997.

102. Interview, 24 July 1997.

103. Interview, 15 July 1997.

104. One such source in Chicago is *Catalyst: Voices of Chicago School Reform*, a news monthly devoted solely to the city's schools. This award-winning publication was often identified by informants as the "most reliable source of information" about the school system.

105. Interview, 16 July 1997.

Chapter 2

BOSTON:
THE STARS FINALLY IN ALIGNMENT

Michael Usdan and Larry Cuban

Recent educational governance changes in Boston have provided the city's schools with a political stability that they have not enjoyed in decades, but serious problems persist. Although the Boston schools have been the subject of numerous studies,[1] our objective here is not to discuss in any detail the important role of the Boston Compact,[2] the volatile history of school desegregation,[3] the current efforts of the Annenberg Challenge/Boston Plan for Excellence, or other specific groups or issues. These matters have been described in great detail elsewhere. Our objective is more limited. It is to analyze how and why macro governance changes have occurred, how new relationships have evolved among the school system, the appointed local school board (in Massachusetts called the "school committee"), and the mayor, and, most important, how these changes are linked, if at all, to the transcendent issue of improving students' academic performance.

In other words, we do not purport to be presenting a comprehensive analysis of the multifaceted Boston school system. We focus only upon the political changes, particularly the powerful new role of the mayor, that have so dramatically transformed the politics of education at the highest governance levels in Boston and on their possible linkage to students' academic performance. While Boston, like other cities, still confronts serious issues pertaining to low-performing schools, the new governance arrangements have built an infrastructure that at least provides the system with some hope for academic improvement and a political equilibrium that it hasn't enjoyed in decades. Despite some promising signs, it is too early to determine whether these recent governance changes will result in sustained improvement in student achievement. Sufficient data simply are unavailable at this early stage of governance reform to permit such judgments.

A BRIEF HISTORY

An understanding of the current situation must flow from the history of a city that was so racially polarized by the volatile school integration struggles of the 1970s.[4] The educational and governance reforms of the 1990s were seeded several decades earlier.[5] Indeed, Boston's racial travails attracted such negative national attention that business and political leaders vowed that their proud city would never again be "dragged through the mud." This backlash against the racial conflict and the ensuing national embarrassment triggered the early efforts of the city's influentials to press for restructuring school governance.[6] Thus the parallel developments in the 1990s, including the change from an elected to appointed school committee, the hiring of a nationally respected school superintendent, and the deep commitment and unprecedented personal involvement of the mayor, had their origins in long-term efforts by the city's civic, university, and corporate leaders to realign what they perceived to be a dysfunctional educational system. There was mounted in a cosmopolitan city, so rich in history, pride, and tradition, a multipronged effort to change a school system whose improvement in academic achievement was at the core of efforts to revitalize the community.[7]

NEEDED CHANGES IN GOVERNANCE

As early as the 1940s, following recommendations by Columbia professor George Strayer, frustrated critics had advocated abolishing the elected school committee. Since 1975, corporate leaders recognized that the traditional school governance structure had to be altered. The patronage-oriented elected school committee had become an embarrassment and a "joke."[8] Civic and corporate dissatisfaction with the school system's academic performance escalated as the student body increasingly came from poor and minority families, especially after the conflict-laden period of court-ordered desegregation. The business community, recognizing its growing need to have a literate and reliable work force in an emerging high-tech economy, became even more disaffected with the pathologies of the city's schools and the community's unwillingness to change them.[9]

These forces converged in the late 1980s with the development of a coalition of civic and corporate officials pushing for a structure in which the mayor exercised more control over the schools through an appointed school committee and a superintendent who would work closely with the city's chief executive.[10] In 1996 the stars finally were aligned. Boston voters reaffirmed their 1991 decision to replace the elected school committee and in 1993 had elected Tom Menino mayor. Late in 1995 the newly appointed school committee in turn selected a superintendent whom the mayor heartily endorsed: Tom Payzant, most recently U.S. Assistant Secretary of Education and a nationally known superintendent with extensive experience in four other communities including San Diego.

A business leader who cochaired the selection committee for superintendent at the invitation of Mayor Menino commented that "if the school system couldn't do it now, it never would."[11] The city's economy was bustling, downtown construction was burgeoning, the mayor's commitment was unequivocal, the teachers union and the private sector were supportive, and the appointed school committee provided a legitimate supportive authority for the new superintendent.[12]

The Changed Role of the Boston School Committee

The shift in the process of how school committee members were selected has dramatically altered the texture of educational governance in Boston. The "circus," as some described the modus operandi of the old elected boards, has been replaced by an appointed body that has been depoliticized and concentrates upon schools and instructional issues. The current members reportedly do not have a personal or political agenda other than school improvement. They are not, unlike their predecessors, preoccupied with running for reelection, patronage, and strategies to use committee service as a stepping-stone to climb the ladder to higher political office. They express an interest in public policy and creating a modern school system that works effectively both educationally and operationally.[13]

The present committee is comfortable with its policy-setting role and seldom engages in micro-managing the system. Nor is the committee a rubber stamp for the superintendent. Although respectful of Payzant's professional leadership and that of the professional staff, it questions both on staff recommendations. The members reportedly view themselves as representing the entire city and not special or single interest constituencies.[14]

Indeed, since Payzant's arrival in 1995, relatively little "sensationalized" news coverage has been devoted either to him or the committee, which unlike its predecessor bodies is content to be in the background and does not crave public attention. Payzant is the system's chief spokesperson with the Boston media on school matters.[15] For example, the appointed school committee was largely invisible in the difficult negotiations with the teachers union during 2000. The mayor, who personally and frequently absorbs media and public criticism of the schools, played an important role in these negotiations. While the unions were essential allies to candidates for the old elected committee,[16] current appointed committee members do not need this dependence in a city where organized labor wields enormous influence. Indeed, there is little doubt that the political strength of the Boston Teachers Union (BTU) has been diluted vis-à-vis the appointed committee. The BTU no longer lobbies individual members who in the past needed their votes and campaign support to win reelection. Currently, the BTU has to go directly to the less malleable mayor and less powerful city council to elicit needed fiscal and political support.

Our interviewees largely agreed that an appointed school committee is desirable at this time with Mayor Menino, who is willing to be accountable and judged on the basis of school success. While the time demands and incessant political controversies make it quite difficult, if not impossible, to recruit to the school committee very senior corporate executives and top civic influentials (so many of whom do not reside in the city) to serve on even an appointed board, the school committee consists of able, educated citizens who have a trusteeship and not a special interest, constituent service, or political orientation toward their responsibilities.

Thus far we have offered only the positives of a mayorally appointed committee in the current political context in which the Boston school system operates. There are, however, negatives as well. Many critics of the appointed school committee believe that members are less engaged than they should be in the city's grassroots communities. There is persistent anxiety about neighborhood access and representation.[17] Appointed board members, interviewees said, lack a feel for the perspectives of local neighborhoods. Elected officials, on the other hand, must be responsive to the needs of constituents if they are to be elected or reelected to office. Appointed boards, it is alleged, often do not pay sufficient attention to neighborhood or community concerns and are less successful in involving parents at the school or local level. Many community and constituency concerns are now dealt with by the city council and not the current appointed board.

This criticism that the appointed committee has lost its feel for grassroots concerns is exacerbated in the minority neighborhoods where there remains a feeling of disenfranchisement and that their voice is unheard on school issues even though there currently are three blacks, three whites and one Latino on the school committee. Some grassroots critics view the appointed committee as not credible, accusing them of serving as a tool for the city's power structure impaneled to meet the needs of the civic and business establishment and not their youngsters.

It is extremely difficult in any large system to maintain the necessary responsiveness to grassroots concerns. In Boston, the situation appears to be relatively positive and differences somewhat muted because the mayor works quite well, for example, with the black community and its influential clergy. The mayor's strong community development push has delivered both jobs and extensive neighborhood improvement projects throughout the city.

The Critical Role of the Mayor

Boston's Mayor Menino, like a growing number of his counterparts in cities around the country, believes that his success or failure will be determined by the quality of the schools and their ability to either retain or attract young families with young children.[18] Yet historically, city schools have been viewed politically as "no win," the Vietnam of urban politics. Reform mayors often have been badly bloodied if they became directly involved in controversial issues such as desegregation, decentralization, collective bargaining, finance, and church-state relationships.

Menino and his counterparts in growing numbers of cities like Chicago, Detroit, Oakland and Cleveland, however, are no longer distancing themselves from their schools.[19] They recognize that the schools must be a major priority as they deal with interconnected social, economic and political issues. They are aware that the schools must improve if cities are to remain economically viable and vibrant.[20] Students must be given the chance to achieve academically and perform in an increasingly competitive and technological workplace. Mayor Menino's popularity is based not on the quality of the Boston Symphony and the dynamic downtown renaissance, but upon the sense that the schools gradually might be improving. Boston voters, in essence, reached the conclusion that improved schools are more likely to happen under the aegis of a caring populist mayor than under the supervision of a patronage-ridden school committee.[21]

There is now a sense that the mayor's deep commitment has wedded him to the school system. An environment and set of expectations have been created that would make it impossible for the mayor to walk away from the schools in the very unlikely event he would be so inclined. Anchoring the middle class in the city will not be possible without offering quality education for young families, a literate workforce for employers, and affordable housing for those who want to remain in the city. These are bedrock factors for the rationale that schools and general-purpose government must have closer relationships in Boston and elsewhere.

While there is no assurance that the recent mayoral involvement in Boston or elsewhere will translate into enhanced student achievement, there is little question, at least in Boston, that the stronger leadership role being played by the mayor has stabilized the system and established the essential conditions for educational improvement to occur.

Much of the stability now enjoyed in the Boston schools can be attributed to the relatively good relationships being maintained between the new governance structure and the powerful teachers union. While the teachers union certainly has less direct political influence with an appointed school committee than it did with an elected body, the power of unions in a strong labor city like Boston can hardly be underestimated.[22] Although the mayor as an elected official certainly must be responsive to the influential unions that represent teachers, school custodians, and school bus drivers, he certainly has a much broader political base and greater influence than the superintendent. Indeed, in Boston, Mayor Menino supported contractual changes such as weakening seniority provisions and strengthening principal's teacher assignment practices in ways in which the superintendent or school committee alone could not.

The essential proactive role of the mayor has been endorsed and enhanced by an important shift in the role of the influential business community. The Boston Compact is one impressive embodiment of a long-term private sector commitment to educational improvement in the city. In Boston the business role has changed.

Business Role in Schools

While business involvement in school partnership programs and similar efforts was moderately successful and praiseworthy, such initiatives seldom altered the basic structure of the schools or strengthened student achievement.[23] This frustration led to the business community's becoming deeply involved both politically and financially in the successful efforts to change the school committee from an elected to an appointed body.

Business leaders, through the Boston Municipal Research Bureau (a fiscal watchdog group) and the Greater Boston Chamber of Commerce (as well as the Boston Compact), have been bought into the superintendent's reform agenda and now are much more strategic in their support for education. Business investment now is focused upon the Boston Plan for Excellence—a project funded by a large Annenberg Foundation grant—and is no longer afflicted with "projectitis," that is, the funding of separate and isolated programs. Business leaders concentrate on instructional issues and systemic academic improvement.

Private sector investments also are now more focused on the superintendent's overall program predicated on standards-based reform and less oriented to special corporate projects such as middle school athletics.[24] Indeed, Superintendent Payzant's comprehensive Focus on Children initiative,[25] launched in 1996, which specifies the standards and outcomes that the district seeks to achieve, attracted pooled private sector resources. Business leaders raised the required Annenberg match for the schools and some 10 million additional private dollars are now anchored in the school system's new teaching and learning programs. The support of the influential Boston Plan for Excellence in the Public Schools (the local education fund) has been of singular importance to these efforts.[26]

This support from private sector leaders reflects the credibility of the current school system. Hopes are increasingly high that this private support will become so deeply rooted that it will continue well into the future, and will be sustained even when Mayor Menino and Superintendent Payzant move on.[27]

We do not intend to be "Pollyannaish" or to suggest that these governance changes have created a state of nirvana in the Boston Public Schools. They continue to face very serious problems such as pervasive low student achievement, inadequate parent involvement, excessive teacher seniority and assignment constraints, and a still rather fledgling (if not inchoate) accountability system in which standards and assessments are not aligned sufficiently with the school curriculum.[28]

Despite these persistent and rather consequential negatives, there is little question but that the Boston schools have made considerable progress in creating the necessary conditions for school improvement since the governance structure was revamped. The mayor's avowed highest priority is the schools. He articulates that he wants improved education to be his major legacy. He uses the bully pulpit of the mayor's office and city hall to encourage public support. The rhetoric has been supported by tangible action. The city (upon which the schools are fiscally dependent) has pledged new resources in areas like school construction and maintenance and invested generously in expanding the system's technological capacities.

The close alliance and special personal chemistry that exist between Mayor Menino and Superintendent Payzant is *one*, if not *the*, central element of the success of the governance changes in Boston. Indeed, for school improvement purposes they are joined at the hip and have developed an external-internal team approach that has provided a problem-laden urban school system with a remarkably stable fiscal, political, and administrative environment in which reform has a much greater chance to succeed.[29] In essence, the mayor handles much of the external politics. He handles many of the larger union and community issues, and spearheads the efforts to provide the necessary financial resources. The mayor, in fact, has been willing to expend his political capital to provide a buffer allowing the superintendent to establish the infrastructure for student improvement.

We do not mean to imply that the mayor is involved in any way with daily management of the school system. The superintendent runs the system. The superintendent and school committee present the mayor with their detailed budget requests, and he in turn determines how these numbers fit into the city's overall fiscal picture. Although the mayor certainly has made the schools a singularly high priority, he does not interfere in staff appointment processes or become involved in day-to-day school matters.[30]

The mayor, however, undoubtedly provides political cover for the school system. In Boston, educational politics has often been a blood sport in which the mayor and city council have battled school leaders, particularly former elected school committee members, who frequently were viewed as rivals with aspirations to run for higher political office.[31] This divisiveness occurs much less now although the city council still tries to influence school policies and priorities. The mayor will not permit the education leadership team to be undermined or openly attacked.

Superintendent Tom Payzant's reactions to his partnership with Boston's mayor have implications for school governance and administrators everywhere. Payzant is widely viewed as "a superintendent's superintendent" and acclaimed as one of the country's leading school administrators. Payzant also is nationally visible as past chairman of the prestigious College Board on which he still serves.

In his earlier superintendencies, Payzant had relatively little direct connection with municipal or general-purpose government. In the earlier years of his career he commented that while he never explicitly acknowledged how political his job was, he implicitly knew that to get anything done he had to engage in the political process. His experience in the U.S. Department of Education, however, really opened his eyes with regard to the pervasive role of politics in shaping educational policy and practice. Events in Boston, of course, have further strengthened this understanding.[32]

Payzant stated that earlier in his career he would have resented the time he currently spends with Boston's mayor and city council. It would have diverted him from his major responsibilities as an educational leader. Now, however, he willingly spends much time with the city's political leaders recognizing that this is where the clout or influence is and the place from which resources must be tapped.[33]

Payzant reflects that he was more of a purist in the past with regard to the relationship between politics and schools. He now more fully recognizes that to accomplish anything in the public sector an individual must be ready to compromise and engage politically in the broader sense. This is particularly important in older cities like Boston where only 20% of the voters have school-age children. The current governance system in Boston seems to be working not because the new political arrangements provide a structural panacea for school improvement that is universally replicable but because the relatively stable context allows for systemic changes and cooperative relationships.

THE CHANGED GOVERNANCE SYSTEM AND COORDINATED SERVICES

Theoretically, one of the logical advantages of having greater mayoral involvement in school governance is the opportunity it affords to more effectively link education with the health, social services, youth development, and other agencies of general-purpose government that also so significantly impact on the lives of children and their families. There are obvious relationships between a child's health and his or her ability to learn. A hungry child, a child with a toothache, or a child with vision deficiencies who cannot see the blackboard all have diminished learning opportunities.

What forms of cooperation in Boston have occurred as the result of the close relationship between the schools and the mayor's office? There is a clear understanding that the schools in Boston and elsewhere neither have the time, resources, or expertise to meet the multifaceted needs of students and their families. The major function of the schools must be academics, but they also must attempt to assume some responsibility for important student services. In Boston, health services are offered by the schools through school-based and community health clinics in collaboration with the city's Public Health Commission. There are student support coordinators who facilitate the provision of social services and family counseling services with community-based providers in every high school and in most middle schools.

The mayor's "2 to 6" (afternoon hours) initiative has helped expand after-school programming and city hall has assisted community-based organizations to expand programs for 3- and 4-year-old youngsters. After-school programs are situated both in schools and in the community. The superintendent's teaching and learning team provides assistance on curricula issues and teacher training programs for community-based programs.[34]

Recently, the superintendent established a Unified School Services Team to provide coordination of the support services to students. A full-service elementary school recently has been initiated in partnership with Boston College. The schools and the Public Health Commission are working together to make families aware of the federal money available for health insurance coverage for poor youngsters. Superintendent Payzant, as a member of the mayor's cabinet, also has ready access to and improved intersector communication with other city agencies such as the police, social services, and public health. For example, during the past 2 years, collaboration between the school system and police department has increased dramatically with focused initiatives to reduce truancy and improve safety in the schools.

Despite these and other examples of coordinated services being offered between the schools and city agencies, there persists a feeling that the school system is "drowning" with all it has to do to improve instruction and student achievement. At a time when the focus is so heavily on instruction and improving the academic program it is hard to create and implement as a major priority an agenda that seeks to integrate city and school social, health, and recreational services.[35] One would think that in cities like Boston, in which 75% of the students are eligible for the reduced-price school lunch program, ultimately closer linkages will develop between education and related human services.

Although some advocates of coordinated services would like to see much more attention being paid to the issue under the new governance structure, both city and school officials explicitly acknowledge that education cannot stay in an isolated silo and must operate in a larger arena.

THE IMPACT OF GOVERNANCE CHANGES UPON STUDENT ACADEMIC ACHIEVEMENT AND MANAGEMENT

Within the school system much concentration on improving instruction and the special needs of underachieving youngsters occurs. The system is no longer distracted by scandals, patronage concerns, and the political machinations of elected board members.

The primary strategy of instructional improvement is to establish an infrastructure that focuses on staff development and building the capacity of teachers and principals.[36] Payzant's strategy for improving the whole school system, not just a few schools, is based on utilizing coaches, focusing on literacy and mathematics, and targeting school-based professional development to improve classroom instruction. This reform plan, set forth in the Focus on Children initiative, is slowly penetrating elementary and middle schools, but is less accepted in the high schools. Since 1995, Payzant has appointed approximately half of all principals and headmasters.

Boston's main instructional focus is on literacy and mathematics. Elementary schools choose from one of four balanced literacy models approved by the system. Reading Recovery programs provide safety nets for young children who have difficulty learning to read. Secondary schools focus on literacy across the curriculum. Targeted support for students who do not meet promotion standards is offered through a 15-month transition program. Students attend summer school in small classes in reading and mathematics and have double blocks of literacy and math during the academic year working with regular classroom teaching literacy and math specialists. Students also receive extra after-school assistance.

As in other school districts, however, whole-school change in Boston likely will come soonest and easiest in the elementary schools. Although a few high schools have developed School-to-Work and other programs, many secondary schools remain unchanged. Numerous interviewees attested to the difficulty of altering the traditional high school's size, use of time, pedagogy, and formal organization.

Administratively, Payzant eliminated the assistant superintendent position. With teaching and learning now the laserlike focus of the system, there is intense emphasis on school-site instructional leadership. Three deputy superintendents have been appointed. They spend most of their time in schools and have exclusive responsibility with the superintendent for the evaluation of principals. Even the superintendent, chief operating officer, and deputy superintendent for teaching and learning each directly supervise four to five schools.

Since Payzant's arrival in 1995, he has made special efforts to align the system's curriculum with national and state standards. Schools prior to his arrival were largely autonomous. Since then top administrators have worked hard to better align the system's learning standards with the state's curricular frameworks.

All of these efforts, of course, are costly and urban districts like Boston increasingly are dependent upon increased state funding and support.

THE ROLE OF THE STATE

The reform efforts in Boston are driven, linked, buttressed, and legitimized significantly by the state's school reform agenda. In 1993 the Commonwealth of Massachusetts enacted the Massachusetts Educational Reform Act (MERA). As a result of its passage, more money has flowed into the cities, and academic expectations have been raised.

The state's efforts to push standards and assessments and establish greater accountability in education through the Massachusetts Comprehensive Assessment System tests (MCAS) beginning in 1998 are inextricably linked to Boston's reform efforts. The controversy over the MCAS tests (opposed by unions, supported by employers) will have enormous impact in setting the context and policy directions for the city's schools in the years immediately ahead.[37]

Massachusetts has opted from the outset to implement a politically risky high-standards approach with high-stakes testing. Texas, on the other hand, initially set lower expectations in its testing program in an effort to gradually build confidence and mitigate the predictable political fallout caused by the possible failure of huge numbers of students. Massachusetts currently is experiencing a powerful backlash against the high-standards and high-stakes-assessment approach and must soon decide whether it will be politically tolerable to have 50–60% of urban students failing the MCAS and not graduating. It is unlikely that this number of failures will be countenanced politically so many efforts are underway to reduce those numbers. Nor will the Boston schools be caught in this volatile cauldron of being affected by some recalibration of the MCAS. Superintendent Payzant and other urban school leaders fear a reversion to lower expectations for urban students and vigorously oppose proposals that the state back off in its pressure for high standards for *all* youngsters.[38]

State Legislation's Influence on Boston's Schools

There are several very significant components of the Massachusetts omnibus reform legislation of 1993 that have influenced Boston and all of the other school systems in the state. One particularly important element of the legislation pertained to removing school committees from the selection of personnel other than the superintendent. In addition, the 1993 reform act eliminated tenure and other protections for principals, allowing communities more easily to replace ineffective or incompetent administrators.

The business community has strongly supported MERA because of its aggressive goals, standards, and high expectations. In Boston, instruction is being driven by the superintendent's agenda, MCAS tests, and the state's standards thrust.

There are multiple levels of conversation and debate about the MCAS both in Boston and throughout the state. As is true in a growing number of other places in the country, opposition to high-stakes assessments has developed in Massachusetts. Projections are that large numbers of students will not meet the high standards of the MERA and instead fail the vigorous English/language arts and mathematics tests required to graduate in 2003. Although the big urban districts such as Boston are likely to have the largest percentage of student failures, urban superintendents like Payzant, as mentioned earlier, don't want to see MCAS diluted for several reasons. They fear that the cities will lose their leverage for additional state resources and that, by making the students the victims of the test, attention will be diverted from their real needs.

In short, Payzant and other urban school leaders, unlike many of their suburban counterparts, want to keep the heat on their systems and not "dumb down" the standards or dilute MCAS. While the debate over how high standards should be continues to rage in Massachusetts, Virginia, Arizona, New York, and elsewhere, there is little doubt that, whatever the resolution of the controversy may be, the impact on urban school systems will be significant. The real challenge is to raise the bottom end of the distribution in student achievement without penalizing the top end.

GOVERNANCE CHANGES, POLITICAL STABILITY, AND ADMINISTRATIVE EFFICIENCY

There appears to be little question but that the Boston schools have greater stability than they have had in many decades. Mayor Menino, whose pivotal role we have discussed at some length, is extremely popular. He ran unopposed in the 1997 city election, and his approval ratings are constantly in the 70–80% range. The populist mayor purportedly has no aspirations to run for higher office and has great credibility in the city's neighborhoods. His political skills in delivering practical solutions and services for his constituents have earned him the nickname "the urban mechanic."[39]

Mayor Menino has provided the schools with substantial fiscal support and budgetary stability that they have rarely enjoyed in recent decades. In other words, the schools are treated well financially and are not "nickeled and dimed" as they once had been. This stability and continuity in the city's top political leadership have been of vital importance to the new education governance structure's chances for success and sustainability. For example, the mayor's influence was instrumental in forging a multiyear contract in 2000 with the teachers union that assured labor peace for a period of time. The mayor was reelected overwhelmingly in November 2001 with more than 70% of the vote.

Superintendent Payzant has continued to enjoy the unequivocal support of both the mayor and the school committee. His contract has been extended through 2005. His tenure as superintendent in Boston has been the longest since the early 1970s.[40]

Some observers, while acknowledging the improvements of recent years and praising the accomplishments of the mayor, the superintendent, and the appointed school committee, comment that a booming national and regional economy has aided district improvements. They worry about whether recent fiscal support for the schools can be sustained if the current economic slowdown deteriorates into a serious long-term recession. If budgets have to be cut, the schools could become quite vulnerable in a city like Boston vis-à-vis the reportedly greater political influence of groups like the police and fire departments.

There are those in Boston who contend that the stability we have been discussing and implicitly lauding may not be an unmitigated blessing. In other words, maybe there is too much stability, and perhaps the stars are *too* aligned. Some "critical friends" contend that the system may not be moving quickly or aggressively enough to meet the needs of the large numbers of underachieving youngsters attending the Boston schools.

This concern about possible complacency is predicated upon the assumption that there is too little tension or sense of crisis because the mayor, school committee, and superintendent seem to agree almost always on major objectives and priorities for the system. Many, of course, would strongly contest this view after so many years of divisiveness in Boston. Some of this unhappiness with the current situation no doubt is an understandable manifestation of the views of citizens who may feel disenfranchised as the result of the elimination of the elected school committee. Others deplore a lack of urgency for rescuing the many underperforming students, especially at district high schools.

CONCLUSIONS

There seems to be little question but that the new governance arrangements in Boston have provided the schools with a stability they have not enjoyed in many years, if not decades. The community for the most part strongly supports the stars as they are now aligned, namely, the current mayor, the appointed school committee, and the superintendent in their collective efforts to improve education.[41]

There is continuity in the system's leadership, an advantage rarely enjoyed in recent times by urban school systems like Boston. The influential business community has great confidence that resources will not be frittered away and will be utilized for school improvement initiatives. The appointed school committee enjoys credibility that its elected predecessors did not because of actions it has taken such as eliminating the one-million-dollar payroll for school committee "aides." The mayor has reduced Boston's volatile swings in educational politics and solidly supported the policies and practices of a respected superintendent.

Despite this undeniable progress and an era of good feeling that seemingly characterizes the system, some "critical friends" remain guarded about the long-range prognosis for the Boston schools. Although student achievement is inching up, the gains as yet have not been as dramatic as they have been in Houston and elsewhere. While reform efforts have penetrated the elementary grades to quite an extent and to a lesser degree the middle schools, the high schools remain a huge problem in Boston, as in other cities.[42]

In summary, recent Boston school governance changes have succeeded in establishing the necessary political stability upon which large-scale improvements in student achievement must be predicated. The ultimate test in Boston, as in school systems throughout the country, will be how the diverse stakeholders judge the system's product, more specifically, the academic success or achievement of the students.

For example, in Boston, as elsewhere, parental and community dissatisfaction with low student achievement remains persistent. Some critics in Boston maintain that recent improvements are still only "miniscule," and that the mayor has not been held sufficiently accountable for the low performance of the schools.[43] Indeed, Boston's Children First, an organization of parent activists, believe that the school committee has been unresponsive and that control of the system should be turned over to the city council.[44]

We can predict with some confidence that the search for structural panaceas to complex school problems will be sought continuously in urban systems and that the governance issue will continue to churn in Boston and cities throughout the country.

Indeed, in closing this chapter let us comment upon the "powerful reforms" and "shallow roots" themes represented by the title of this book. We have noted the positive changes in Boston's school governance climate and the potential "powerful" educational reform agenda set forth by Payzant. Despite this progress, however, the pressing question remains as to how deeply these changes are currently embedded in the system. What happens if the continuity of the unique leadership team of Menino and Payzant for some reason or another cannot be sustained? What happens if grassroots frustrations or unrest with the pace of change topples the appointed board and the system reverts to an elected body? In the politically volatile world of urban school governance can the stars be aligned indefinitely without stronger evidence than we currently have that the governance changes wrought so painstakingly in cities like Boston can be connected to conclusive gains in student achievement?

NOTES

1. Peter Schrag, *Village School Downtown: Boston Schools, Boston Politics* (Boston: Beacon Press, 1967); John Portz, L. Stein, and Robin R. Jones, *City Schools and City Politics: Institutions and Leadership in Pittsburgh, Boston, and St. Louis* (Lawrence: University Press of Kansas, 1999).

2. The Boston Compact has for many years served as an important catalyst for change. Early in its history it was largely a vehicle for involving the business community that attracted national attention for a number of reasons, not the least of which was its pioneering mutual accountability features. Employers promised jobs to students if test scores rose, the dropout rate diminished, and attendance rates increased.

Currently, it is a broad based coalition seeking school improvement. Its signatories include the mayor, the superintendent of schools, the chair of the Boston School Committee, the president of the Boston Teachers Union, the chair of the Boston Plan for Excellence in the Public Schools and the Greater Boston Chamber of Commerce, the chair of the Boston Higher Education Partnership, the chair of the Boston Human

Services Coalition, the chair of the Boston Cultural Partnership, and the chair of the Boston Private Industry Council.

The 2000 Boston Compact (the Compact must be renewed every 5 years) has three major goals: (1) meet the high standards challenge, (2) increase opportunities for college and career success, and (3) recruit and prepare the next generation of teachers and principals.

3. J. Anthony Lukas, *Common Ground: A Turbulent Decade in the Lives of Three American Families* (New York: Alfred Knopf, 1986).

4. R. Dentler and M. Scott, *Schools on Trial: An Inside Account of the Boston Desegregation Case* (Cambridge, MA: Abt Books, 1981); D. Golden and D. Lowery, "Boston and the Post-War Racial Strain—Blacks and Whites in Boston: 1945–1982," *Boston Globe*, 24 September 1982.

5. Robert Schwartz, interview, 13 December 2000, and Neil Sullivan, interview, 14 December 2000.

6. Wendy Puriefoy, interview, 11 January 2001.

7. H. Jones, "At Last Stars Are in Alignment for School Reform in Boston," *Boston Globe,* 15 April 1997; Wendy Puriefoy, interview.

8. "Political Past Haunts Schools in Boston," *Boston Globe*, 1 July 1982.

9. William Boyan, interview, 13 December 2000.

10. J. Hart, "Mayor Names Panel to Find School Chief," *Boston Globe*, 9 March 1995.

11. Cathy Minehan, interview, 14 December 2000.

12. B. Mooney, "Mayor Gets Wakeup Call on School Committee," *Boston Globe,* 11 December 1995.

13. Joseph Cronin, interview, 13 December 2000, and Elizabeth Reilinger, interview, 16 January 2001.

14. Boyan; interview; Schwartz, interview.

15. Ellen Guiney, interview, 13 December 2000.

16. Edward Doherty, interview, 13 December 2000.

17. Robert Gittens, interview, 13 December 2000.

18. G. Anand, "Menino Pledges Better Schools," *Boston Globe*, 18 January 1996, p. 25. Speaking at the Jeremiah Burke High School, the mayor was quoted as saying about education improvement, "If I fail to bring about these specific reforms by the year 2001, then judge me harshly."

19. Gary Yee, "From Court Street to City Hall: Governance Changes in the Boston Public Schools" (unpublished manuscript, Oakland, CA, 15 August 2000); J. Rakowsky, "Education Efforts Make Menino a Guest of Honor at Mayor's Event," *Boston Globe*, 7 May 1998, p. B9.

20. P. Hill, C. Campbell, and J. Harvey, *It Takes a City: Getting Serious about Urban School Reform* (Washington, DC: Brookings Institution, 2000).

21. "At Last: Schools That Mean Business," *Boston Globe*, 1 November 1996, p. 26.

22. Doherty, interview.

23. Schwartz, interview; Joseph M. Cronin, *Corporations and Urban School Reform: Lessons from Boston*, Occasional Paper no. 12 (Washington, DC: Institute for Educational Leadership, 1991).

24. Boyan, interview.

25. Boston Public Schools, *Focus on Children: A Comprehensive Reform Plan for the Boston Public Schools* (Boston: Author, 1996).

26. Barbara Neufeld and Ellen Guiney, "Transforming Events: A Local Education Fund's Efforts to Promote Large-Scale Urban School Reform" (paper presented at the annual meeting of the American Educational Research Association, New Orleans, LA, 24–28 April 2000).

27. Boyan, interview.

28. Critical Friends, *Status Report on Boston's Public Schools after Two Years of Reform* (Boston: Author, 1997).

29. Thomas Payzant, interview, 14 December 2000.

30. Reilinger, interview.

31. Sullivan, interview.

32. Payzant, interview.

33. For a somewhat more critical view of mayoral involvement, see Richard Hunter, "The Mayor Versus the School Superintendent," *Education and Urban Society* 29 (2): 217–232 (1997).

34. Payzant, interview, provides the basis for this discussion of the relationship between schools and general purpose government in Boston.

35. Payzant, interview.

36. Guiney, interview.

37. The State Education Department in Massachusetts has limited staff supervisory capacity and minimal involvement in Boston's school affairs other than in vocational or special education. The notable exception, of course, is the relatively recent leadership being manifested by the state in the singularly important areas of standards and assessments (MCAS).

38. Payzant, interview.

39. A. Walker, "Menino's Basic Vision Is of a City That Works," *Boston Globe*, 2 July 1995, p. 1.

40. One admirer of Superintendent Payzant likened him to a long-distance marathon runner who would persist in the race for its duration.

41. J. Portz, *External Actors and the Boston Public Schools: The Courts, the Business Community, and the Mayor*, Occasional Paper on Comparative Urban Studies (Washington, DC: Woodrow Wilson International Center for Scholars, 1997).

42. Schwartz, interview; Sullivan, interview.

43. Robert C. Johnston, "Boston Group: Council Should Run Schools," *Education Week*, 28 February 2001, p.12.

44. Ibid.

Chapter 3

A VISION OF HOPE: A CASE STUDY OF SEATTLE'S TWO NONTRADITIONAL SUPERINTENDENTS

Gary Yee and Barbara McCloud

INTRODUCTION

In recent times, the urban superintendent's job has been described as one requiring a "miracle worker"[1] or the "Lone Ranger."[2] These mixed images create only a slightly exaggerated composite of the modern-day school leader—a highly principled man or woman with unusual courage, who is unafraid to do battle (usually with the teachers union, or the bureaucracy, or special interest groups), and who is willing and able to pass swift, often ruthless judgment. In district after troubled district, the quality of superintendents' leadership is often measured by their willingness and ability to act quickly to fire incompetent principals and central district bureaucrats, to rally teachers and administrators around a common educational vision, to present a balanced budget, and in the process to raise student achievement.

Within a few short years, urban districts seem to quickly lose momentum, and school boards and their superintendents become mired in intractable policy debates at interminable board meetings. Tumultuous tenures and tenuous public support, with little recognition, seem to be the common working conditions experienced by superintendents in each large city school system. In district after district, that same leader who seemed to be everywhere at once in the beginning is castigated for failing to produce significant change. With diminishing political support, the superintendent's tenure frequently ends in a rancorous dismissal or resignation, to be followed by recrimination and blame and a search for a replacement. The public no longer sees the superintendent as the "messiah," but instead the superintendent becomes the "scapegoat."[3] Where their arrival brought a fresh breath of hope, each departure leaves teachers and the public at large with a sense of hopelessness.

If one assumes that every superintendent requires a reasonable length of time in order to develop and implement a districtwide school improvement agenda, different questions arise about leading an urban district. Does it require a knowledgeable insider, who comes up through the ranks of teacher, principal, and central office administrator, or a seasoned administrator with a proven track record of success as a superintendent in another, usually smaller district? Could someone from another sector succeed? Could a CEO from industry lead a school district? Could an investment banker? Could a general?

While the urban superintendency has for many decades represented the pinnacle of a long, successful career for public school educators, more recently urban school boards have selected candidates with little formal training in education, and little if any professional experience teaching in, let alone managing, a school or a school district. In the 1990s, the Seattle Public Schools' board of education did exactly that, by selecting not one, but two, nontraditionally prepared superintendents. In 1995, the school board selected General John Stanford, its first noneducator superintendent and its first African American. After his 3-year tenure was tragically shortened by a terminal illness, the board promoted the man Stanford had selected to be his chief financial officer, Joseph Olchefske, to be his successor. Unlike other urban superintendencies, Stanford's ended with an affirmation of the public's strong belief in schools, and Olchefske's appointment confirmed the optimism that the "dream" of educational excellence could be fulfilled.[4]

In this chapter we examine the actions of Stanford and Olchefske as case studies of the leadership behavior of two nontraditionally prepared superintendents—what they have accomplished and achieved, and under what conditions. We begin by reviewing the context of Seattle's schools within its city and its cultural identity. We document some of the major initiatives begun under these two superintendents. We report on the general sentiment that surrounds their work, as reported by Seattle educators, policy makers, community leaders, and other stakeholders. And we consider whether or not there are distinctive characteristics of nontraditional superintendents that make them particularly appealing, or perhaps uniquely suited, for leading urban school districts across the country, as opposed to candidates who have climbed the long traditional educational ladder, from teacher, principal, central office staff, to superintendent of a small "starter" district, to the urban superintendency. Finally, we ask whether their leadership will produce better schools and better outcomes for children.

For our data sources, we relied extensively on published newspaper reports and articles, several research studies that have been conducted on various aspects of Seattle's schools, reports produced by the Seattle Public Schools, and interviews with Seattle Public Schools administrators, teachers, and school board members, former Seattle Education Association leaders, and community and business activists and leaders.[5]

THE CONTEXT OF THE SEATTLE PUBLIC SCHOOLS

Seattle itself does not fit the stereotype of a decaying urban center with a majority population of largely poor and minority residents, served by a troubled school system that fails most of its students, and epic board–superintendent–teacher union battles played out in the press and in political campaigns. Compared to the other cities in this study, Seattle is the smallest, and it has the lowest unemployment rate, the lowest poverty rate, the smallest proportion of African American and Latino residents, the fewest high school dropouts, and the lowest percent of children who live in distressed neighborhoods.[6]

The largest city in the Pacific Northwest, Seattle's population consists of about 500,000 residents; whites continue to be in the majority, with Asian Americans the second largest population group, followed by African Americans and Latinos. Seattle continues to grow slowly in population, possessing both quaint, tree-lined neighborhoods, and a city center booming with high-rises, redevelopment, and new, luxurious housing that takes advantage of the sweeping views of bays and lakes and mountains. The city has a reputation among its residents as a prosperous, cultured, liberal city of and for the middle class, a place where people from the surrounding countryside come, if they can afford it, not the other way around. Seattle politics are described by residents as generally civil.[7]

Historically, Seattle's citizens were proud of their public schools.[8] While Seattle's total population continues to grow slowly, its student population has remained fairly steady over the past decade at about 45,000 students, a significant decrease from its high water mark of 100,000 students in 1962. Approximately 40% of all students receive free or reduced lunch support; about 15% of white students and 64% of black students qualify. About 13% of the students are considered limited English proficient. Best estimates are that 35% of children in the more affluent north-end Seattle neighborhoods attend private schools, while only 10% in the poorer south end do.

Over the past decade, Seattle's students have consistently performed at or above the national average on the California Achievement Test (CAT), a nationally norm-referenced, standardized test administered and scored by the district. In 1990 through 1995, scores were consistently above the national average in reading, language, and mathematics for each year, at the elementary, middle, and high school levels.[9] In 1996, the district replaced the CAT with the Iowa Test of Basic Skills (ITBS). Students performed at about the same level as indicated on the CAT—at or above the national average—and in the elementary grades, students showed significant gains in 1998 and 1999, with average performance at about the 60th percentile.

Despite establishing a generally favorable climate of fiscal and political support for its schools, Seattle residents have also struggled to address three pressing issues that have surfaced time and again throughout the last 50 years with respect to their public school system: the significant disparities in student achievement levels across the city's schools; the negative effects in schools of racial isolation based on housing patterns and neighborhood characteristics; and the development of prudent and coherent strategies to close underutilized schools and upgrade aging and overcrowded ones.

Seattle's schools have historically been relatively successful for most of the city's children. High school graduates have been able to find work in the aircraft and shipping industries, and more recently in the large telecommunications and computer companies and related support infrastructure that has emerged in the nearby suburbs. Using the nationally normed, standardized tests as an achievement indicator, over the last 5 years, from 1996 to 2001, Seattle's students have scored at or above the 50th percentile at most grade levels in the core content areas. The national percentile ranking of the "average" Seattle third grader has increased by about 10 percentile points over the past 4 years (47th percentile to 57th percentile in reading; 48th percentile to 65th percentile in math).[10] In a television interview, businessman-turned-school-board-member Don Nielson said, "We have a city that's not broken, we have a system that's not broke; we're not as we used to be, but it's not broken, but it needs to be better."[11]

However, when performance is disaggregated by ethnic groups, there has been a persistent, 20 percentile points difference between the overall achievement level of white students and the achievement level of African American and Latino students. While all ethnic groups have shown academic improvements over the past 5 years, the achievement gap has stubbornly persisted. In 1999, while white and Asian American students, who make up about 65% of the student population, perform well above the national average, Native American, African American, and Latino students lag behind. White students perform as a group at the 70th percentile level; African American students perform at about the 30th percentile level overall.

The efforts of the Seattle school district to address issues of racial segregation in schools generated significant tension and debate during the 1960s, as it did for urban school districts across the country, and during that time in Seattle, there were numerous demonstrations and even a student boycott. In contrast to many other urban centers, however, Seattle chose to voluntarily adopt a mandatory busing strategy to desegregate schools and provide more balanced enrollments from overcrowded south-end schools to underutilized north-end schools.[12] This policy resulted in sporadic recall efforts of board members that failed, and other challenges, but busing essentially remained in place until the late 1980s, when it was replaced with a "controlled choice plan." In 1995, after seeing that for every north-end student who rode a bus to a south-end school, 10 south-end students were bused to north-end schools, Superintendent Stanford decided that he needed to end busing, declaring, "I don't have to sit next to someone of another color to learn."[13]

The need to modernize some schools but close others due to shifts and declines in enrollment also created many acrimonious debates centered on schools as sources of pride and identity for many neighborhoods and severe drains on limited district resources. Influential and highly vocal neighborhood activists were able to keep schools open, despite very small enrollments and very expensive-to-maintain facilities. Others questioned why the district would spend money on rebuilding schools in neighborhoods where children were being bused in to maintain enrollment, while schools in the "less desirable" inner-city core were left to decay. Despite elaborate planning rubrics designed by district staff, politically mobilized neighborhood groups put great pressure on the school board, creating divisions based on narrow neighborhood issues and delaying all school closure decisions for a decade. As one researcher put it: "School communities were extremely upset when their schools were named for closure and argued that those schools belonged to them and the citizens of their neighborhoods."[14]

Desegregation and school closure policies were inextricably intertwined; underutilized schools in the north end were kept open by busing students from the south end, and while this served to help desegregate those schools, north-end students rarely accepted busing to the minority-majority schools in the south end. The local school helped to define each neighborhood community, so when the district adopted the mandatory school busing strategy to desegregate its schools, not only did this exacerbate fears of ethnic conflict and misunderstanding, but fears arose that it would sever friendships among neighbors and separate neighborhood children from each other.

Ironically, most of the excess classroom space was available in mostly white neighborhoods, so mostly minority children rode the buses to schools outside their district and white children stayed in their neighborhoods. By some accounts, 10 black children attended schools in white neighborhoods for every white child who was bused to a school in a black neighborhood. Schools in white neighborhoods with enrollments of under 200 children were recommended for closure, but those recommendations were fiercely resisted by neighborhood residents who feared that their children would then have to be bused into other, "less desirable" neighborhoods.

These tensions were ever-present through the 1970s and 1980s, and the school levy system, which required the district to go before voters for reauthorization every 2 or 3 years, served as a referendum that reflected public support for, or irritation with, the school district administration, especially with respect to school desegregation efforts and/or school closures. Levies required a super-majority of 60% of the numbers of voters in the previous election, so votes taken after a national election required widespread support across the city, from traditionally active neighborhoods in the north end to the less active south end. Unsuccessful campaigns were often followed by the dismissal or departure of the superintendent during that period.

THE PRESENT ERA: JOHN STANFORD (1995–1998) AND JOSEPH OLCHEFSKE (1998–PRESENT)

By most accounts, William Kendrick's 10-year tenure as Seattle's superintendent ended with a soft thud in 1994. With a student assignment plan in place that included busing, with school closures completed, and with the student population stabilized at about 45,000 students, informants barely remember anything about his tenure, except that the schools were bureaucratic black holes, where ideas and resources and reforms never really took hold. Kendricks was remembered as a "nice" superintendent, but hardly one to lead a world-class school system. His last years were remembered as "without energy," but even worse, Seattle's school board meetings were remembered as sessions of bickering, name-calling, and promotion of narrow interests. In 1994, another tax levy failed to pass, and after that defeat, Kendricks chose to retire, a decision, many suggest, was welcomed by his board.[15]

Those we interviewed unanimously recall the charisma and charm that General John Stanford brought to his interview for the superintendency in 1995. A member of the interview committee remembered that General Stanford stood formally beside the table that was provided for each candidate and never sat down or referred to notes. There was some concern about his lack of educational experience and his military background, but in the end, he impressed the entire committee as a person who could unite and mobilize the entire community. In a televised interview conducted shortly after his death, teachers and city leaders reported that every Seattle child knew who John Stanford was, and they loved him because they knew he was sincere. A parent and city official remarked: "He convinced us as a community that schools were getting better and that they could be great. We don't know if that's true, but we believed him, and that was just as good."[16]

Perhaps most significant, the business community felt very comfortable and familiar with Stanford, and he felt comfortable with them. In his former roles as head of logistics for the U.S. Army and chief executive of Fulton County, Georgia, Stanford had been accustomed to working with business executives. The Alliance for Education, a business group that consolidated most other business groups in Seattle, was able to mobilize important and credible political backing for Stanford's superintendency and financial support for his initiatives.

Historically, the business community had always viewed support for schools as a civic duty, but business leaders usually sponsored only one school or project at a time through small, one-time grants to schools and corporate sponsorship for various ad hoc projects. Some businesses participated in Adopt-a-School programs, and there was a formal monthly meeting that brought the chief executive officers of major Seattle corporations together with city and district leaders. But in the 1990s, the private sector and civic leaders grew increasingly concerned that the district's graduates were not being adequately prepared for the increasingly technical jobs being created in the technology-rich environment of the new economy. During this time, there was a collective sense that the district as a whole had begun to lose momentum, no matter who was superintendent.

Business leaders sought changes in the governance and the leadership of the school district. They decided that schools would never improve unless a different type of board member were chosen. They increasingly believed that ineffective school board members were micromanaging district efforts. Forming a political action committee, Step Forward, they identified civic leaders interested in running for the school board and actively campaigned for their election. Subsequently, in 1993, two new board members were elected, both with strong business connections.

Unlike other cities where mayoral selection committees chose a nontraditionally prepared superintendent, Seattle's mayor did not play a significant role in the selection process in Seattle. Instead, much of the impetus came from school board members themselves, who wanted to widen the pool of candidates to be considered. Stanford was chosen over one other finalist, also an African American, a superintendent from a midwestern city school district, who by most accounts would have been an excellent choice, if Stanford had not been available. Some city leaders questioned whether Stanford's lack of education experience would limit his effectiveness, and whether his military background would fit into Seattle's liberal, "process-driven" political process. Seattle, after all, was a city that had declined to host a Gulf War parade.[17] Nevertheless, having just experienced a long-term, traditionally prepared superintendent and a micromanaging school board, the community as a whole seemed ready for a strong, take-charge, highly visible superintendent like John Stanford. As superintendent, Stanford's first senior appointment was Joseph Olchefske, an investment banker whose work experience and professional training was also not in education, but in finance. They had met in an elevator and struck up a friendship, just as Stanford was beginning his superintendency. Stanford believed not only that Olchefske's fiscal and business acumen was necessary to solve a serious budgetary shortfall, but that his intelligence and commitment to developing a systemic strategy for improving Seattle's schools would lead to districtwide gains in students' academic performance.

Stanford himself acknowledged that the district's goals as developed under Kendricks were fine; what was missing, Stanford argued, was an implementation strategy to achieve those goals and a community-wide campaign to engage and find support for those goals.[18] He agreed with Kendricks on two basic academic priorities—to raise student achievement for all and to close the achievement gap between white and minority students throughout the district. As reported in his own published book, Stanford freely drew on his military experience in developing his management style as superintendent, but that style was far different from the stereotypical one of the autocratic military leader whose commands are followed without question. Stanford's leadership style was to empower everyone to follow his lead.

Stanford outlined his strategic plan as follows:

Increase academic achievement for all students.

Close student achievement gaps.

Attract, develop, and retain an excellent multicultural workforce to provide students with successful role models.

Provide students with a healthy, safe, and secure learning environment.

Provide stable and adequate funding to assure that students will receive a high quality and consistent education.

Meet diverse student and parent needs to attract and retain students.

At the very beginning of their tenure, Stanford and his chief financial officer, Joseph Olchefske, immediately confronted a looming budget deficit that would have derailed any curriculum and instructional reform effort. According to their analysis, the district would need to cut $35 million from the budget over a 3-year period, and they would need to mount another levy campaign not only for operational enhancements but needed facilities modernization. Stanford believed that he needed to create a business plan focused on student outcomes, retool the district's infrastructure to overcome system lethargy, and reengage the community and the district's rank and file. Those plans will be discussed in greater detail in the next section.

Two years into his tenure, Stanford announced that he was being treated for leukemia. He vigorously fought the illness, and because he was convinced that he would recover, he continued to stay at the helm of the district. While the board and most staff continued to operate, key central office administrative positions began to turn over, especially in the leadership of the critically important academic areas. This was particularly significant because of Stanford's own inexperience with the specifics of curriculum and instruction. Arlene Ackerman, his chief academic officer, became superintendent in Washington, D.C., and the directors of academic achievement and curriculum and educational reform also left. While board members urged him to fill those vacancies, they did not press him to replenish his leadership team, and Stanford left the positions unfilled.

Stanford's untimely death in November 1998 left the board members with the significant problem of executive succession. They considered three choices: They could appoint Olchefske, who had assumed most of Stanford's executive responsibilities during his illness; they could conduct a national search for a replacement; or they could reconfigure the position of the superintendent. The third option would allow the board to create a dual superintendency, with a chief academic officer and a chief operations officer who would both be chosen by the board and report to it. This strategy was seriously considered in order to take advantage of Olchefske's knowledge of the budget and the organizational changes undertaken under Stanford, while supplementing them with the educational experience of a senior educator. According to press reports, principals, the teachers union, and other veteran staff were in favor of the second option, a national search, not because they disliked Olchefske, but because they wanted to underscore the need for more academic leadership.[19]

In February 1999, the board chose the first option and decided to appoint Olchefske. They were impressed with the leadership he had shown during the interim term, and they did not want to lose the positive momentum that had been created under Stanford. Olchefske declared, "I own this—I've been part of shaping the path we're on. Clearly, we have to move beyond into the next phase; we like the path we're on, but the work is far from done."[20]

Satisfaction with Olchefske's appointment was confirmed in four influential sectors. First, the Bill and Melinda Gates Foundation pledged $26 million to Seattle schools to further school reform efforts, and the members of the business-driven Alliance for Education pledged to raise additional resources from a broad spectrum of the community as a sign of its commitment to Stanford's legacy. Second, an annual survey of Seattle's parents and residents reported their belief that the schools were improving and indicated their continued support for and satisfaction with the new superintendent. Third, the school board praised Olchefske's performance in his second annual review, and in October 2000 raised his salary, commending him for strengthening his senior staff with the hiring of June Rimmer, a veteran of the Indianapolis School District. They also noted that he had acted to remove ineffective principals.[21] Finally, in February 2001, the city's voters passed two levies that raised additional funds for the Seattle schools, an indication of the community's willingness to tax itself to support the schools and, by association, the new superintendent.

Two campaign messages vividly illustrate the linked focus and work of these two nontraditional superintendents. The first, which describes Stanford's commitment to systemic reform, is taken from the district's 1997–1998 annual report: "The vision: to build a world-class, student-focused learning system."[22] More recent district documents articulate an operational goal, established during Olchefske's tenure: "Delivering on the Dream: academic achievement for every student in every school."[23]

KEY FEATURES OF THE EDUCATIONAL REFORMS

New Academic Content Standards for Every Grade

Stanford and Olchefske outlined their vision for the Seattle school system in the following way:[24] "to create the highest possible standards for students, teachers and principals—and then hold our people to them . . . to focus our entire operation on our children . . . to get the community involved in making our district successful."[25]

With the state adoption of the Washington Essential Academic Learning Requirements in 1993 as a guide, Stanford's and Olchefske's notion of a systemic transformation began with a focus on student learning, not on the practice of teaching and instruction. The Washington Requirements outlined the performance standards expected of students, not teachers. By 1999, the Office of Standards and Assessment, working with administrators and teachers, converted those state standards into academic standards for each grade level, in each of four content areas. In future years, professional development, and the adoption of new curriculum materials and assessments will be driven by these standards. Olchefske hoped that those standards would be highly visible at every school, in every classroom; in visits to three schools, large posters highlighting the key content standards were evident in classrooms, bulletin boards displaying children's work had elements of the standards connected to them. Work has begun to connect those standards in explicit ways to teachers' lessons plans, and it is viewed as a priority area by Rimmer, the chief academic officer.

A New Student Assignment Plan and a Subsequent End to Mandatory Busing

In order to restore widespread public support for schools, Stanford and others believed that Seattle had to eliminate mandatory busing, a process they believed drove many white families from the public school system and frustrated African American parents whose children required long and wasteful bus rides across town, with little proven academic benefit. Stanford's staff created a neighborhood school assignment policy which offered students a preference for attending a school in their own geographic region but options to attend other schools if their parent so chose. An economist by training, Olchefske believed that continuing to offer school placement choices to parents used market forces to stimulate school competition for students.

Only by increasing the visible quality of all schools could they avoid accusations that the neighborhood school policy would result in unequal education based on housing patterns. Olchefske wanted schools to adopt appealing programs, create visible marketing strategies, and publicize results, all of which he believed would attract students and families to their neighborhood schools. If any school had more students applying than it had capacity for, students would be chosen based on a complex series of "tiebreakers" that included preference for students who were from an ethnic group that was underrepresented at the school. By staff estimate, over 80% of all students have been offered their top selection.

The shift to neighborhood schools may result in a resegregation of schools, reflecting the historic geographic concentration of minority families in certain neighborhoods across the city, and the choice of parents to keep their children close to home. One third of the elementary schools now have 80% or more minority students.[26] Nevertheless, the great majority of parents, when given a choice of schools, have been consistently choosing schools near their homes, an indication of general approval of the neighborhood schools of choice strategy. To ensure that the neighborhood schools policy worked for all and provided adequate resources for schools where students had greater needs, Olchefske's strategy used fiscal incentives that assigned a value, through a weighted student formula, that apportioned dollars based on the needs and programs that a student was entitled to.

Weighted Student Formula

Olchefske believed that creating meaningful competition for students among schools could encourage districtwide improvement, but there was concern that schools would try to recruit only the most academically gifted students. There needed to be incentives to recruit all children, even those with special needs or from lower income communities in the vicinity of some of the schools. In order to address fears that the new student assignment plan would create a world-class system for the affluent north end and a second-class system for the poorer south end, Stanford and Olchefske sought a strategy to redistribute limited school resources to schools that would see an influx of new students returning to their schools in the south end. The resource allocation system they developed, the Weighted Student Formula, was drawn from a similar program that they had observed in Alberta, Canada.[27] Olchefske assigned more resources to needy students, and tied those resources to the school that the students attended, making them relatively more financially "valuable" to the receiving school.

Schools that gained enrollment as a result of the Weighted Student Formula (see below) have added extra services, including full-day kindergartens or smaller class sizes, and that has meant that the schools needed more classrooms. Thus the initial benefits from the Weighted Student Formula are sometimes compromised because schools are forced to erect portable buildings to handle the additional classrooms, as students return to their neighborhood schools or select highly attractive schools.

In addition, while it is true that additional funds followed students to their new schools, those funds came from compensatory sources, such as Title 1 and Special Education, and reflected the additional needs that these students already had. The basic general-purpose support that students carried with them remained the same, and so in most cases, movement of a student from one school to another simply meant a gain in funding to the school based on increased enrollment, plus a smaller "weight" gain if the student qualified for special funding based on need. For a school, most of the increased funding translated into additional teaching staff to accommodate the increased enrollment, so there was little "value-added" impact that accompanied these student transfers.

More recently, researchers at the Center for Reinventing Government at the University of Washington identified significant, unintended imbalances in funding that continued to favor some schools serving wealthier communities, despite the weighted student formula.[28] According to them, if one calculates the total budget for a school, including the actual salaries of staff, then many in fact cost more to operate, per student, than do schools serving lower income communities. This is because the teaching and administrative staffs at schools in wealthier communities were in general more highly experienced and therefore were more highly paid. A teacher with 11 years experience was paid about 50% more than a new teacher; their experience level placed them higher on the salary scale. The Center's analysts support the concept of the Weighted Student Formula, but argue that it should be fully implemented to reflect the actual cost of teacher and administrative salaries. While there is ongoing discussion about this apparent issue, the Weighted Student Formula remains as a district policy.

Higher Professional Standards for Principals

Stanford and Olchefske believed that principals needed to be treated as chief executive officers of their schools. That meant principals should have more discretion over their budgets, selection of new teachers, and school-site professional development programs. Stanford established a principal's leadership institute in his first year, which was funded by the Alliance for Education, and every principal participated. He suggested that principals knew how to educate, but that they needed additional skills "in inspiring, motivating, and guiding their diverse communities of students, teachers, and parents."[29] While all principals who were serving at the time participated in the yearlong training, there has been a great deal of turnover in the administrative ranks, and it is a priority to provide ongoing professional development opportunities for each new group of principals, as well as for principals serving in new schools.

According to press reports, a departing personnel director had suggested that 25% of the principals were ineffective. Stanford immediately defended the principals and resisted calls for more drastic transfers and demotions.[30] The reporter suggested that Stanford, like the superintendents before him, seemed reticent to remove or fire principals; according to the reporter, Stanford had not begun to formally evaluate his principals until December 1998, more than 2 years after he had assumed the superintendency. In response, Stanford noted, "Because I am a general, people wanted me to come in here and fire people. That's not my style. My style is to love 'em and lead 'em."[31] In the same interview, Olchefske pointed out that the pool of principals was so thin that it constituted a "people crisis." During his tenure, Stanford had personally assigned nearly 70 principals, but most were veterans from within the system who had been transferred from one school to another or promoted from within. While his transfer policy had benefited some schools when he replaced a weak principal with a more success-

ful one from another school, the school that lost its successful principal sometimes experienced a drop in test scores.

Olchefske's tenure has already been shaped by his willingness to demote and
transfer ineffective principals. Within his first year as permanent superintendent,
he demoted four principals and hired five principals from outside the district,
indications, he said, of his determination to have "a high-quality principal as a
leader for every school."[32] It was later announced that a longtime principal of
a high school had been forced to resign that spring, but was allowed to receive a
large severance package. "I [Olchefske] wanted to move and move aggressively.
If it cost some money to move that way, I was willing to pay something."[33] In
the case of the high school principal, parents and teachers had campaigned for
over a year to have the principal removed. More recently, Olchefske removed a
controversial director of special education but allowed him also to receive a severance package.[34]

Appointment and replacement decisions have been restricted to the superintendent, and those actions are highly visible symbols of a superintendent's
willingness and ability to exercise authority. But they are also among the most
desired decisions that school-site staff and parents want to make. This reflects
the tension inherent in efforts to increase responsibility and autonomy at the
school site, without jeopardizing working rights of administrators, the independence of their managerial authority, or the oversight responsibility of the superintendent for each school site.

Site-Based Management and a New Trust Agreement with Teachers

A key feature of Stanford's efforts to stimulate change systemwide, but especially at the grassroots school-site level, was treating principals as CEOs and
shifting more decision-making authority to the school site. Part of that shift
entailed a new, more positive working arrangement between the district and the
Seattle Education Association (SEA). The SEA had already initiated, in negotiations with then Superintendent Kendricks, a peer review evaluation program
called STAR (Staff Training Assistance and Review) program, which matched
new teachers with experienced teachers who act as mentors.[35]

The standard collective bargaining contract between the teachers association
and the district expired, and, following the model of the labor-management trust
agreement that had been signed by General Motors and the United Auto Workers for their Saturn division, the SEA and the district agreed to sign their own
trust agreement. Stanford acknowledged the SEA's leadership in urging this form
of labor agreement, and union leaders of that movement underscore Kendrick's
important foundational work.[36] The underlying principle of the agreement was
that at the site level, staff and administration would create a common vision, with
an "authentic" decision making role for teachers. The trust agreement that went

into effect during the 1996–97 school year reflected the positive operational relationship between Stanford and Olchefske and the SEA. The final collective bargaining arrangement was driven by "interest-based bargaining," a process that emphasizes problem solving rather than position-based negotiations, spearheaded by the city's chief labor negotiator. The contract is now in place, and includes:

A shared, decision making role for teachers in their schools with respect to budget, strategic planning, curriculum, and professional development, through the establishment of a leadership team selected by the site as a whole.

More hiring flexibility and teacher input on hiring decisions; revisions in the teacher transfer policy, through site-hiring teams, with seniority retained as a factor but not the decisive factor in hiring, transfers, and layoffs.

A new teacher evaluation policy, tied in part to student achievement, with measures of achievement jointly determined by administration and staff.

Development of a New Student Accountability System Based on a Value-Added Measure of Success.

Seattle recently hired William Sanders, a Tennessee statistician who had developed a "value-added" technique that tracks student performance from one year to the next for students, and then compares that growth with students from similar background characteristics, and against other children in a class.[37] The important contribution this can make is that it focuses on student progress over a school year, not simply a single snapshot of student performance. Sanders' system has been used in Tennessee to calculate the average improvement that can be attributed to a teacher's effort, and could provide the beginning of a system for Seattle that uses student performance as a measure of teacher effectiveness, although that has not yet taken place.

Teachers and their organizational representatives have usually objected to using student achievement as part of teacher evaluation because students begin with different academic skills and have access to different sets of community and family assets. To compare one teacher to another, or even to a standard expected level of student achievement or student growth, requires a capacity to control for those variables. Tying teacher evaluations to student achievement requires a capacity to assess the effect of the teacher's classroom performance on student achievement, irrespective of the impact of demographic factors, and even irrespective of the quality of instruction in preceding years. If the student progress of an entire class can be measured as Sanders suggests, then it is possible to compare the "teacher effect" in one class to that of another.

Some objections to this effort have arisen. First, the focus on standardized test score performance, on a test not tied to the standards, might detract from more important efforts to develop assessments tied directly to the content standards. Second, the cost and complexity of the assessment system is an expense that could be better spent elsewhere, and in different ways. More important, some critics question whether the quality of teaching is best evaluated by this kind of measurement of student outcomes. According to a Seattle principal, principal evaluations now include a component that focuses on schoolwide improvements in student outcomes.[38]

ANALYSIS

It is clear from the review of Stanford's 3-year tenure within the context of what Seattle wanted and needed, that there was a combination of person, place, and circumstances that created strong incentives for positive change. While people complained about "an educational malaise" that existed in Seattle prior to his arrival, and despaired of the low quality of some of the schools, in fact, there was no significant labor unrest, test scores were higher than in most cities of its size, and through elections the district was governed by a corporate-style board of directors. Executives of the SEA reported an amicable, positive, and productive relationship with Kendricks that focused on teaching and learning, including 10 years of management-labor cooperation.[39] The city's political and business leadership, while unhappy with school performance, was nevertheless not interested in taking over the schools, something that has occurred in other cities. Nevertheless, the struggle to pass the levy signaled that Seattle's voters were not satisfied with the school system as it was performing.

What everyone wanted was a superintendent who could restore the community's confidence in its school system, and who would reinvigorate the schools. There was no mandate to choose a nontraditionally prepared superintendent, but the community wanted new and different leadership, and there was little resistance when a superintendent candidate was found who had no professional school experience.

Stanford created a powerful media campaign on behalf of children that challenged everyone to work together to create better schools. His personal high visibility in the schools during his 3-year tenure produced much positive public enthusiasm for the schools and substantial concrete support for the school district as a whole by the business community and residents who personally invested in the Alliance for Education. While most attributed the dramatic turnaround to Stanford, others pointed out that many of the pieces were in place before he arrived: an orderly succession process; strong and visionary teachers' association leadership; a vibrant and growing local economic base; organized support from the business community; and a solid school board. These are the very factors that have often subverted and undermined new superintendents from the day they arrived.

Stanford emphasized the importance of a fundamental shift from a system focused on adult issues to one focused on children's achievement, and he repeatedly articulated this as his system reform strategy. He personally led the campaign with his high visibility in interacting with children. Yet most of the significant changes that characterize his tenure focused on adult issues—school funding, school assignment choices for parents, a new labor contract for teachers, new site-based decision-making structures, and the principal as the school's CEO. These changes were all shaped and directed toward the goal of improving student achievement. They certainly set the stage for improved use of teaching and learning resources. However, they had yet to address the technical core of education—teaching and learning—in a particularly strategic way. In fact, there seems to have been little in the way of actual definition and change in terms of what was actually being taught and how, at the end of Stanford's tenure, it was clear that the district needed academic leadership, and that appointment became Olchefske's top priority when he succeeded Stanford.

Olchefske's appointment was in large measure an endorsement by the board of the direction of Stanford's superintendency and an unwillingness to take chances with another search. In 2002, Olchefske enters the fourth year of his tenure as permanent superintendent. One can view his tenure as an extension of many of the initiatives begun under Stanford's tenure, while at the same time it is clear that Olchefske has firmly planted his own imprimatur and is the district's CEO. The work that remains involves extending the curriculum changes into the classroom, or as Olchefske would say, into every classroom.

As research has repeatedly shown, uniform classroom implementation of district-level policy changes is a very complex enterprise.[40] It includes several aspects: seeing that teachers adopt and accept the new standards as applying to every child; developing and utilizing classroom practices that support the academic standards; providing adequate support to meet the needs of underperforming students; ensuring that resources, especially qualified and committed teachers, are adequately deployed in the schools with the neediest students; and maintaining public support for the entire school system, even as parental attention is now refocused primarily on the local neighborhood schools where their children attend.

Two areas in which Stanford received some criticism—that his instructional program was unfocused and that he failed to remove ineffective principals—were among the first actions on Olchefske's agenda. Within 6 months, Olchefske hired an academic officer, and the board had adopted a set of learning outcome standards as well as a broad exit criteria for high schoolers. Less than a year after his appointment, the press announced that Olchefske had demoted 4 principals.[41] But recent difficulties with filling several key high school principalships have also created some public questions about both the selection process and the final appointments.[42] He also continues to refine the Weighted Student Formula as a way to provide differential support to schools. But as he noted in our interview, the curriculum has not yet changed as much as he desires.

Stanford and Olchefske have developed tremendous community support for their leadership and avoided organized challenges to the directions they undertook. The support of the business community will in all likelihood be sustained. It remains to be seen whether the deliberate implementation of standards-based instructional strategies and accountability systems will succeed in raising student achievement and closing achievement gaps. The purpose of returning to neighborhood school assignment was to improve opportunities for minority children and to reconnect parents to their neighborhood schools. Most parents seem to be pleased with the new assignment policy, but there are persistent challenges from parent groups to the race-based assignment priorities.[43]

The educational reforms initiated in the past 6 years by Superintendents Stanford and Olchefske are significant for the Seattle Public Schools, but they are not significantly different from others that have been proposed and implemented in other cities by more traditionally trained superintendents. The systemic approach of aligning standards, assessments, curriculum and instruction, and professional development has been advocated for more than 10 years.[44] As increased attention is given to formal teacher and administrator evaluations tied to student performance—high-stakes evaluations—there may be significantly more tension that emerges. In contrast to Stanford, Olchefske has increased his central office staff's responsibility for the evaluation of principals and has tied student performance to that evaluation. He has shown a willingness to reassign, demote, and dismiss school principals. Whether and how staff will respond to, or resist, efforts to increase overall accountability at the classroom level, and whether Olchefske will be able to identify and place highly skilled leadership at school sites is also a challenge that superintendents across the country face.[45]

With the current high level of community and professional support in place, there is reason to believe that Olchefske and his leadership team will continue to make steady progress in implementing a standards-based educational reform agenda, in partnership with the SEA, although the teachers' association itself has undergone a significant leadership changeover.[46]

The standard that Olchefske has set for himself, to significantly reduce the achievement gap between ethnic groups, will be the greatest challenge, since the district is now concentrating on teaching and learning in the classroom, and the gap still has persisted (although every ethnic group has made steady gains). The test results to date suggest that closing the gap will continue to be a difficult enterprise and more resources will be needed, especially an expanded pool of talented, well-trained, and committed teachers and administrators. The board and superintendent will need to monitor the achievement of African American students, especially with respect to the achievement gap, to ensure that both the neighborhood school assignment plans and the educational reforms have had the anticipated effect. Disparities not only in achievement, but in district application of suspension and discipline policies, may also lead to increased scrutiny of the effect of the system reform policies implemented over the past 6 years. As these complex problem areas emerge, Olchefske and his team will be judged by their willingness and ability to effectively manage these policy dilemmas.[47]

CONCLUSION

The charismatic persona that Stanford publicly communicated, that captured the imagination of the community and moved it to action, seems to have been at least as important as the management skills that he actually brought, the initiatives that he proposed and supported, and the authority that many associate with a military leader. Stanford was fondly remembered as an "idea-a-minute" manager, meaning that he floated many ideas and left it to staff to figure out how to implement them. Some interviewees suggested that he failed to address low-performing administrators, either through a more deliberate evaluation process or through the outright removal of ineffective principals. It must be remembered that Seattle schools were performing at a level that would be the envy of many other urban districts. It is also difficult to identify the specific teaching and learning strategies that were implemented during his brief 3-year tenure.[48]

Still, the notion of restoring hope and confidence, convincing parents and the business community that the Seattle schools could be "world-class," and refocusing attention on academic achievement for all children, was a valuable outcome of his tenure and in all likelihood will be his most important legacy. Other superintendents have declared such goals, but most have simply not been able to convince their communities that it was really possible and mobilize residents and business and political leaders toward positive action. The benefits to the district cannot be simply measured in gains in efficiency or academic achievement; they are gains in goodwill, in a sense of community participation in the education of the next generation, in the possibilities and expectations of high-quality education for all children.

If raising community optimism about its schools and its neighborhoods is one of the most important roles of the superintendent, then boards of education responsible for the selection process may well want to include candidates from outside education who have been similarly inspiring in their work settings, for example, writers, religious leaders, community and labor organizers, and politicians. At the same time, we should not exclude educators who may possess the same charisma, simply because they have chosen to develop their leadership skills in the schools. There is a danger in believing or assuming that only generals, or noneducators, can ignite such optimism within a community. Thirty years ago in Oakland, California, an African American from Philadelphia arrived on the scene as superintendent of schools, and generated similar energy and hope; his name was Marcus Foster, and he was a longtime veteran public school educator.[49] And educators who were interviewed, who remembered the tension and suspicion that occurred when Seattle's teachers went on strike in 1985, recall with admiration the healing that occurred and the optimism that was generated by then newly hired superintendent, William Kendrick.

The lesson here is that the ability to work with the external environment in which schools are embedded is an essential ingredient to a successful superintendency.[50] That environment includes political activists who speak for disadvantaged and disempowered communities, neighborhood activists and parents who choose to live in certain communities and desire to maintain the quality of life for themselves and their children, and a business community whose support provides significant additional resources and political legitimacy to the district's efforts. Stanford seemed to have been at ease, well respected, and successful in all of these areas, even if all sectors did not always agree with him. This is an important quality that superintendents, whether they are traditionally prepared or come from another sector, need to possess and convey, and as Kendrick's 10-year tenure suggests, it is an ability that is affected by time and circumstance.[51]

Joseph Olchefske possesses the kinds of fiscal and administrative expertise and entrée to the business community that most educators lack. Those talents, and the fortuitous meeting with Stanford as he began his tenure, gave him the initial position as CFO for a major school district without any professional school experience or exposure. Stanford's extended illness and untimely death subsequently gave him the opportunity to lead the district on an interim basis. But Olchefske's own skills are the product of significant and demanding academic preparation as well as real-life experience. His technical skill in identifying the looming budget crisis and controlling the budget process helped to drive creative solutions to differential funding in schools. Olchefske gained large-system management experience in the interim period when he was able to assume operational authority for the entire district. When the board's search committee decided on Stanford's successor, Olchefske was chosen in part because he was now the "insider." This confluence of opportunity and expertise are uncommon, but it also took a strong sense of self-confidence, adventure, and civic duty to take on such complex challenges when they were presented.

To his credit, Olchefske was willing to serve in a highly political position paying considerably less than he was making as an investment banker. He was also wise enough to realize the professional limitations of his background, and he quickly hired two highly qualified educators—one a local superintendent, and the other a strong instructional leader—to serve as a leadership team. Focusing on student achievement as measured by standardized tests has many detractors, but one thing is certain: When a superintendent is a noneducator, such measures provide a straightforward and logical way to measure district performance and are clearly understood by business, political, and community leaders. This is a lesson that is applicable to traditionally trained superintendents as well.

In the end, Seattle's residents and educators seem to be well satisfied with their choice of John Stanford and Joseph Olchefske. However, sustaining systemic change requires an understanding of how teachers and school staffs work to make the school improvements that are necessary conditions for high achievement for every child in every school. Even with standards and accountability instruments in place, there are many questions about whether instructional classroom practice will change sufficiently for comprehensive school improvement, and whether fiscal and human resources are sufficient to provide opportunities to learn for every student in every school, no matter where those schools are located. For that to occur, experienced professional educators in the district office and in schools, who possess deep personal knowledge of instructional practice in real school settings, must offer instructional leadership. More than any other actions, Olchefske's selection, support, and evaluation of principals for school sites and central office administrators will establish his instructional reputation, and his managing of competing neighborhood interests with respect to student assignment strategies will demonstrate his political skills.[52]

There will be some who will invoke Stanford's legacy to support narrow, parochial interests, or as justification for challenging difficult decisions that the superintendent must make. To some extent, the community's recollections of Stanford suggest that he was the Lone Ranger and the Miracle Worker, and at this time, neither he nor Olchefske has yet been made a martyr or scapegoat. Yet it must be remembered that the success of these nontraditionally prepared superintendents builds on the tenure of their predecessor, William Kendricks, the support of enlightened teacher leadership, the generous financial support of the community in an era of significant economic expansion, the general achievement level of Seattle's students, and the professional expertise of senior, traditionally prepared educators. Their tenure brings hope not only that Seattle schools can improve but that urban school improvement is possible and that it can occur within the context of cooperative and ethical political, managerial, and instructional leadership that draws together all of the strengths of educators and the community. That hope is remarkable because it was expressed eloquently throughout the entire city in words and action.[53] What remains to be seen is whether or not it can be sustained and mobilized through community action long enough without fracture so as to fulfill the dream—academic achievement for every child in every school.

NOTES

1. Mark Starr, "Miracle Workers Wanted," *Newsweek*, 14 January 1991, 40–44.

2. *Seattle Post-Intelligencer*, 5 May 1975, quoted in Stephen Rowley, *School Closure in Seattle: A Case Study of Educational Decision Making* (Ph.D. diss., Stanford University, 1984).

3. Hugh Scott, *The Black Superintendent, Messiah or Scapegoat?* (Washington, DC: Howard University Press, 1980).

4. "We can call Stanford HOPE." A quotation from seventh graders Jackie Lopez and Mutanda Kwesele, a *Seattle Times Special Section*, 3 December 1998, p. C2.

5. Initial interviews were conducted over a 2-day period in Seattle, 24–26 January 2001, using a semistructured interview protocol. Interviewees included Seattle Public Schools superintendent Joseph Olchefske, veteran and newly hired central office administrators, Seattle public policy researchers, and Seattle civic and political leaders. Subsequent interviews were also conducted with school principals and teachers on 17 April 2001 in a visit to three Seattle Schools, and on 28 April 2001 with a former Seattle Education Association leader.

6. For a detailed comparison of the social context of schools, see the Annie Casey Foundation's *City Kids Report, http://www.aecf.org.*

7. This is a consistent response from our interviews.

8. Rowley, *School Closure.*

9. Student Information Services Office, *Data Profile: District Summary, 1996,* Report 95-1 (Seattle: Seattle Public Schools, 1997).

10. Seattle Public Schools, *Data Profile: District Summary, November 1999,* Report 99-1 (Seattle: Seattle Public Schools, 2000).

11. John Merrow, *The Tale of Three Cities: The Mayor, the Minister, and the General* (New York: The Merrow Report, 1998 [*http://www.pbs.org/merrow*]). Don Nielson quote is in program.

12. Stephen Rowley, *School Closure.*

13. Ruth Teichroeb, "End to Forced Busing Creates New Problems for Seattle's Schools," *Seattle Post-Intelligencer*, 3 June 1999 (*http://seattlep-i.nwsource.com/local/race03.shtml*).

14. Rowley, *School Closure*, p. 171.

15. Interviews with school administrators, 24–26 January 2001.

16. John Merrow, *Tale of Three Cities.*

17. Interviews with civic and political leaders, 25 January 2001.

18. John Stanford, *Victory in Our Schools* (New York: Bantam Books, 1999).

19. Ruth Teichroeb, "Olchefske's First Priority: Find Academic Officer for City Schools," *Seattle Post-Intelligencer*, 11 February 1999 (*http://seattlep-i.nwsoruce.com/local/skull11.shtml*).

20. Ibid.

21. Keith Ervin, "Superintendent Earns Good Marks from Board," *Seattle Times*, 19 October 2000 (*http://archives.seattletimes.nwsource.com*).

22. Stanford, *Victory in Our Schools.*

23. Seattle Public Schools, *Good News: A Quarterly Publication of the Seattle Public Schools Community Relations Office*, no. 2 (fall 2000).

24. See Paul Hill, Christine Campbell, and James Harvey, *It Takes a City: Getting Serious about Urban School Reform* (Washington, DC: Brookings Institution, 2000).

25. Stanford, *Victory in Our Schools*, p. 15.

26. Ruth Teichroeb, "Two Schools Illustrate North-South Divide," *Seattle Post-Intelligencer*, 3 June 1999 (*http://seattlep-i.nwsource.com/local/skul03.shtml*).

27. Stanford, *Victory in Our Schools*, p. 186.

28. Marguerite Roza, "Policy Inadvertently Robs Poor Schools to Benefit the Rich," *Seattle Post-Intelligencer*, 24 September 2000 (*http://seatlep-i.nwsource.com/opinion/focus24.shtml*).

29. Stanford, *Victory in Our Schools*, p. 65.

30. Ruth Teichroeb, "Weak Leaders Threaten John Stanford's Goal of 'World Class' Schools in Seattle, Critics Say," *Seattle Post-Intelligencer*, 13 July 1998 (*http://seattlep-i.nwsource.com/awards/principal/princl.shtml*).

31. Ibid.

32. Debera Harrell, "Demotions of Principals Send Message to Improve," *Seattle Post-Intelligencer*, 17 May 2000 (*http://seatlep-i.nwsource.com/local/prin17.shtml*).

33. Keith Ervin, "Rainier Beach Principal Paid $173,500 by District to Resign," *Seattle Post-Intelligencer*, 18 September 2000 (*http://archives.seattletimes. nwsource.com*).

34. Rebekah Denn, "Special Education Chief Quits," *Seattle Post-Intelligencer*, 3 March 2001 (*http://seattlep-i.nwsource.com/local/resign03.shtml*).

35. Seattle Education Association, *Seattle Education Association and Seattle Public Schools Launch Mentor Program*, undated flyer to SEA membership.

36. Interview with former Seattle Education Association leader, 28 April 2001.

37. William Sanders and Sandra Horn, "The Tennessee Value-Added Assessment System: Mixed-Model Methodology in Educational Assessment," *Journal of Personnel Evaluation in Education*, 8 (3): 299–311 (October 1994).

38. Interview with principal, 17 April 2001.

39. Interviews with principals, teacher, and former union leader, 17 April 2001, and 28 April 2001.

40. Michael Fullan, *The New Meaning of Educational Change* (New York: Teachers College Press, 1991).

41. Debera Harrell, "Demotions of Principals."

42. Rebekah Denn, "Garfield High Again Seeks Principal after Day Reconsiders," *Seattle Post-Intelligencer*, 26 May 2001 (*http://seattlep-i.nwsource.com/local/24816_garfield26.shtml*).

43. Rebekah Denn, "Parents Challenge Seattle Schools' Race Rule," *Seattle Post-Intelligencer*, 29 March 2001 (*http://seattlep-i.nwsource.com/local/parents29.shtml*).

44. Marshall Smith and Jennifer O'Day, "Systemic School Reform," *Politics of Education Association Yearbook, 1990* (1991): 233–267.

45. Institute for Educational Leadership, *Leadership for Student Learning: Reinventing the Principalship*, Report of the Task Force on the Principalship (Washington, DC: Institute for Educational Leadership, October 2000 [*http://www.iel.org*]). Rebekah Denn, "Seattle Schools See Need to Hire 2000 New Teachers," *Seattle Post-Intelligencer*, March 9, 2001 (*http://seattlep-i.nwsource.com/local/staffing09.shtml*).

46. Interviews with teachers and principals, 17 April 2001.

47. Larry Cuban, *How Can I Fix It? An Educator's Road Map* (New York: Teachers College Press, 2001).

48. Interviews with teachers and principals, 17 April 2001.

49. Gary Yee, *Miracle Workers Wanted: Executive Succession and Organizational Change in an Urban School District* (Ph.D. diss., Stanford University, 1995). See also Marcus Foster, *Making Schools Work* (Philadelphia: Westminster Press, 1974).

50. Barbara McCloud and Floretta McKenzie, "School Boards and Superintendents in Urban Districts," *Phi Delta Kappan,* 75 (January 1994): 384–385.

51. Other cases include Waldemar Rojas (San Francisco and Dallas); Ramon Cortines (San Francisco and New York City); and Laval Wilson (Berkeley and Boston).

52. Larry Cuban, *The Managerial Imperative and the Practice of Leadership in Schools* (Albany: State University of New York Press, 1988).

53. Marc Ramirez, "Keeping His Vision Alive," *Seattle Times,* 3 December 1998, p. C3.

Chapter 4

FAST AND TOP-DOWN: SYSTEMIC REFORM AND STUDENT ACHIEVEMENT IN SAN DIEGO CITY SCHOOLS

Larry Cuban and Michael Usdan

If dramatically changing a school system is like turning around an aircraft carrier, Alan Bersin, San Diego school superintendent and former U.S. Attorney and "Border Czar" for the Southwest region, said in his first year, "the carrier hasn't changed course yet, but it's shimmying." By the fourth year, amid stormy weather, the carrier had clearly changed direction.[1]

This chapter details the San Diego story of a noneducator leading the eighth largest school district in the nation's largest state where governors, state superintendents, and legislatures have mandated reforms unrelentingly over the past 2 decades.[2]

Four years into the superintendency of a former U.S. Attorney (appointed by a Democratic President) in a largely conservative city dominated by Republicans and business interests, key features of Alan Bersin's tenure include:

- Gained support for a $1.5 billion bond referendum to build and repair schools (78% voted for it).
- Renovated district bureaucracy to realign staffing, budgets, and practitioner roles at the district, school, and classroom levels to be consistent with the stated mission of improving "student achievement by supporting teaching and learning in the classroom."
- Established district expectations and mechanisms for teachers and principals to keep learning as professionals, gaining further expertise to concentrate on improving student performance in literacy and math.[3]

Continual conflicts between the superintendent and the school board minority and between the San Diego Education Association (SDEA) and the superintendent have altered both the substance and pace of the changes. Since the early months of his superintendency, Bersin has managed to retain a slim 3–2 majority on key votes authorizing new programs, reorganizations, and reallocation of funds and personnel. Union leadership has been at loggerheads with Bersin over the lack of collaboration or even consultation since the superintendent launched a fleet of changes within the first 6 months of his tenure. As the SDEA president said: "It is reform being done *to* us, not *with* us." Bersin, predictably, sees the situation differently: "SDEA leadership, virtually from day one, has greeted reform here with the unremitting hostility of a 'Khrushchev's Nyet.'"[4]

Amid the unremitting conflicts, the superintendent has received strong and abiding support from the city's business and civic leaders, who had originally engineered the choice of the former prosecutor.

These substantial victories and disruptive conflicts have exacted a high price. Fear and mistrust of Bersin's motives and the reforms persist among many administrators and teachers, the very people who are responsible daily for improving student performance. Major demonstrations drawing thousands of teachers organized by the union to protest how teacher-coaches were to be chosen and the firing of 600 teacher aides testify to the open antagonism that has erupted. Moreover, high school faculties' and administrators' sluggishness for the reform has left secondary schools, as is the case in most cities, in the backwater of the district changes.[5]

Thus a new superintendent's swift moves have grafted onto a large urban district powerful reforms that show signs of sprouting the desired fruits. Yet in 2002 it still remains a frail growth with shallow roots.

The San Diego story poses tough questions about the prevailing assumptions and wisdom of governance trends in big city school districts vying to improve students' test scores. These questions challenge corporate leaders, civic officials, and educators in other cities committed to wedding business support and expertise to political clout in squeezing better teaching out of urban practitioners and higher test scores out of low-performing students. Questions for other urban districts that arise from the San Diego reforms (1998–2002) are these:

1. Can a noneducator superintendent establish a new infrastructure for teaching and learning and create a professional culture that concentrates on improving academic achievement of low-performing students?
2. Can a noneducator's top-down, fast-paced strategy of implementing a new infrastructure for teaching and learning instill the necessary commitment among practitioners to sustain the reform while erasing their initial fears and mistrust over this centralized, accelerated approach to change?[6]

In this chapter we will describe the key features of the San Diego reforms noted above and offer answers to the questions just listed. We begin with the choice of Alan Bersin to lead the system, a decision orchestrated by civic and business leaders frustrated by the system's inability to raise student achievement.

CHOOSING A NONEDUCATOR

Interviews, newspaper accounts, and research studies strikingly converge in telling the story of how in 1998 a Democratic appointee who had cracked down on border crime got named as the new superintendent in a city historically controlled by the Republican party.

By the mid-1990s, among civic and business leaders, there was a growing sense of a paralyzed school system controlled by a sclerotic bureaucracy more concerned about the square footage and number of windows in their offices then students' academic performance. "It was a system," one administrator said, "built to satisfy adults, not serve children." A teachers' strike in 1996 revealed to these civic and corporate elites that the then superintendent, a veteran popular educator who had risen through the ranks, was no longer in control of the system. Committed to a strategy of decentralization, five clusters of schools led by assistant superintendents at the "Ed Center," as the headquarters of the district was called, varied greatly in academic performance. Moreover, the system's prior leadership had been committed to school-site management (as had the teachers' union that had negotiated the concept into the contract), further decentralizing management of the district. It seemed to these civic and business leaders that neither the bureaucracy nor the union attended adequately enough to students' academic performance. The *San Diego Union Tribune* put it bluntly: The district "was run by bureaucrats who had become numb to the public at the same time [as] the public has clearly grown anxious for major reforms in education." These elite groups (Business Roundtable of the San Diego Chamber of Commerce, corporate foundations, and civic officials) wanted an "agent of change."[7]

What needed to be changed and why did these changes matter? These local leaders were close to unanimous in their answers: Install a fearless manager who knows how to run a large organization. Dismantle the bureaucracy that smothered progress in schools and classrooms. Concentrate on raising academic achievement, particularly of those students who have been performing poorly.

But why should the district concentrate on improving student achievement? Again, our sources largely agreed on the reasons for this focus. Corporate leaders sought to maintain a vital downtown and avert satellite cities springing up elsewhere like their neighboring megalopolis to the north. Moreover, unless the city retained its unique and sizable white and minority middle and upper-middle class (estimated at better than a third of the city) and had a literate workforce ready and able to step into twenty-first-century jobs in an information-based economy, San Diego would become just another decaying city. Community leaders wanted public schools that would keep young families in the city. Employers wanted schools they could point to with pride in recruiting managers. Both wanted schools that prepared students with entry-level job skills or for further education. Public schools were the linchpin in the larger urban strategy of keeping San Diego a thriving city.[8]

In 1997, the school board hired a search firm to generate candidates for the superintendency. In reviewing applicants, the company used a "white paper" drafted by a small committee drawn from the Chamber of Commerce's Business Roundtable that clearly left open the option of a new superintendent being a noneducator. The board then appointed two committees. One was composed of five civic and corporate leaders without professional educators or union members (the head of the city's YMCA, a wealthy businessman, an African American former city councilman, a university president, and a Latino community leader). This committee was charged to interview and recommend finalists to the school board adhering to the strictest confidentiality in the process. Another committee, composed of 32 community members and educators (teacher union members refused to participate on this committee because of their exclusion from the smaller one), developed "profiles" of expectations for a new superintendent. They played no role in recruiting, interviewing, or naming the finalists. The smaller civic and corporate committee recommended two candidates, Peter Negroni and Alan Bersin, to the school board. After interviewing both, the board voted 4–0 (with one abstention) to appoint Bersin. Named as the incoming superintendent in March 1998, Bersin created a transition team and spent 3 months visiting schools and community groups, and gaining intelligence about the district. Just before formally assuming all duties as superintendent, Bersin named Anthony Alvarado, then superintendent of District #2 in New York City, as Chancellor of Instruction.

In New York City, Alvarado had, for over a decade, orchestrated multiple changes in principals and teachers, a great deal of professional development, and, with close ties to the United Federation of Teachers, a district office committed to helping practitioners teach and students learn. Test scores in the district had risen over that period. Alvarado became Chancellor of Instruction under Bersin in June 1998 with the express charge to apply what he had learned in District #2 to San Diego, a district almost five times larger, and to do so in less than a decade. Basically, Bersin and Alvarado were betting that the scale and time issues could be managed.

In creating a bifurcated superintendency, Bersin split a school chief's customary three roles, delegating control of instruction to Alvarado and assuming the political and managerial roles himself.[9]

We now turn to the main features marking the initial 3 years of the San Diego reform.

ACTIONS TAKEN

A top-down, fast-paced reform strategy jolted the entire system (18,000 employees for 146,000 students spending nearly one billion dollars a year) into achieving notable gains. Within 6 months, Bersin had gained voter approval for $1.5 billion in bonds to build new schools and renovate older ones and scrapped the 15-year-old decentralized managerial and instructional organization of the district.

Reaching out to the larger community and cementing relationships with business and civic elites, the newly minted superintendent scored a stunning triumph in securing an unheard of 78% approval for the bond measure. Internally, Bersin sought managerial control. In place of the old organization, Bersin reorganized the Ed Center to centralize authority in his office while creating an Institute for Learning under Alvarado that concentrated on converting the district's assistant superintendents and principals from managers into instructional leaders and focused teachers' attention on literacy.

The reorganization of the Ed Center involved cutting staff by 18% and produced $8.3 million in savings during the first 2 years. The savings went to the new Institute for Learning and the seven Instructional Leaders (ILs), all recruited from the ranks of principals and Ed Center staff, who were responsible for 175 schools. A few months later, Bersin sent shock waves through administrative ranks by reassigning 15 school administrators to other posts including classroom teaching. After a bruising struggle with the SDEA and a 3–2 school board approval, Bersin and Alvarado placed 85 peer coaches (drawn from the corps of teachers and funded by the savings from headquarter's reorganization) in over 115 schools, particularly those with students scoring in the lowest quartiles on standardized tests. These teacher-coaches helped teachers and principals implement literacy (and later math) strategies in their classrooms. Following much school board and public criticism over the new superintendent's failure to implement a 1997 school board policy on ending social promotion, Bersin and Alvarado drafted a districtwide Blueprint for Student Success in a Standards Based System that included strategies for preventing student academic failure, interventions and remediation when students performed poorly, and retention policies. For the Institute of Learning, peer coaches, principals, and teachers working on literacy and math, the Blueprint became an essential trail guide to follow.[10]

All of these initiatives spilled across the system in 18 months. As Bersin said, "There was no other way to jumpstart systemic reform. You don't announce it. You've got to jolt the system. I understood that. . . . [I]f people don't understand you're serious about change . . . the bureaucracy will own you." In the same vein, Alvarado said:

> There has to be a boom . . . in large-scale reform. . . . The boom doesn't have to be a political boom, but it has to be an organizational boom. . . . [and] after you go boom,

you need to adjust how you pace and organize . . . so there becomes a regularity and that people know what to expect.[11]

Unrelenting top-down managerial direction at an accelerator-to-the-floor pace (Bersin's phrase for the pace was "not reckless but fearless") captures both the theory and action of these district reformers.[12]

Certainly, other big city superintendents and school boards have boasted about a reform bonanza in a compressed time period. The crucial test for those who brag, however, is seldom the announced initiatives, but rather evidence that the reforms have the necessary resources and are being implemented in schools and classrooms. In establishing the Institute for Learning as a vehicle for converting all principals into instructional leaders, recruiting and training peer coaches, and offering the broadest array of opportunities for teachers to learn literacy and math practices that San Diego had ever seen, Bersin and Alvarado converted words swiftly into deeds. They mobilized political and economic resources to consolidate the reforms they had so swiftly launched.

Our interviews with staff developers, principals, and top administrators, Amy Hightower's dissertation, and reports from independent evaluator Barbara Neufeld, who was hired by the district, suggest strongly that the reorganization of the bureaucracy, the reallocation of funds, the creation of the Institute for Learning with seven newly appointed Instructional Leaders, reassignment of principals, teacher coaches, the Blueprint for Student Success—all amid stormy conflict with the teachers' union—have indeed changed the aircraft carrier's course toward the desired port. Insofar as we can interpret the limited evidence, we see the beginnings of a genuine district culture of professional norms that concentrates upon teaching and learning and raising students' academic performance. Considering the history of urban school reform in the last quarter-century, such outcomes, if they are consolidated and sustained, represent notable successes for a big city school district.[13]

Continual conflicts between the superintendent and the school board and between the San Diego teachers' union and the superintendent, however, have produced accommodations in both the substance and pace of the changes.

If the electroshock treatment applied by Bersin and Alvarado to the San Diego system sufficiently jarred the system for the superintendent and his chancellor to secure rapid successes, disruptive conflicts accompanied each victory. Certainly Bersin and his allies outside of the system expected conflict to occur. Rapid changes of the magnitude that Bersin sought guaranteed a certain level of active resistance from those who believed that they were already doing their best under trying conditions and those who wanted to protect their interests. Both Bersin and Alvarado knew that in splitting the roles that superintendents customarily perform, Bersin's job was to buffer Alvarado from external and internal political conflicts for the latter's instructional design to take hold. Conflict is inevitable when a new superintendent is hired to be "an agent of change" and is "fearless" in hammering his agenda onto an entire system.

Yet two conflicts that emerged at the very beginning of Bersin's tenure have persisted through 4 years. A continuing 3–2 division on the school board and the teachers' union's aggressive opposition to Bersin's agenda threaten the survival of the instructional reforms. We discuss each of these conflicts briefly.

THE 3–2 SCHOOL BOARD SPLIT

In San Diego, the five-member elected board is independent politically and fiscally of the mayor and city council. Both the mayor and council appear to be only marginally involved in school matters and certainly are not major players.

As the independent, elected school board, it appointed Bersin on a 4–0 vote with one abstention. Frances Zimmerman, the member who chose to abstain, joined John de Beck to become early critics and then, with teacher union support, opponents of the superintendent's agenda ever since. Ron Ottinger, Sue Braun, and Edward Lopez have largely endorsed the direction Bersin was taking the district. On key appointments and major initiatives proposed by Bersin since 1998, from hiring Alvarado to the Blueprint for Student Success, board members have debated, sometimes acrimoniously, and then eventually split, giving the superintendent a slim margin of victory.[14]

Occasionally a 3–2 vote on a matter was shaky because one member of the majority expressed reservations about the decision. Staff members told us that this divisiveness and predictable split, over time not only made presentations to the board difficult but also shaped their recommendations to Bersin and Alvarado. Moreover, both the superintendent and chancellor had become more cautious and accommodating in their responses to opposition either on the board, or among administrators and teachers. Their comments to us suggested that their institutional radar picked up potential conflicts far better than in the initial years and they could now make midcourse shifts in developing new policies and implementing existing ones to avoid some out-and-out public fights over noncritical issues.[15]

Board members disliked the rancor and the personalizing of conflicts. When three incumbent board members ran for reelection in 2000, including Frances Zimmerman, a persistent critic of Bersin, the bitterness escalated. A private group of business leaders and supporters of the Bersin administration recruited a candidate to oppose Zimmerman. They raised substantial amounts of money (over $500,000) far exceeding what is customarily spent on school board elections ($40,000) and ran ads that urged voters to reject Zimmerman because of her opposition to the superintendent's agenda. Media opinion and interviewees felt that the ad campaign was overkill and the huge amount of money for a school board election put Zimmerman in an underdog situation, contributing to her victory, albeit one in which she barely edged out her opponent. Ed Lopez and Ron Ottinger, the other incumbent board members, were reelected by wide margins reflecting the broad support Bersin's reforms have garnered in the San Diego community.[16]

The 3–2 majority supporting Bersin remains intact following the election. The next election is in 2002. The rancor has even increased over the errant E-mail sent by board president Sue Braun suggesting, tongue-in-cheek, that both of her colleagues be shot dead. Braun's apology and resignation as board president, but not from the board itself, hardly diminished the heated exchanges. The *Union-Tribune*, supportive of Bersin's reform agenda since his appointment editorialized that the board behaves in public meetings "like a dysfunctional family locked in an endless vendetta."[17] No one can predict with any certainty whether the majority will continue after 2002, grow to 4–1, or shift against Bersin. For two of these three possibilities in the immediate future, board-superintendent conflict deepened by past animosities remains a given. There is little question in our minds that should events transpire that produce a majority against Bersin, he and Alvarado would depart and the direction of the reforms would unalterably shift.

SAN DIEGO EDUCATION ASSOCIATION VS. BERSIN

The struggle between the teachers union and Alan Bersin also mirrors the fault line for divisions within the school board. Conflict arose shortly after the ex–U.S. Attorney's appointment. The SDEA had worked closely with Bersin's predecessors in planning and implementing school reforms over the previous decade. The union had favored school-site decision making and had negotiated the reform into the contract. The 1996 teachers strike, however, convinced business and civic leaders that a major change in the district's direction had to occur. In appointing Bersin, the city's business leaders took the initiative and the union was relegated to the sidelines. Within 3 months of Bersin's entering the Ed Center, SDEA leadership realized that the earlier collaboration with the administration and the union in reforming schools would no longer be the case. "SDEA," Bersin later said, "no longer held or wielded veto power over changes proposed in the status quo. This meant a fundamental shift in relationships that union leaders could not and would not accept."[18]

After 3 years of sharp-edged tension that most observers—including ourselves—would agree has become both polarized and personal, there is little hope that the SDEA and the superintendent would drop their swords and beat them into plowshares to till the district together. Acrimonious exchanges between SDEA President Marc Knapp and Alan Bersin have ebbed and flowed during and after the conflicts over selecting and placing peer coaches, firing 600 teacher aides to fund a portion of the Blueprint for Student Success, and numerous other controversial episodes. The SDEA rallied thousands of teachers to oppose the superintendent's selection of peer coaches and firing teacher aides. The *SDEA Advocate*, the union newsletter, provided a monthly pulpit to president Marc Knapp for pointing out how the superintendent's reform agenda harms teachers. One example taken from his remarks on the Institute for Learning in the November 1999 issue gives the overall flavor of his columns:

> What amazes me most about the Institute's Fix-The-Broken-Educator-And-You-Will-Fix-The-Child scapegoat approach is that it is misguided and ignores problems like poverty, attendance, health care, second language learners, etc. . . . Why in the name of all that's sane, would the Institute heap mounds of unwarranted criticism on educators and believe that it would be able to attract anyone to a profession that already depends on the personal self-sacrifice from all its practitioners? We may be naïve but we aren't stupid.[19]

Yet the SDEA agreed to a 2-year extension of their contract in mid-2000. In the light of this intense conflict-ridden history, how could this cooperation occur? According to the superintendent, "sustaining and enhancing the instructional strategy in place, over time, will attract most teachers sufficiently to gain their loyalty to the reform. A more cooperative union leadership stance will then follow." Thus, the SDEA sought the extension to protect benefits for 2 years while avoiding a showdown it did not believe it could win with the administration. To the union leadership, however, extending the contract was a smart move because they believed that Bersin and company will have exited after 2002 or, in the angry words of one union leader, the "bozos will be gone."[20]

We cannot determine which version best explains the agreement. We do know that the conventional wisdom about reforming big city schools is that for reform to succeed, the local union has to work closely with top administrators and the board of education. Alvarado's experience in New York City with unions leads him to agree with the popular wisdom, but he raised an important question:

> Everybody almost assumes that all the players have to be on board in the reform. One of the reasons why it is so hard is because you can never get all of the stars aligned, and, therefore, that's why you don't get reform. The real question is: is that really true? I . . . have always said that the union has to be on board. I actually believe that [having] the union on board makes it easier and may even result in more powerful implementation of reform. The question is: if one of the players is not on board, can you still do reform?[21]

Bersin and Alvarado are gambling that the answer is yes. It is risky. Much less of a gamble in this conflict with the SDEA, however, is retaining the loyalty of the San Diego business community, which is not particularly supportive of unionism.

Eites' Support

The city's business and civic leaders who brought Bersin to San Diego continue to support him. Interviewees and media opinion agree that Bersin has moved with dispatch in reforming the city's schools and is making solid progress. Although some individuals expressed dismay with the aggressive styles of the superintendent and his chancellor, the deeply personal conflicts with the teachers' union leaders, and the annoyances of noisy school board opponents, most praised the superintendent for his leadership and managerial effectiveness in such a brief time. Few doubt—including Bersin and Alvarado—that without the explicit and, in some instances, covert support of these business and civic elites, the district reforms would last no longer than an April morning's dew on a beautifully manicured lawn at Point Loma.[22]

Tangible support from these elites for Bersin became public at the time of his appointment. Since then constant conflicts with the school board over administrative decisions made it apparent to many corporate and civic supporters of school reform that the thinness of a 3–2 majority jeopardized reform momentum. But the group's effort to unseat Frances Zimmerman, a vocal opponent of the superintendent, failed. Revealing the limitations that business elites face in influencing district policies, the school board still remains divided. Bersin asked the board in December 2000 to reappoint Alvarado until 2004. The superintendent glowed in his remarks: "The improvements we have seen across the board in student achievement during the past 2 years are directly attributable to the reforms that have been put in place, in large part through the efforts of Chancellor Alvarado." The board's response was the customary 3–2 vote in favor of the superintendent's recommendation.[23]

Another instance of business leaders' open support for Bersin occurred when Bersin initially chose Alvarado to become his chancellor. A number of thorny issues arose concerning the New York native's living arrangements in San Diego. During his first 18 months, Alvarado commuted weekly from the East Coast. Costs for all of this air travel and maintaining dual apartments for this period had to be covered. Using public funds to supplement Alvarado's salary would have been unseemly so a small group of businessmen stepped in and raised private funds to subsidize these costs until Alvarado moved to San Diego permanently in the fall of 2000.[24]

Both Bersin and Alvarado recognize that support from the city's political and business leaders has been essential in their quest for broad and deep systemic reform to improve student achievement. Yet both also realize that they have paid a price for this support and for the swift pace of their reform agenda. The costs exacted from continual conflicts with the school board and the SDEA have already been noted. Less clear is the collateral damage to morale and trust.[25]

FURTHER DAMAGES FROM CONSTANT CONFLICT

Fear and distrust of Bersin's motives and the reforms persists among many administrators and teachers, the very people who do the daily work of running schools and teaching students. In the first 2 years when Bersin reassigned Ed

Center administrators, transferred principals, openly tangled with the SDEA over peer coaches, fired 600 teacher aides, and reorganized the instructional side of the district into the Institute for Learning under Alvarado, morale deteriorated greatly, according to many interviewees, newspaper reports, and a series of in-depth reports from Barbara Neufeld, an independent evaluator hired by the district. Neufeld, who had conducted evaluations in the district's middle schools since 1993, drew the following conclusions from extensive interviews with middle school principals and teachers in June 1999: Although most of the teachers and principals she spoke with endorsed the direction and content of the reforms,

> they objected to the top-down process, the speed with which they were to make sig-nificant changes, the increased sense that their work was being monitored for com-pliance more than for support, and, in light of this, the fact that the professional development they had received was insufficient to enable them to effectively imple-ment the new strategies.

Former elementary school principal Ernie McCray agreed: "While there have been some positives under Alan, he's introduced an undercurrent of disrespect that is corrosive."[26]

Yet a year later, Neufeld and her colleagues interviewed 42 middle school teachers and found that:

> Teachers reported that although the reform remains top-down and is being imple-mented quickly, staff developers [coaches] provide real, appropriately focused pro-fessional development support and they have opportunities to make local adjustments to the strategies in light of their own and their students' needs.[27]

When we asked our interviewees who swore that morale was low among teachers and administrators for evidence of this loss in spirit and spread of fear, they mentioned the increased departure of experienced educators from the dis-trict, the large rallies of teachers protesting superintendent decisions, and dif-ficulties in implementing reforms, particularly in San Diego high schools. Interviewees reported that such exits were common but when we asked for sources to confirm the apparent trend, we only heard stories of several highly regarded individual teachers and principals leaving for posts elsewhere in San Diego county. We did receive data from the superintendent's office and other sources on teacher departures and retirements. The data could neither confirm nor reject the inference that teacher morale had declined, improved, or remained stable since Bersin's appointment.[28]

Thus the evidence we have is both ambiguous and fragmentary in determin-ing how widespread and deep the mistrust of the superintendent's motives and the reforms are in 2002. Much is heavily dependent upon who renders the opin-ions, when the opinions have been offered over the past 4 years of school reform, and which aspect of the reform is being judged.

There was more evidence on high school reform. In speaking of high schools both Bersin ("they are really difficult places to change") and Alvarado ("high schools are bastions of inaction") openly expressed concern over the pace and scope of reforms being implemented after almost 4 years. A top administrator at the Ed Center and veteran of the system who works closely with ILs and principals estimated that of 16 high schools, only 2 "have bought into the reforms." There is evidence beyond these assertions to support the notion, in San Diego as well as in other urban districts, that high schools have been far slower than middle and elementary schools in embracing the K–12 reforms.[29]

In a survey of all San Diego principals (147 responded) conducted by Stanford's Center for the Study of Teaching and Policy in September 2000, high school principals differed substantially from their peers in elementary and middle schools. On the impact of monthly professional meetings for administrators (the"Principal Learning Communities") 96% of elementary school principals gave the innovation high marks while high school principals registered 54% support. On the monthly Principal Conferences, like the Learning Communities an opportunity for professional development, 89% of the elementary school principals rated it highly while 46% of the high school principals did so.[30]

Again, interpreting these figures is dicey. How much of this apparent resistance is due to reactions to Bersin, to the substance, pace, and direction of the district reforms, or due to the very nature of high schools as large, bureaucratic organizations that have a history of independence from district office mandates, or some combination of these factors? Whatever the source of opposition, it is clear that the secondary school piece of the K–12 reform agenda, even with recent efforts to restructure the ninth grade in both curriculum and longer class periods, has still a very long road to travel in getting implemented.[31]

Also clear to us was that the trauma of the initial year apparently left deep marks on those within the system—when administrators were transferred and dismissed, when Ed Center reorganizations uprooted familiar faces, and when reform initiatives spilled over the schools raising expectations that both principals and teachers would alter daily practices in schools and classrooms. We heard from interviewees many stories of victories over entrenched interests within the system, and we heard from the same people stories of casualties and damage. We sensed that the retelling of these stories to us, literally strangers to them, had transformed facts into mythic sagas that reform supporters relished and opponents abhorred.

Still unclear to us is whether the consequences of the "boom" theory of changing the system in the initial year have left raw, unhealed wounds that will continue to fester and undermine both the direction and institutionalizing of these reforms or whether the agenda of change has taken hold among principals and teachers sufficiently for the initial trauma to heal, leaving a few unpleasant but distant memories that will fade as new cadres of teachers and principals enter the system. It is too early to answer this key question.

QUESTIONS THAT NEED ANSWERS

Whether or not there is sufficient commitment to sustain a district-driven reform among the very people who run schools and teach students is, of course, a major question that arises from the San Diego experience, one that bears greatly on urban school reform aimed at improving student academic achievement elsewhere in the nation. We alert readers that our answers to such questions after only 4 years of district-driven reform in San Diego are both tentative and, in some instances, speculative.

1. Can a noneducator superintendent swiftly establish a new infrastructure for teaching and learning and create a professional culture that concentrates on improving academic achievement of low-performing students? For San Diego after 4 years, the answer is yes. In Bersin's splitting his roles with Alvarado to the managerial reorganization of the Ed Center to the allocation of resources—the laserlike focus is on raising academic achievement, particularly of those students in the lowest quartiles. By explicitly delegating to Alvarado exclusive reign over the instructional domain while the superintendent managed the system and shielded his deputy from political fire, Bersin established a bifurcated superintendency. Bersin managed the business, facilities, and operations side of the organization while Alvarado designed and implemented an instructional infrastructure. The Institute for Learning with each of the ILs (one now specifically assigned to high schools) working with approximately 25 principals to be instructional leaders in their schools assisting teachers to implement new programs in literacy and math is in operation. Peer coaches work as staff developers with principals and teachers across the system. Extensive courses for teachers and principals are offered during the year and in the summer. Teachers and principals, mostly in elementary and middle schools, speak the same language when literacy is discussed: "Read Aloud" and "Independent Reading" are part of the vocabulary and teaching repertoire. Walk Throughs and Portfolio Assessments (begun in the early 1990s) are becoming institutionalized forms of accountability that San Diego educators use.

In short, there is now in place an instructional infrastructure sharply focused on helping teachers and principals concentrate on literacy and math with their students. In place also are a Literacy Framework and Principles of Learning that shape how each day is organized, what teachers and principals are expected to do, and expected outcomes for student achievement. In establishing the infrastructure and process, Bersin and Alvarado have also begun to create districtwide norms crucial for an emerging professional culture/In providing coaches for principals and teachers, offering a rich array of literacy and math courses from local, state, national, and international experts, and creating learning communities of principals and teachers the outlines of a district professional culture permeating most San Diego elementary and middle schools has begun to emerge.

The test of this new infrastructure, process, and culture, of course, is whether this combination of elements will, indeed, achieve what Bersin and Alvarado seek: all schools concentrating on teaching literacy and math and the numbers of low-performing students on state tests shrinking as overall achievement in reading and math rise for the district.

After 4 years, much variation in implementing the instructional reforms exists among schools. High schools have already been mentioned. Among middle schools, Neufeld suggests there is more acceptance and action, at least as reported by teachers and principals. Among elementary schools there has been the greatest progress, and even here there is much variation. There are a few schools where the principals are clearly instructional leaders, where the focus on teaching and learning is sharp, the staff has been winnowed and cultivated, and classroom practices and student work are consistent across grades. Then a large group of schools—probably the majority—show improved principal leadership, display reasonable progress in instructional improvement, are deeply involved in professional development, and have in many classrooms high-quality student work. These schools are in the early-to-middle stages of reform.[32]

Finally, there are a small number of schools where academic performance is unsatisfactory. Their staffs vary in eagerness to improve. They have some semblance of principal leadership, and on occasion seek out ways of gaining more knowledge and skills to better educate their students. The ILs spend far more time with these schools because they have the longest distance to travel and are targets for the most improvement. Such variation among schools is expected.[33]

There has been test score improvement and Bersin's supporters have eagerly sought to attribute the gains to the reforms. In July 2000, after the state released SAT-9 scores and there were distinct improvements in elementary school scores for San Diego City Schools, board of education president Edward Lopez said: "The improved test scores reflect the hard work and dedication of teachers and students. Our reforms implemented over the past 2 years are improving the quality of instructional programs across the district." Alan Bersin said: "We are moving in the right direction with our efforts. But we still have a long way to go and we must not forget that."

The Superintendent is correct. It is premature to make a case for the reforms succeeding, particularly after a plateauing of scores in 2001. At his first "State of the District" address, Bersin promised the 700-member audience of teachers, principals, and parents (with 150 protestors picketing outside of the auditorium) that he would pull 29 schools out of the bottom of the state rankings, every student in the class of 2005 would pass California's high school exit exam, college attendance would increase and drop-outs would decrease. Implicitly, Bersin acknowledged that after 5 or more years of state testing, district patterns of students' academic achievement at elementary and secondary levels will emerge far more clearly. For now, to district and school leaders sustaining the infrastructure, process, and culture and its taking hold in San Diego high schools remain the challenge.[34]

2. Can a noneducator superintendent's top-down, fast-paced strategy of implementing a new infrastructure for teaching and learning instill the necessary commitment among practitioners to sustain the reform while erasing their fears and mistrust over the centralized, accelerated approach? Our answer is: We don't know. The strong feelings of fear, anger, and dismay among teachers and administrators generated in the first year of mandates spilling forth from Bersin's and Alvarado's offices have seemingly eased with time, and the opportunities for learning afforded the instructional staff have grown. We note that the emerging culture of professionalism, varied across elementary and secondary schools, has also lessened some of the mistrust. But a large residue remains.

We were surprised by the lack of questions or even interest in Bersin being a noneducator. His quickness in learning the terrain and eagerness to make decisions allayed many concerns of critics outside of the system. His appointment of Alvarado and dividing up the customary roles between him and his deputy has erased many of the doubts about the inevitable stumbles that a noneducator would make.

The question that did dominate our interviews and for which no one had an answer is: How long will Bersin remain as superintendent? It is the crucial question because if the history of urban school reform demonstrates anything, it is that stability in tenure is an essential condition for reforms to be initiated, consolidated, and institutionalized. Five to 7 years is a sufficient amount of time to begin to see emerging patterns of what works, what needs to be dropped, and what needs amending. And, of course, to sample whether the initial fears and distrust have melted away or have congealed into deep opposition. In that period of time, the direction of the Institute for Learning and concentration on teaching and learning will have been sharpened, consolidated, and possibly become self-renewing. Of course, 7 to 10 years (2005 to 2008) offers the optimum chance for a superintendent, staff, parents, and city elites to see what occurs after an entire cohort of students have moved through the grades experiencing the reforms. Judging whether the reforms have had their desired effects after a decade becomes much easier.[35]

In interviews with Bersin and Alvarado, both expressed fierce determination to stay the course, that is, serve beyond 2005. After all, Alvarado's New York City experience in District #2 took a decade for the desired results to become apparent to even the most nearsighted of observers. Were Bersin to fulfill his pledge to remain, the political uncertainty stemming from a split board and fierce union opposition that could cripple the instructional and organizational changes would have had time to dissipate. In recognition of the length of time urban school reform takes, two national foundations in 2001 gave the San Diego schools $22.5 million to underwrite the systemic reforms that the superintendent had launched, but attached a highly unusual condition to the grant: Both Bersin and Alvarado had to remain as school officials during the disbursement of the funds.[36]

In April 2002, the school board extended Bersin's contract to 2006. Yes, the vote in favor of extension, a salary increase and bonuses for meeting performance goals was approved by the all-too-familiar 3–2 division. The school board election later in the year, of course, not this contract extension, will determine whether Bersin and Alvarado do have the time to consolidate the reforms they have launched to improve teaching and learning.

Were a board hostile to Bersin to take office in 2003, it would mean that he would eventually leave before fulfilling his pledge. New school leaders would have little difficulty in pulling up the roots of their predecessor's programs and repeating the familiar, but sad, cycle of urban school reform.[37]

NOTES

1. Tony Perry, "San Diego Schools Hit by Whirlwind," *Los Angeles Times*, 24 June 1999, pp. A1, 25.

2. Marshall Smith and Jennifer O'Day, "Systemic School Reform," *Politics of Education Association Yearbook, 1990* (1991): 233–267; Diane Massell, *The District Role in Building Capacity: Four Strategies*, Policy Brief, RB-32-September (Philadelphia: Consortium for Policy Research in Education, University of Pennsylvania, 2000); Policy Analysis for California Education, *Crucial Issues in California Education 2000: Are the Reform Pieces Fitting Together?* (Berkeley, CA: Author, 2000).

3. Bess Keller, "In San Diego, Pace Is Quick under Bersin," *Education Week*, 4 August 1999, p. 19; mission statement from San Diego City Schools website (*http://www.sandi.net*). We wish to acknowledge the help of Jamie Ginsberg, a parent in the San Diego city schools who sent us many articles from local newspapers and magazines. She is, however, in no way responsible for the interpretations or conclusions in the chapter.

4. Marc Knapp, interview, 19 December 2000; Alan Bersin, phone interview, 28 March 2001.

5. Descriptions of the teacher protests can be found in chapters 5 and 6 of Amy Hightower, "San Diego's Big Boom: Changing District Bureaucracy to Communities of Learning" (Ph.D. diss., Stanford University, 2001). We are indebted to Amy for permitting us to quote from her study of the initial years of Bersin's administration. Concerns over fear and mistrust in addition to mounting attrition came to us from interviews with Alan Bersin, 18 December 2000; Marc Knapp; Robin Whitlow, 19 December 2000; Anthony Alvarado, 20 December 2000; and Charles Nathanson, 19 December 2000.

6. See Richard Elmore and Deanna Burney, *The Challenge of School Variability: Improving Instruction in New York City's Community District #2* (New York: National Commission on Teaching and America's Future: Consortium for Policy Research in Education, 1998).

7. Interviews with Scott Himelstein, 19 December 2000; John Johnson, 19 December 2000; Ron Ottinger, 19 December 2000; Nathanson, 19 December 2000; Terry Smith, 20 December 2000; George Mitrovich, 20 December 2000; and William Lynch, 20 December 2000. Quote from *San Diego Union Tribune*, 10 March 1998, is cited in Hightower draft dissertation, chapter 2, p. 8.

8. Ginger Hovenic, interview, 20 December 2000; Bersin, interview; Hightower, "San Diego's Big Boom"; Neil Peirce and Curtis Johnson, "Growing San Diego's Future Workforce," *San Diego Magazine* 52(1): 89–99 (1999).

9. Ottinger, interview; Knapp, interview; Hightower, "San Diego's Big Boom," pp. 8–19. For an analysis of the superintendent roles, see Larry Cuban, *The Managerial Imperative and the Practice of Leadership in Schools* (Albany: State University of New York Press, 1988), chapter 5. Alvarado had created a sterling reputation as a vigorous, conceptually astute administrator of his high-poverty K–8 community district in New York City. After almost a decade, he had created an instructional infrastructure and professional culture that supported teaching and learning. Academic achievement had climbed from one of the lowest scoring districts to second in the city by 1997. See Elmore and Burney, "Challenge of School Variability."

10. Interviews with Bersin; Alvarado; Ann Van Sickle, Debbie Beldock, Stacy Jones, Staci Monreal, 19 December 2000; Kathy Ford, Wendy Ranck-Buhr, and Cherissa Krieder, 20 December 2000. Tamar Lewin, "Educators Are Bypassed As School System Leaders," *New York Times*, 8 June 2000, pp. 1, 20; Bess Keller, "In San Diego," pp. 1, 19; Maureen Magee, "Major School Overhaul Proposed," *San Diego Union-Tribune*, 14 December 1999, pp. 1, 13; Perry, "San Diego Schools."

11. Bersin quote is from chapter 1 of Hightower, "San Diego's Big Boom"; Alvarado "boom" quote also in Hightower. In 1984, Ross Perot, appointed by Governor Mark White to lead a reform task force to overhaul the state school system, announced that "we've got to drop a bomb on them, we got to nuke them—that's the way to make changes in these organizations" (quoted by Linda McNeil, *Contradictions of School Reform: Educational Costs of Standardized Testing* [New York: Routledge, 2000], p. 186; see also pp. 153–188).

12. Bersin, interview.

13. See Frederick M. Hess, *Spinning Wheels: The Politics of Urban School Reform* (Washington, DC: Brookings Institution, 1999), chapters 1, 4, and 8; see also Richard Elmore, *Building a New Structure for School Leadership* (Washington, DC: Albert Shanker Institute, 2000).

14. Tensions among the split board heated up even more in mid-October 2001 when board president Sue Braun, one of the three-member majority, in an E-mail following an especially contentious 8-hour board meeting, suggested humorously that civility at board meetings might increase if both members were shot: "I was thinking

of a way to get them both with one bullet, but now think they are each too heavy for that to work." Coming on the heels of shooting deaths at a county high school and growing anger at the board's incivility at meetings, the ensuing uproar over the publication of the E-mail message led to Braun's apologies and resignation from the presidency of the board, although she retained her position as board member. Ben Fox, "San Diego School Official's E-mail Suggests Colleagues Be Shot," *Sacramento Bee*, 8 October 2001. Subsequent media attention and an avalanche of editorials and letters to the *San Diego Union-Tribune* editor calling the board a "civic disgrace" led to proposals for the mayor of San Diego to intervene with the board and save Bersin's reforms ("Fix School Board, Mayor Murphy Can Play Vital Role," editorial, 17 October 2001).

15. Interviews with Monreal; Bersin; Smith; Ottinger; and Fran Zimmerman, 19–20 December 2000.

16. Tony Perry, "Ads Spark Backlash in School Race," *Los Angeles Times*, 17 October 2000; Barbara Whitaker, "Business Groups That Back Superintendent Spend Big in San Diego School Board Race," *New York Times*, 25 October 2000, p. A16; Maureen Magee, "Zimmerman Wins Tight Race with Dubick," *San Diego Union-Tribune*, 8 November 2000, p. 1; interviews with Johnson, Lynch, Himelstein, and Mitrovich.

17. Editorial, "Dysfunctional Family," *San Diego Union-Tribune*, 17 October 2001.

18. Interviews with Knapp, Whitlow, Bersin, Nathanson, and Ottinger.

19. Interviews with Bersin, Smith, Zimmerman, Knapp, and Whitlow; San Diego Education Association, "Presidents [sic] Column," November 1999 (*http://www.sdea.net/column_pres/1199.html*).

20. Interviews with Bersin, Smith, Alvarado, Nathanson, and Knapp. Phone interview with Bersin.

21. Hightower, "San Diego's Big Boom."

22. See editorials, "Bersin's Rookie Year," *San Diego Union-Tribune*, 6 August 1999, and "A Brilliant Pipe Dream," *San Diego Union-Tribune*, 19 December 1999; interviews with Bersin, Alvarado, Nathanson, Ottinger, Lynch, and Mitrovich.

23. Interviews with Johnson, Zimmerman, Himelstein; quote on Alvarado comes from San Diego City Schools Communications Office, "News Release," 12 December 2000.

24. Interviews with Bersin, Lynch, and Mitrovich.

25. Interviews with Bersin and Alvarado.

26. Barbara Neufeld and Judy Swanson, *San Diego City Schools Update Report* (Cambridge, MA: Education Matters, 1999), p. 2; McCray quote is in Perry, "San Diego Schools," p. A26.

27. Barbara Neufeld, *Implementing Standards-Based Reforms in San Diego City Schools Update Report* (Cambridge, MA: Education Matters, 2000), p. 3.

28. We asked Superintendent Bersin for data on whether the rates for teachers and administrators leaving the system since 1998 was stable, increasing, or decreas-

ing. We received a table listing retirements of teachers, principals, and other staff between 1996–2000. The number of teacher retirements had more than doubled (from 64 in 1997–1998 to 146 in 1999–2000). Not only are these figures a tiny fraction of the teacher corps, but without data from the 1980s and early 1990s and information about the age profile of district teachers and state and local incentives for retirement, it is premature to attribute increases in retirement to a new administration. Teacher resignations increased from 196 in 1996–1997 to 347 in 1999 and then dropped to 273 in 2000–2001. Again, without information on prior years and the age profile of the teacher corps, connecting increases for resignations to Bersin is, at best, dicey. The number of principals retiring dropped from 8 in 1996–1997 to 4 in 1999–2000 (memo from Bersin to Cuban and Usdan, 10 April 2001). Data on teacher retirements and resignations, 1996–2001, are in Joanne Gribble, "Unbridled Passion or New York Pushiness?" *San Diego Metropolitan, http://www.sandiegometrocom/2001/sept/coverstory.html* (2001).

29. Interviews with Bersin, Alvarado, and Monreal. Phone interview with Bersin.

30. Milbrey McLaughlin, Joan Talbert, Amy Hightower, and Jeannette LaFors, *San Diego Principal Survey Summary* (Stanford, CA: Stanford University, Center for the Study of Teaching and Policy, 2000).

31. For the uproar over the introduction of a physics course that all ninth graders must take, see Maureen Magee, "S.D. Schools Delay Plan on Physics Requisite," *San Diego Union-Tribune*, 24 April 2001, p. 1. See also Maureen Magee, "San Diego Granted $8 Million to Reform High Schools," *San Diego Union-Tribune*, 12 October 2001, for a grant from the Carnegie Corporation and the Bill and Melinda Gates Foundations that gave the city schools and six other cities funds to revamp their high schools by working directly with students about curriculum, instruction, and school organization.

32. Neufeld, *Implementing Standards-Based Reforms*; Monreal, interview.

33. See Elmore and Burney, "Challenge of School Variability."

34. San Diego City Schools Communications Office, "News Release," 17 July 2000. Bersin's address is summarized in Jill Spielvogel and David Graham, "First 'State of the District' Speech Fails to Placate Foes," *San Diego Union-Tribune*, 5 April 2002, p. 1.

35. Michael Fullan, *The New Meaning of Educational Change* (New York: Teachers College Press, 1991); Hess, *Spinning Wheels*; Gary Yee and Larry Cuban, "When Is Tenure Long Enough? A Historical Analysis of Superintendent Turnover and Tenure in Urban School Districts," *Educational Administration Quarterly*, 32 (Supplement): 615–641 (1996).

36. Maureen Magee, "School Reform Gets Private Boost," *San Diego Union-Tribune*, 6 November 2001. The two funders are the Bill and Melinda Gates Foundation and the William and Flora Hewlett Foundation.

37. Interviews with Bersin and Alvarado.

Chapter 5

A TALL ORDER FOR PHILADELPHIA'S NEW APPROACH TO SCHOOL GOVERNANCE:

Heal the Political Rifts, Close the Budget Gap, *and* Improve the Schools

William Lowe Boyd and Jolley Bruce Christman

Perhaps the job of superintendent is too much for any one individual. With the exception of Connie Clayton, most of Philadelphia's school superintendents have left under a cloud of shame.
              Editorial, *Philadelphia Daily News*, 14 August 2000

Whatever our failures, they're not for lack of a good educational plan. Children Achieving is one of the best in the country. Our challenges are a lack of public will to educate our city's children and a lack of capacity to successfully implement our plan. . . . David Hornbeck is the most thorough and thoughtful school reformer in the country. But I've learned that knowing what you need to do is not the same as getting it done. It's a matter of the huge scale. For example, our school district has the second largest transportation system in the state. We're looking at the business model of leadership. It appeals to me. I want someone who has experience running a big, complex organization and who will allow educators to do their job.
Pedro Ramos, Philadelphia Board of Education President, 5 March 2001

In 1994 David Hornbeck came to Philadelphia determined to do what "no city with any significant number and diversity of students" had ever done before: help "a large proportion of its young people achieve at high levels."[1] In his 6 years as superintendent of the seventh largest school district in the country, Hornbeck aggressively implemented an ambitious and controversial standards-based reform plan called Children Achieving. His message, "All students can achieve at high levels," his complex plan, and his passionate style made public education a frequent front page story in a city where "there used to be despair and no attention [to schools]."[2]

Unfortunately, Hornbeck's success in getting people's attention, improving student achievement on standardized tests, and making accountability the centerpiece of his reform plan was offset by his lack of political skill in dealing with key constituencies. Like all urban superintendents, of course, he faced many problems—political, financial, and educational. But his confrontational approach in dealing with his key funders—the state legislature and Republican governor Tom Ridge—and his failure to inspire and engage frontline school staff—teachers and principals—increasingly exasperated even those who admired his vision and persistence. Ultimately, in the face of a huge budget deficit and declining political support in the Philadelphia business and civic community, Hornbeck resigned, on 5 June 2000, rather than oversee the dismantling of his vision for improving the achievement of all Philadelphia children.

This case study examines how Philadelphia shifted its approach to governing the school district in order to cope with its political and budgetary problems and the increasing threat of a state takeover. Philadelphia's shift to a corporate model of district management plus greater mayoral involvement in school governance paralleled patterns in a number of cities. But features of the proposed state takeover were unique, especially the possibilities of overall management of the school system by a for-profit firm (Edison Schools) and/or dividing the system into tiers of schools, in one of which schools would be managed by partnerships between community and for-profit organizations.[3] We address the following central questions: What factors and actors drove the modifications in district governance and leadership, including the unprecedented proposals from the state? How did key players and constituencies negotiate their roles and relationships during the transitional months? What were the early effects and consequences of the initial governance changes?

Although Hornbeck's weaknesses in negotiating political relationships and in managing the district and its budget were the most visible factors leading to a stronger mayoral role and the adoption of the corporate governance model, deeper currents of change were also significant:

A greatly increased role for state government in local districts.
The turn to market forces and school choice as a remedy for dysfunctional schools.

A new urban economy that has changed the city's corporate community and
   its relationship to civic life.

We begin with a chronology of key events that shaped the story of what
happened in Philadelphia during these years. We then turn to a more detailed
discussion of the issues and principal actors and groups involved in the new governance system before the state takeover of the system.

OVERVIEW OF MAIN DEVELOPMENTS

• 1993: The state freezes its funding formula for school districts and adopts
yearly funding adjustments for districts that do not reflect changes in enrollment
or social needs. This development contributes to the increasing financial difficulties of urban and property-poor school districts.

• 1994: Hornbeck arrives in Philadelphia and prepares to launch his ambitious Children Achieving Plan, which requires a huge increase in funding.

• 1995: Philadelphia receives a $50 million Annenberg Challenge grant,
which is matched by $100 million from Philadelphia corporations, foundations,
and federal grants. This still provides only part of the needed funds, leading
Hornbeck to fully implement Children Achieving in only 6 of 22 neighborhood
"clusters" of schools in the reorganized district.
   The city council denies the district's request for increased funding to schools.
Mayor Ed Rendell and council president John Street remain firm in their commitment not to increase the tax burden on Philadelphia residents. They join with
Superintendent Hornbeck to request more funding from the state.
   Philadelphia files a federal civil rights lawsuit against the state over alleged
inadequate funding.

• 1998: Hornbeck threatens to adopt an unbalanced budget, if the state does
not provide the needed funds, which could lead to the schools closing before the
end of the school year.
   Governor Ridge and the legislature respond to Hornbeck's threat and pass a
draconian state takeover law, Act 46, aimed at Philadelphia.
   Hornbeck and the district "balance" the budget at the eleventh hour to avert
state takeover, but with borrowed money from banks.
   Street is elected mayor and a referendum is passed which strengthens the new
mayor's role in education by allowing him to appoint a new school board with
terms identical to his own.
   Mayor Street appoints a Secretary of Education for the city, Debra Kahn,
who is charged with leading the district's team in negotiation of a new teacher

contract and working to mend fences with state leaders in an effort to get increased state funding.

• 2000: The Pennsylvania legislature passes the *Education Empowerment Act* (Act 16 of 2000), a state reform and "takeover" bill targeted at eleven urban school districts (including Philadelphia) with high student failure rates.

The threat of a state takeover crisis in the district during the Republican Convention in Philadelphia is averted by a financial settlement between the district and Governor Ridge. Still facing a deficit, the school board cuts the budget, and Hornbeck resigns in protest.[4]

The decision by the board of education to adopt a corporate style of district management is made public. Deidre Farmbry, a veteran Philadelphia educator, is named chief academic officer.[5] The chief operating officer and chief financial officer were appointed in May.

Philip Goldsmith, a lawyer and journalist, is named chief executive officer, with a one-year interim appointment. (Goldsmith had been considered by the state as a possible CEO for the district in the event of a state takeover.)

A teacher strike over a weekend is settled with help from Mayor Street and pressure from Governor Ridge, who threatened a state takeover of the district.

• 2001: The state accepts Philadelphia's plan for improvements, required under the *Education Empowerment Act*, to avert a state takeover of the district.

The proposed 2002 district budget reports a $234 million deficit. It is unclear how the district will deal with this deficit, as the state had proposed only a small increase in its funding for Philadelphia.[6]

As an economy measure, the district's 22 clusters are replaced by eight academic offices, reducing administrative costs and reassigning some cluster staff to teaching positions. The school board adopts a budget with a $216 million deficit, creating a new fiscal crisis with state takeover of the district possible.[7]

Mayor Street and Governor Ridge sign a Memorandum of Understanding providing for state funding to keep the district operating, but indicating the state will takeover the operation of the Philadelphia schools at the end of October if no agreement between the city and state has been reached to resolve the budgetary crisis.

Governor Ridge gives Edison Schools a $2.7 million contract for a 2-month study to make recommendations about the financial and educational problems in Philadelphia.

The deadline for the state takeover is postponed until the end of November at which time Governor Ridge leaves Pennsylvania to take up his federal responsibilities as head of Homeland Security.

Ridge's successor as governor, Mark Schweiker, releases the Edison report, triggering controversy over its recommendations, especially that failing schools and the central management of the school system would be contracted out to for-profit firms.

Mayor Street and community groups adamantly oppose for-profit management of the system, and Governor Schweiker, bowing to political pressure, agrees to remove this idea from negotiations over the proposed plan.

Opposition and street demonstrations continue and a 3-week extension of the deadline is given, to provide more time for negotiations to work out the necessary agreements between the state and the city to avoid a "hostile takeover."

Governor Schweiker and Mayor Street announce an agreement to enable a "friendly" takeover, commencing the next day. In the unwritten agreement, both sides, but especially the state, made concessions.

BACKGROUND FOR SUPERINTENDENT HORNBECK'S SYSTEMIC REFORM PLAN

Due to a drastic decline in the number of jobs available and to a changing economy, Philadelphia's population decreased dramatically from the 1970s to the 1980s, as did its middle-class tax base. When David Hornbeck began his tenure as superintendent in 1994, the city was still recovering from a serious fiscal crisis in which it was forced to borrow $150 million from its employee pension fund just to stay afloat. With its credit ruined, the city had to pay more than $5 million to obtain the loan, a fee equivalent to a 24% interest rate.[8]

During his 8-year tenure, Democratic mayor Ed Rendell brought Philadelphia back from financial collapse, creating a small budget surplus before he left office in 2000.[9] Not giving in to demands of striking city workers early in his administration, he ultimately negotiated a contract that provided more discretion for management. Perhaps more importantly, Rendell made Philadelphians proud of their city. He put tourism at the center of Philadelphia's economic renewal and unceasingly and flamboyantly promoted "the city that loves you back." This was no easy feat given the image many Americans had of Philadelphia and its city government: a city block in flames after Mayor Wilson Goode and his managing director dropped a bomb on the headquarters of the radical group MOVE. Rendell worked with Republicans in the state to bring jobs to Philadelphia, and by 1997 economic prosperity had even trickled into Philadelphia when the city showed a net gain in jobs and reversed a trend of decades.[10]

In school district matters, however, Mayor Rendell was a "silent partner." One civic leader quipped, "Frankly, there were years when Ed Rendell didn't even mention schools in his State of the City address."[11] Rendell certainly did not lack for opportunity to be a player in public education. Like his predecessors, he had the power to appoint school board members as vacancies arose.[12] Still, because the mayor was not able to appoint the entire board when he assumed office, the accountability of the board to the mayor was considerably diluted. The board had the responsibility for setting policy and spending priorities. But although the school district had its own budget, the board had no taxing power; the city council levied taxes.

In the 30 years previous to Hornbeck's arrival, Philadelphia had two reform superintendents: Mark Shedd and Constance Clayton. In 1965 Shedd, a national figure in education, brought to Philadelphia a progressive approach to teaching and learning. Under his administration, the district launched alternative schools, open classroom education, team teaching, and an early version of service learning. Like other districts across the country, Philadelphia experienced its share of political unrest during this period. In fact, one notable confrontation was between Police Commissioner Frank Rizzo and a group of student and adult activist protestors who advocated African American studies in the district's curriculum. A leader of that protest was David Hornbeck, who at the time was a civil rights lawyer and activist in the city.

Philadelphia had two "insider" superintendents, Michael Marcase and Matthew Costanzo, during the 1970s when union rancor and fiscal crises prevailed. A series of bitter and disastrous teacher strikes rocked Philadelphia. One 51-day strike in 1973 left particularly deep wounds.

In 1980 Philadelphians elected their first African American mayor and shortly thereafter Constance Clayton became both the first African American and first woman superintendent. Clayton made labor peace and financial stability the first order of business in her plan to improve public education, and was largely successful in these areas. During Clayton's decade-long tenure there were no teacher strikes, and the district both balanced its budget and improved its bond rating.

Clayton's education reforms included a standardized curriculum that offered an academic scope and sequence for all grades and subject areas. A citywide testing program aligned test items with discrete curriculum objectives and provided schools with a tool to monitor student progress toward achievement goals specified in their School Improvement Plan.

Unfortunately, Clayton's strategy for improving the academic achievement of students reaped disappointing results. A special section of the *Philadelphia Inquirer* published in 1994—2 years after Superintendent Clayton retired—painted a dismal portrait of student achievement in the school system. According to the *Inquirer*,

> Over half of the city's public school students were failing to master basic skills. Fifty-one percent had failed the state reading test as compared to 13 percent statewide, and 50 percent failed the state math test as compared to 14 percent statewide. Seventy percent of African Americans and 75 percent of Latinos failed one or both parts of the state test.
>
> Forty-nine percent of ninth graders failed to earn promotion to the 10th grade.
>
> On any given day one in four students was absent from class, and in the average year, nearly one in four students was suspended from school.[13]

City corporate and civic leaders seized Clayton's retirement as the moment to influence the direction of Philadelphia public education. Under Clayton, the participation of the private sector in public education had increased. Higher education, foundations, and private sector partners had created PATHS/PRISM (Philadelphia Alliance for the Teaching of Humanities/Philadelphia Renaissance in Science and Mathematics) which aimed to professionalize teaching through professional development activities and minigrants for classroom teachers. And in 1986 the Pew Charitable Trust had heavily invested in local public school reform through its $13 million grant to restructure Philadelphia's neighborhood high schools. Civic elites, however, believed that Clayton had sought their support, but not their input, on matters of substance. They were disillusioned with a district administration that was not forthcoming with data on whether students were actually making progress.[14] So, they established the Partnership for Public Education, which worked with the mayor and board of education, to recruit a superintendent who would put accountability at the center of the district reform agenda. By this time, the Pew Charitable Trust had assumed a prominent role in the national standards movement. The foundation hoped to recruit a leader committed to that brand of reform.

Philadelphia found its man in David Hornbeck. Although trained as a minister and lawyer, rather than as an educator, Hornbeck had previously served as Commissioner of Education in Maryland and had been the primary architect of the Kentucky Education Reform Act (KERA). KERA's emphasis on standards, accountability, and comprehensive change resonated with city leaders.

Two factors forged an early alliance between Hornbeck and the business community. First, business leaders believed that the district's contract with the teachers union, the Philadelphia Federation of Teachers (PFT), was a major obstacle to improving public schools. Convinced that management needed more control over teacher assignments and noninstructional time, they wanted the new superintendent to wrest contract concessions from the PFT. Second, shortly after the Philadelphia school board adopted Hornbeck's reform plan, the Annenberg Foundation designated Philadelphia as one of a small number of American cities to receive a 5-year, $50 million Annenberg Challenge grant to improve public education.

Among the conditions for receiving the grant were the requirements to produce two matching dollars (i.e., $100 million over 5 years) for each one received from the Annenberg Foundation, and to create an independent management structure, preferably located in the city's corporate community, to provide program, fiscal, and evaluation oversight of the grant. Hornbeck turned to Greater Philadelphia First, an association of chief executives from the region's largest companies to establish the Children Achieving Challenge. As we will discuss below, the broad scope of Children Achieving distinguished it from other Annenberg sites. It was the "only city that attempted to leverage the Annenberg (and matching) dollars to redesign the whole school system—all 257 schools, 13,000 teachers, and 215,000 students."[15]

In hindsight, the key differences between Kentucky and Philadelphia are obvious: Kentucky's ambitious reform carried the clout of state legislation; it also was accompanied by a significant increase in state funding for public education. Neither of these would be the case in Philadelphia.

CHILDREN ACHIEVING: COMPREHENSIVE AND AMBITIOUS EDUCATIONAL REFORM

In 1995 Superintendent Hornbeck launched Children Achieving, a 10-point reform agenda that was based on the assumption that previous attempts at reforms have largely failed because they were too incremental, too piecemeal, and too narrowly framed, and because they did not attempt to alter the "system" itself.[16] In contrast, Children Achieving intended to offer a coherent and comprehensive reform design. As a systemic reform effort, it sought to raise student achievement and improve teaching and learning through implementation of standards for student performance and a strong accountability system, the empowerment of schools by moving authority for instructional decisions away from the central office, and increased capacity by providing strong supports for teachers and students. Content standards outlined the knowledge and skills that Philadelphia students should acquire. The accountability system assessed schools' performance annually and rewarded progress or sanctioned decline every 2 years. Decentralization offered new organizational structures—clusters, local school councils, and small learning communities—that moved instructional decision making closer to local neighborhoods, schools, and classrooms. Clusters were composed of a comprehensive, neighborhood high school and its feeder middle and elementary schools. There were 22 clusters in the district, and local school councils were envisioned, but few materialized that had any real effect. Small learning communities were created in schools to offer teachers and students smaller and more intimate environments for teaching and learning. They were made up of 200–400 students and their teachers.

Evaluators of the reform effort noted the complexity of the reform in their articulation of Children Achieving's theory of action:

> Given high academic standards and strong incentives to focus their efforts and resources; more control over school resource allocations, organization, policies, and programs; adequate funding and resources; more hands-on leadership and high quality support; better coordination of resources and programs; schools restructured to support good teaching and encourage improvement of practice; rich professional development of their own choosing; and increased public understanding and support; the teachers and administrators of the Philadelphia schools will develop, adopt or adapt instructional technologies and patterns of behavior that will help all children reach the district's high standards.[17]

Children Achieving offered a powerful set of ideas to guide educational improvement in the city. These included the following:

Primacy of results: Results are what matter; how they are achieved is less
    important.
Equity is paramount: The School District must be an advocate for the poor
    children it serves. Equity—of academic expectations, learning opportu-
    nities, and achievement outcomes—is a paramount objective.
School personnel need autonomy: Those working closest to students know
    what's best for them, and want and need the freedom and authority to
    act on their decisions in order to meet their students' needs.
Strong incentives are necessary: To spur action at the cluster and school level,
    strong incentives must be developed.
Do it all at once: Reform in all aspects of the system must occur simultaneously
    and immediately to achieve significant results.[18]

High standards and high expectations for Philadelphia's educators and students were the hallmarks of Children Achieving. School district leaders argued that, typically, adults' expectations of students have been too low and this has contributed to the consistently low achievement levels in Philadelphia's schools. As one district leader explained,

> In its most essential form, Children Achieving is a set of values about how
> a school district serves and honors children and families. . . . Some of the
> important things that have been a part of Children Achieving are the
> focus on rigorous standards, and rigorous standards for all children. It
> may take differentiated instruction and different amounts of time for
> children to reach those standards, but we can't start with an assumption
> that there are different standards for different children.[19]

The evaluators of the Children Achieving Challenge, in a summary report to Mayor Street on the progress of educational reform, pointed out a lack of consensus around the important values underlying Children Achieving, "particularly those that demand reexamination of deeply held beliefs, radically new behavior, persistent follow-through, and additional resources."[20] They offered the example of opposition to Superintendent Hornbeck's proposal to remove admissions criteria for student selection into special programs and schools. In a rare appearance at their meetings, Mayor Rendell successfully urged school board members to leave the criteria in place. He argued that dismantling these programs would further increase the tide of middle-class parents leaving the city in search of strong academic programs.

Children Achieving did not initially promote a particular set of recommended practices for schools. As mentioned earlier, the architects of the reform envisioned the decentralization of decisions about curriculum and instruction. They originally intended that neighborhood clusters, local schools, and small learning communities would customize educational practices to meet the needs of their students and utilize the resources of their communities. But as achievement gains leveled off, district leaders became convinced that school staffs needed more guidance about curriculum and instruction. In addition, the urgency of the reform's principle "to do it all at once created pressure on central office staff simply to 'roll out' the reforms and move on to the next priority."[21]

Not surprisingly, people in schools, particularly principals, felt overwhelmed and confused by the overall complexity of the reform and by the number of district and cluster mandates. Over 4 years, the central office directed schools to

> Reorganize into small learning communities.
> Implement the comprehensive support process and the school-to-career program.
> Receive training on a new set of standards, assessments, and curriculum frameworks.
> Adjust to a new administrative structure.
> Respond to new accountability policies.
> Adopt new graduation and promotion requirements.

Research is clear that a sustained focus is essential to substantive educational improvement, but in Philadelphia, reform overload was a strong contributor to school staff's inability to focus their efforts around clearly defined and manageable instructional priorities. Furthermore, unfunded mandates resulted in rampant frustration and alienation among principals. They felt angry, disempowered, and disrespected as they received one directive after another that had not been shaped by their input and that was not accompanied with the necessary supports for implementation.

CHILDREN ACHIEVING'S HIGH PRICE TAG

Children Achieving came with a high price tag. Its full implementation required significant additional funding from either the city or the state. In fact, its initial design was based on the assumption that more funding would be forthcoming. When Hornbeck became superintendent in August 1994, he had reason to believe that he had the political support needed to win more funding from the state. He began his tenure with a Democratic governor, Democratic majorities in the state legislature, and a Democratic mayor, and he had strong backing from business and civic leaders in Philadelphia. It appeared as though all the right players were in place. The prevailing view was expressed by a local foundation staff member: "We believe that if not now in Philadelphia, then when?"

Children Achieving can be viewed as a calculated risk.[22] In this view, Superintendent Hornbeck was betting that the Annenberg Challenge grant and its matching funds could be used to improve performance, and that improved performance would generate the political will to obtain increased city and state funding, either through the courts or the legislature, thus allowing the reforms to be institutionalized and continued.[23] It turned out that this was a bad bet. Just 3 months into his administration, the political landscape in Pennsylvania and Philadelphia changed dramatically. The state elected a Republican governor and Republican majorities in the state legislature who were committed to reducing government spending.

Nor was the mayor or city council willing to risk the financial jeopardy or political heat that increased city funding to schools would generate. When Hornbeck came seeking additional money for his reform plan, they argued that the city had "stretched its taxing ability to the limit" and refused to provide significant additional resources for Children Achieving.[24] By 1997, the superintendent, the board of education, the city council, and the mayor were in agreement that it was the state that was failing to provide a fair share of the costs of educating Philadelphia's students—students who had many social, emotional, and academic needs.

Philadelphia's spending for these students was well below what was spent in its surrounding counties, as much as $5,443 per student. Teacher salaries were also higher in suburban areas. Starting salaries in the suburbs averaged more than $3,500 higher than starting salaries in Philadelphia and maximum salaries were more than $9,000 higher.[25]

The funds the state of Pennsylvania provides to each school district are supposed to be based on a funding formula that takes into account the number of pupils, the special needs of the district, its ability to raise local taxes, and other factors. However, the state froze the formula in 1993, which meant that state aid to the district after that date did not rise in response to increases in enrollment. On a per-pupil basis adjusted for inflation, the real value of state education funds coming to Philadelphia actually decreased by 5.9% between 1993 and 1998.[26]

Relationships between the state and the district became tense when the new governor pushed vouchers and charter schools as remedies for poor student performance and entrenched bureaucracy and reached a boiling point when David Hornbeck alleged that state funding policies were racist. With inadequate political support and personal antagonisms between state representatives and the superintendent, the school district was unable to persuade Pennsylvania state officials to significantly increase funding. Despite two court cases against the state and threats by the superintendent to adopt an unbalanced budget and close schools early in 1999, the governor and legislative leadership were unwilling to alter the school funding formula or provide the money requested. They believed that funds were being used inefficiently in Philadelphia and that the district's teacher contract was a major obstacle to improvement. In their view better management and a better contract were prerequisites for additional state funds. The state did provide Philadelphia with some one-time grants, but these were small in comparison to what the school district said was required to continue with the Children Achieving reform agenda.

In addition to refusing to provide significant additional school funds for Philadelphia, the state passed legislation granting itself greater power and authority over public education in the city. In response to Hornbeck's threat to close schools early during the 1998–99 school year, the state passed Act 46, a draconian bill aimed directly at Philadelphia that would allow the state to take over the district if Hornbeck pursued his threat. All the unions opposed this bill, but it passed easily, despite its numerous incendiary features, such as provisions for replacing the school board and superintendent, suspending the teachers' contract, laying off teachers, and, in the words of the PFT, "unilateral school closings and privatization by converting public schools to charter schools without approval by teachers and parents."[27] It was then Philadelphia's turn to be "motivated" to find a way to avoid school closure and state takeover. Rather than cutting the proposed school budget, an eleventh-hour solution was found when two local banks issued the district letters of credit enabling it to borrow $250 million to keep operating through June 1999.[28]

A NEW ROLE FOR THE MAYOR IN SCHOOL GOVERNANCE

In November 1999 Philadelphia voters elected a new mayor, Democrat John Street, who supported Superintendent Hornbeck and his Children Achieving reforms. They also approved a change to the City Charter, which allowed the new mayor to appoint all of the board of education members concurrently with his term of office.

Street, an African American and former community activist, who had served as city council president during Rendell's administration, ran with the powerful endorsement of Mayor Rendell. He faced strong opposition from Republican Sam Katz, a government finance consultant. Both candidates said that public education would be a top priority in their administration, but they had very different visions for how to improve city schools. Street believed in the Children Achieving reform plan and said that he supported David Hornbeck. Katz called for the removal of Hornbeck and looked to school choice reforms—vouchers and charter schools—as the only solutions with enough muscle to improve the dismal achievement of Philadelphia students.

Governance of public education was a key issue in the mayoral primaries and election, as noted in the *Philadelphia Inquirer*:

> In a departure from past mayor campaigns, when the schools barely rated a mention, this year's crop of candidates is talking often and avidly about public education. And in keeping with the national trend, many of the prescriptions center on changing how the school system is run and financed.[29]

All of the candidates, with the notable exception of Street, favored a stronger role for the city's chief executive in the governance of its public schools. They all supported a change in the city's Home Rule Charter which would enable the mayor to appoint a new nine-member school board all at once (to serve the same 4-year term as the mayor) and to fire members at will. (Previously, there had been 6-year staggered terms with the mayor only able to make new appointments as terms expired. This meant that a mayor might not gain full control of the board until well into a second term.)

City councilman Michael Nutter introduced the proposal to the council to include the amendment on the November ballot. Philadelphia good government groups, like the Committee of Seventy, had been pushing for a change in the charter for more than 2 decades. Rendell supported the change as did Ted Kirsch, president of the Philadelphia Federation of Teachers.

As a candidate, John Street was skeptical about increased mayoral responsibility and accountability for public schools. But as mayor, Street increasingly signaled his willingness to lead. In his first year he created a cabinet-level position, Secretary of Education; held town meetings on public education in all 22 cluster areas; exerted a strong influence on teacher contract negotiations; began to craft a new conciliatory strategy in the city's dealing with state government; unveiled a plan aimed at keeping working- and middle-class families in the city, which included attacking neighborhood blight, bearing down on predatory lenders, and improving educational options through strong magnet programs and charter schools.

Street appointed Debra Kahn, a former advisor of Mayor Rendell, to fill the position of Secretary of Education. She described her role as putting a "face on Street's education agenda," while the mayor said that her immediate tasks would be to seek more funding from the state, lead a panel that would nominate new board members, and play a key role in the district's negotiating team for a new teacher contract. Street's board appointments were generally held in high regard. Pedro Ramos, an attorney and Philadelphia public school graduate and parent, served as president of the board. Dorothy Summers, a leader in the African American community and a former middle school principal was vice president. The nine-member board also included a former city budget director, a black clergyman, a retired district administrator, and several civic leaders including the executive director of the United Way.

While Street proclaimed that David Hornbeck was his choice for superintendent and that Children Achieving was the right reform plan for Philadelphia, the mayor's actions signaled to some that he was ready for a change. As one union leader put it, "Street loved Hornbeck to death."[30]

Mayor Street wanted a new strategy for handling the politics of public education. David Hornbeck was confrontational and the mayor wanted something different. He and his secretary of education and the president of the board decided to look for a CEO type to deal with the political and financial issues.[31]

The political impasse between the district and the state came to a head again in the summer of 2000 when the district faced a budget deficit of $205 million. Under pressure from the state takeover law to balance the budget, the Philadelphia board of education made cuts and adopted a budget of nearly $1.6 billion, which contained no new money for the programs the superintendent felt were required to fully implement the Children Achieving reform agenda. As a result, Hornbeck postponed the implementation of new promotion and graduation requirements and reduced the number of days allocated for teacher professional development. Not willing to remain to oversee the piece-by-piece dismantling of his reform agenda, Superintendent Hornbeck announced his resignation on June 5, 2000.

THE BUSINESS COMMUNITY

> David believed you could make a social contract with the business community, but he looked up and they were gone. I don't think the corporate community is playing a healthy, visible constructive role in public education. But they carry tremendous weight. It's a combination of factors. So few businesses are local now. And there are some leaders who came through the Archdiocese system. They want to keep taxes down and have vouchers.[32]

Initially, the corporate community was enthusiastic about Hornbeck's arrival and his bold plan for reform. Greater Philadelphia First (GPF) helped raise the Annenberg matching funds and, in fact, by June 1996 Philadelphia had outdistanced all other Annenberg cities by raising more than 90% of the required $100 million.[33] Midway through Hornbeck's tenure as superintendent, board leadership at Greater Philadelphia First changed. (By June 2000 only 4 of Greater Philadelphia First's founding 23 CEOs remained.)

The turnover of leadership at GPF was a symptom of major shifts in the city's economic life. Nicholas Lemann offered this description of what happened in Philadelphia (and is happening in cities across the country): Despite increased financial prosperity and a city government that inspired confidence, the new urban economy was altering its civic life in ways that had repercussions for the role of the business community in public education. Multinationals took over regional institutions such as Scott Paper and Smith Kline pharmaceuticals. More important, the local banking industries vanished. These changes have increased the wealth of stockholders but Lemann argues that they have not reaped long-term benefits for cities. One consequence of these changes has been diminished participation of the corporate community in public life.

[The] complaint is that First Union and the other new outside companies don't care about the civic life of Philadelphia. People told me that you can't fill a nonprofit board of directors in Philadelphia these days.[34]

A funder of reform agreed with that assessment:

What happened was a rapid transformation from businesses led by Philly people to businesses without a vested interest in Philadelphia, or an understanding of the city. And there was an expanding ambivalence about the ability of school systems to reform. And third, there was the trepidation of any business leader to oppose a popular governor who continued to support economic development in the city.[35]

Disappointed that school district officials had not won major concessions from the teachers' union during contract negotiations in 1998, GPF began to withdraw its support of the district's reform agenda:

Hornbeck and [David] Cohen [Chief of staff during Rendell's first term and a lead city negotiator in the PFT talks] promised us they were going to negotiate some changes. They made a commitment and on the strength of that promise, the business community raised the match for Annenberg. We kept our end of the bargain, but they didn't. We wanted the right to assign people to schools without going by seniority, the right to make hiring decisions at the school level, some control over how prep time is used, and several other changes, but we got none of them.[36]

GPF was also sympathetic to Pennsylvania's pro-business Republican governor, Tom Ridge, and to his proposals for school vouchers and more charter schools. By this time Ridge had become engaged in a highly personalized battle with the district and Hornbeck, in particular, over two issues: the state funding formula and school choice. A GPF staff member described what happened:

The corporate community at the beginning, and along the way, had competing interests. I think that there was a struggle between the educational issues they knew to be critical to city's long-term health and their own economic health and wanting to support an accountability, standards-driven agenda. There was also a conflict between the economic stance and support of the governor, and his educational agenda. It was a constant tug of war. Later, David's personality made even more difference for them [corporate leaders]. The governor's commitment to economic development is pretty solid from the business community's perspective. While I was there (at GPF), I watched the scale start to tip and split the business community. Being inside, I saw where it came from, even if I didn't like it.[37]

Community leaders were disheartened by the erosion of business support for Hornbeck and their withdrawal from the arena of public education. One explained that business leaders' orientation made it difficult for them to be patient and persist in the face of serious social problems:

> The business community thinks short-term. They think in terms of quarters—the furthest into the future they might look is 2 years. They pulled back because there were not results soon enough. Even though there was improvement on tests, people in the business community don't care about tests. They haven't seen results in the kids who are coming to them looking for jobs out of high school, and that's what they're really looking for.[38]

Others were harsher in their assessment of the business community's role, asserting that the governor's voucher plan comported with corporate leaders' support for parochial schools. They were cynical about the potential of the business sector as a catalyst for improving education for poor children of color.

> Right now this corporate community gets off the hook. It skates. It's having too good a party right now. Maybe when Wall Street crashes, they'll realize what's going on. It stands to lose eventually. We've allowed the development of ways for the education of the labor force to come from elsewhere and government brokers for corporate interests.[39]

A former GPF board member described his frustration with Governor Ridge and his disillusionment with GPF at the time of the threatened state takeover:

> I went to Harrisburg to talk to Governor Ridge. The message that I was trying to get across to the state was, "We know that the district is not perfect. But we have a man running it today who is most unusual because he believes that he can fix it. This is an incredible asset for you. What do we have to do to link arms with you?" Honestly, Ridge believes that you can't fix the Philadelphia public school district. He'd rather skirt it by building an alternative system. In defense of Ridge, even if he had wanted to support Philadelphia schools, he might not have been able to politically because of opposition in the House of Representatives.
> I dropped out of GPF when they decided to support vouchers. I thought it was a big card to play, and should have been worth $50–100 million from the state. And I think that this last round—getting $15

million for dropping the deseg case was a sellout. They thought they'd get $65 million. I knew they wouldn't.[40]

As this discussion has shown, business community support for the school district has declined. Yet, its influence on the district remains significant, as demonstrated by the school board's adoption of the corporate governance model and its selection of an interim CEO in 2001 with credibility in the business community. Later, when Governor Schweiker and Mayor Street were in a standoff over the terms of the state takeover, business leaders intervened, with some effect, to urge them both to return to the negotiating table.

PRINCIPALS AND TEACHERS

Like other urban districts, Philadelphia faces serious shortages of high-quality personnel to guide and support the reforms. The district is at a disadvantage in recruiting and retaining qualified school leaders because its salaries are the lowest in the region, and because state legislation has made retirement an attractive option for many. Studies show that many prospective and current teachers are being lured to positions outside of the city, where salaries are higher, class sizes are smaller, and teaching conditions are generally more appealing.[41]

The school district's relationships with its professional unions, the Philadelphia Federation of Teachers (PFT) and the Commonwealth Association of School Administrators (CASA) were strained over the course of Children Achieving. Both the PFT and CASA sought salary schedules that were more competitive with the surrounding suburbs. And they offered strong objections to key components of Children Achieving, particularly to its accountability provisions. Alleging that the pay for performance system for school principals was not objective, CASA brought suit against the district. The PFT repeatedly questioned whether the district's standardized assessment, the Stanford Achievement Test, ninth edition, was well aligned with the content standards and charged that the Professional Responsibility Index (PRI), the formula used to assess schools' progress towards their accountability targets, was invalid and unfair. They also criticized the clusters as increased bureaucracy, and argued that money would be better spent on early childhood education, smaller classes, and a district curriculum that would provide more direction to teachers.

In addition, the school district, under heavy pressure from the state and the business community, sought major changes in the teacher contract's work rules in the negotiations that began in January 2000. Specifically, district officials wanted three things:

A longer school day and school year without explicitly paying teachers for the additional time. The teachers' work day was already one hour less than the state average.

A change in how teachers were assigned to schools. Rather than rely on seniority, the district wanted to give principals a greater voice in hiring and the ability to assign the most qualified teachers to schools with the most need.[42]

A pay for performance system. Under the current contract, teachers' salaries are based on years of service and their educational attainments. The district would like salary increases to be based on classroom performance.

The PFT was adamantly opposed to asking teachers to take on additional burdens without commensurate increases in compensation, and they were reluctant to give up work rules fought for and won in earlier contracts, much less agree to using test scores to determine salary increases.

The PFT and the school district worked for 10 months to negotiate a new contract. For the majority of this time, Mayor Street played a background role in the contract talks. But in the last 2 months of negotiations, Street became a far more visible and aggressive player, driven in part by the power given to him in Act 46. Street's first surge of authority came when the teacher contract expired on 1 September 2000. According to Act 46, the terms of the contract could not be extended past this date, and the state was given the power to take over the school district at any point they deemed necessary. Rather than risk a state takeover, teachers worked without a contract with hopes of settling quickly. For more than 3 weeks Street refrained from asserting his authority to impose a new contract. But on September 27 he did so, stating, "The PFT understandably is more than willing to indefinitely continue the status quo, and the status quo is the one thing that I cannot accept for public education in Philadelphia." He explained that it was his responsibility as mayor to be "very aggressive in representing the interests of the students, families and businesses that depend on the city."[43] Street received the public support of Governor Ridge who promised more state aid only if Philadelphia teachers would agree to contract concessions. Ridge also said that the state would consider a "friendly takeover" of the school district, if the teachers struck. When the teachers went on strike after classes ended on Friday, 29 October 2000, Street sat at the bargaining table until early Monday morning, 31 October, when the district and PFT finally reached an agreement.

THE LEGACY OF CHILDREN ACHIEVING

In an interview study of more than 40 business and civic leaders, community activists, and parents,[44] almost all agreed that there had been progress under Children Achieving. Gains in student achievement and greater citizen engagement in the dialogue about public education were the two most frequently cited legacies of the reforms. However, interviewees mitigated the test score progress by arguing that the scores didn't improve fast enough, or weren't high enough, across all schools, or might not even be real gains in learning:

There's no denying there's been improvement. The test scores have gone up. Not just the district's tests. If you look at the *Inquirer*'s analysis of the state tests, Philadelphia made more progress than anyone. It's encouraging, but it's not fast enough. (Foundation leader)

There's been some improvement. Scores are up but not enough and not fast enough, but at least we're headed in the right direction. (Newspaper reporter)

I think the single most important accomplishment is that David has focused people on the bottom line—what kids can do. For whatever reason, maybe because of the test or whatever, people believe that kids need to be able to do more in school. I think he was way ahead of the curve on that issue. In spite of every obstacle imaginable, student achievement gains have been made at least in some schools. The issue is how do we transfer those gains to all schools. (Member of mayor's cabinet)

The scores went up. The bottom line is student performance. The reforms seem to be making progress. But what I worry about is what children are learning. Maybe it is just teaching to the test. I hope not. I want to believe that there has been some real progress. (Business leader)

The second most frequently cited improvement was the fact that public education in Philadelphia has become a more public issue over the past 5 years. One parent and community activist said:

Education is much more on people's minds. There used to be despair and no attention. It is now widely understood that problems need to be addressed. Also there is more open sharing of data, and we can look at where schools are working.

Supporters of this view also asserted, however, that the school district still has a long way to go in solving the problems that have now become public. As one community representative explained:

I do see progress. I think the ability to have a running conversation about achievement for all kids for 4 years running is a huge accomplishment. I think that people on the street have something to say about the education crisis we're facing because of David's efforts. It gives us something to build on, but we have to remember that it takes a long time.

CONCLUSION

Mayor Street's increased role and control of the school board, plus the corporate management structure the school district adopted, increased the centralization of control over the system. Further, steps taken to reduce the budgetary deficit, notably the decision to replace the 22 cluster groupings of schools with eight academic offices, reduced the decentralization of the system.[45] But, as the summer of 2001 approached, both the new governance and leadership relationships were still being worked out, and some ambiguity remained about who really was in charge.

The board's appointment of Philip Goldsmith as a *one-year interim* chief executive officer *after* its appointment of the chief academic, operating, and financial officers blurred his authority. Several "insiders" we interviewed expressed concern, based on what they had seen so far, about who was, or would be, actually exercising leadership within the corporate structure. The very active role being played in decision making by the school board and by Mayor Street's secretary of education, Debra Kahn, introduced further uncertainty. Some informants perceived them, at times, to be engaged in micromanaging the district.

Additional uncertainty revolved around the attitude of school administrators and teachers in the district, as well as that of the Philadelphia Federation of Teachers. Many administrators and teachers felt burnout and low morale as a result of the 6 years of pressure (and, some perceived, disrespect) from Hornbeck in his aggressive push for reform and accountability for results. With retirements, difficult working conditions, and lower wages than in the suburbs, attracting and retaining sufficient qualified educators in the school district of Philadelphia continued as a huge challenge.

One change was quite evident: Mayor Street had taken a vigorous and prominent role in supporting public education and, indeed, made it virtually his top priority. He had been much more active in this regard than his predecessor, Mayor Rendell. Street visited all 22 clusters of schools in his early days in office. More important were his actions and the influence he had wielded, for example, in working closely and compatibly with Governor Ridge, and in helping abort a brief teacher strike. Although he is a Democrat, Mayor Street had been quite visible and successful in collaborating with Republican Governor Ridge and even with President George W. Bush, who called attention to Mayor Street in his 2001 State of the Union address, in regard to faith-based "charitable choice" initiatives thriving in Philadelphia. It was widely hoped that Street's "charm offensive" with Governor Ridge (in contrast to Hornbeck's acrimonious relationship) would lead to substantially more state financial aid, to stave off the district's budgetary crisis and avoid the threatened state takeover of the district.[46]

In another important development, Mayor Street's strong support of charter schools in Philadelphia signaled an important shift in the attitude of the city's leadership toward school choice and charter schools. It was further evidence of Street's desire to reach out to Republicans, including especially Governor Ridge, whose main ideas about school reform revolved around vouchers and charter schools. Mayor Street's support of charter schools also very much reflected his belief that the improvement of public education options for families in Philadelphia was a key to attracting and retaining middle- and working-class families in the city.

By contrast, the district and school board had been very critical of the rapid growth of charter schools in Philadelphia, and the board had been considering not renewing some of the charters they had granted. Without desiring it, the district had about half (34) of all the charter schools that now exist in the entire state. As Debra Kahn noted in testimony before the Senate Education Committee in February 2001, "Charter schools [now] comprise 6.5% of [Philadelphia's] public school enrollment. Taken alone, those 14,000 students would constitute the sixth largest school district in the Commonwealth." She added, further, that "Charter school costs are projected to total $79.2 million for the Philadelphia School District in the current school year, or about 5% of total operating expenses."[47] A report by the Pennsylvania Economy League, commissioned by the Greater Philadelphia Urban Affairs Coalition and released 2 June 2001, called for greater state funding of the charter schools, which the district blamed for more than half of the $216 million deficit in the budget it adopted for 2001–2002.[48]

Many public educators view charter schools with great suspicion. They see them as a threat, draining funds and students away from the district. But the board and public education establishment have been unable to stop the growth of charter schools in the district because they are very popular with parents and, as a result, with the state and local legislators representing these parents. The board knows that even if they reject charter school proposals, they are quite likely to be approved by the state's Charter Schools Appeals Board. That, plus strong support from influential state legislators, a number of whom are seen as "sponsors" having their own charter schools, causes the board to be reluctant to reject charter school proposals, unless they are obviously inadequate.

In August 2001 the pace of developments toward a state takeover of Philadelphia's school system accelerated greatly. Controversy began to mount as it became clear that Governor Ridge was envisioning a takeover that could include significant steps toward privatization through the involvement of Edison Schools, the nation's largest for-profit educational management organization. As the state authorities became more aggressive, and the threat of substantial privatization loomed ever larger, Mayor Street abandoned his "charm offensive" and hopes evaporated for a cooperative partnership between city and state authorities. During the fall of 2001, acrimony escalated rapidly, as actors in Philadelphia increasingly perceived the state engaged in a "power grab" and a "hostile takeover" that should be resisted by all possible means, including street demonstrations and lawsuits.[49]

The rapid flow of events and thrusts and counterthrusts throughout the fall between the contending parties became the subject of almost daily newspaper articles in the *Philadelphia Inquirer* and the *Philadelphia Daily News*. A synopsis of the main events will suffice here.[50] To begin with, the Memorandum of Understanding that Mayor Street and Governor Ridge signed on July 30 established provisions to try to solve the district's fiscal and educational crisis by the end of October.[51] The state agreed to advance funds to enable the district to pay its bills and meet its payroll until the end of October. The district agreed to cooperate fully with an outside study the governor would commission to present a plan by the end of September to solve the crisis. Further, it was agreed that during October the city and the state would try to agree upon a mutually acceptable version of this plan, but that if no agreement could be reached, the state would take over the operation of the district at the end of October.

The week after the memorandum was signed, Governor Ridge announced that Edison Schools was being commissioned to do a $2.7 million study over 2 months, in order to present a plan for resolving the district's fiscal and educational woes. Speculation was rampant that Edison Schools, already controversial in other cities, would propose (and the governor would support) a large role for itself in Philadelphia. Opponents of Edison Schools, and of for-profit management in education, began to organize and campaign against both.

In September Governor Ridge's appointment by President Bush to oversee Homeland Security caused a month's extension of the timetable set in the Memorandum of Understanding. Ridge's successor, Lt. Governor Mark Schweiker, pledged to carry forward Ridge's plans concerning Philadelphia.

A major flash point came on October 23, when the state legislature rushed through a bill in one day to strengthen Act 46 of 1998, the bill that had been passed to facilitate a state takeover of Philadelphia's schools. The new provisions strengthened the governor's hand by enabling him to appoint four out of five members of a new board that would rule the schools under a takeover. The mayor's one appointee would serve for 3 years, but most of the governor's appointees would serve much longer (two for 7 years, one for 5 years, and one for 3 years), and well beyond his own term of office. Mayor Street called this abrupt move "disrespectful" and Philadelphia school advocates denounced it as a "naked power grab." City leaders, who were Democrats, were still smarting from a recent seizure by Republicans of control over the Philadelphia Parking Authority and its rich patronage resources. They saw the legislature's actions as a further Republican power grab.[52]

The next flash point came with the release of Edison Schools' report, which sparked immediate controversy and opposition to it. The most explosive features of the plan were provisions for the central management of the school system by a private operator (most likely Edison Schools), and a division of the system's schools into three groups, based on performance: the 60 worst-performing schools, which would be run by Edison or other private firms in partnership with community groups; the 34 best-performing schools, which would be supervised by the district's private operator, but essentially left alone; and the 170 remaining schools, which would receive special assistance, such as curriculum improvements and teacher training.[53]

Mayor Street responded to the report by stating that he would not begin negotiations with Governor Schweiker until the proposal for central management by a private firm was dropped. Moreover, as the *Philadelphia Inquirer* reported, "In a symbolic move Mayor Street yesterday opened an office for himself in the Philadelphia schools administration building and vowed to fight total privatization of the district in the legislature, in the courts, and in the streets."[54]

Similarly, Philadelphia's board of education denounced the plan, noting that Edison's proposal combined "inexperience [in managing a large urban district] with conflict of interest" since, as the central managers, Edison would be able to enter into contracts with itself.[55] Edison's report also came in for scathing criticism from the Council of Great City Schools for both its cost ($2.7 million) and quality. Michael Casserly, the executive director of the council, said that "One could have conducted a review of the school system that would have been more objective and detailed for a lot less money."[56]

In the face of widespread opposition and street demonstrations by community groups and students adamantly against for-profit management of the school system, Governor Schweiker ultimately bowed to political pressure and agreed on November 20 to remove this item from negotiations over the proposed plan. Under his revised plan, Edison would still play an important role as a consultant and service provider.[57]

Facing the deadline at the end of November, with street demonstrations continuing, the state agreed to give a 3-week extension of the deadline, in order to provide more time to achieve the necessary agreements (especially over financial matters) between the state and the city to avoid a "hostile takeover." But political hardball continued. The governor's office next said that it "would not give the district a $70 million advance so that it could meet its December 21 payroll." Governor Schweiker wanted to split the amount and have the city pay $35 million that it had promised but never given to the district.[58]

The gulf was actually increasing between the state and the city about the financial contributions each should make for the resolution of the district's budget crisis. The state had proposed that the city and state each contribute $75 million in new money for the first year. The city's latest offer was $15 million against $110 million from the state. After 5 years, this proposal would have the city contributing $100 million and the state $900 million. Referring to this 9 to 1 ratio, the governor's spokesman said, "The mayor [earlier] called our proposal 'Fantasyland.' This is not even in Fantasyland's ZIP code."[59]

To make matters worse, on successive days it was learned, first, that during the negotiations the state had already proposed a $101 million, 6-year compensation package to Edison, with substantial cuts to be imposed on the school system, and, second, a secret 67-page report to the mayor with legal advice on how to fight or undermine the takeover was leaked to the press. These two developments infuriated leaders for both the city and the state. Philip Goldsmith, the district's interim CEO, resigned in protest. A "friendly" takeover seemed further away than ever.[60]

Nevertheless, on December 21 Governor Schweiker and Mayor Street announced an agreement that would permit a takeover of the school district, to commence the next day. To enable a "friendly" takeover, a number of important concessions were made, mainly by the state. Mayor Street agreed that the city would give $45 million more per year toward the operation of the schools, while the state would contribute $75 million more. This still left a gap of $80 million to be covered through unspecified economy measures. Governor Schweiker agreed to give Mayor Street two appointees, rather than just one, to the five-member School Reform Commission that would run the district. Further, Schweiker agreed that at least a 4 to 1 vote by the commission would be required for four kinds of decisions: the selection of the system's CEO and its legal counsel, and decisions to incur debt or change bylaws. Finally, Schweiker also agreed that any decisions to hire for-profit educational management firms would have to be made by the whole commission, after it was appointed.[61]

The unwritten agreement announced by Schweiker and Street left unclear the role that Edison Schools might play in assisting with the management of the district or in operating an unspecified number of schools. On one hand, the governor and the interim chairman of the School Reform Commission he appointed, James Nevels, spoke very favorably about Edison Schools. On the other hand, opposition to privatization by a coalition of public employee unions and citizen groups continued.[62]

In an insightful commentary on the takeover, *Philadelphia Inquirer* education reporter Dale Mezzacappa asked why, of all the troubled urban school districts, Philadelphia had become the largest to be taken over. She observed that "Outside Pennsylvania, Philadelphia is seen as an urban district that has made some progress and is nowhere near the bottom nationwide. In the state, however, it is seen as a total, abject failure, immune to improvement from within and in need of drastic, historic intervention." Mezzacappa then showed how a compelling case can be made that the state itself caused most of Philadelphia's increasing school budget deficit by suspending its school finance formula in the early 1990s, and then allowing the state's share of the funding to dwindle in subsequent years.[63]

Despite the agreement for a state takeover, along with solving the budget deficit problem, one of the greatest challenges facing Philadelphia for the rest of the decade will be obtaining the needed leadership and public support for its public schools. Will the state be able to recruit a strong CEO to replace interim CEO Goldsmith? And, even if a strong CEO can be attracted, will the school system's new leadership be able to elicit sufficient civic and business community support? Whoever is leading the school system will be facing a business community in Philadelphia that has reduced its activity and engagement with public education and that increasingly is characterized by absentee ownership. With globalization and multinational corporations, not just cities but, indeed, nation-states find themselves unable to count on the support and loyalty of major corporations. In *It Takes a City*, Hill, Campbell, and Harvey argue eloquently for strong and sustained civic coalitions as the critical component for successful urban school reform.[64] Unfortunately, cities increasingly find it harder to mobilize business leaders for this purpose. This will be a critical test for the future of Philadelphia's schools, however they are managed.

About a less controversial set of strategies, Kirst and Bulkley observed that "A key issue is whether mayoral control can improve classroom instruction and the everyday lives of teachers and children." They noted that governance change usually has had little effect on classrooms, but that Chicago and Boston demonstrate that it can make a difference with the right leadership and policies.[65] Finding this combination of attributes, while operating under fiscal constraints in a state takeover likely to involve privatization, will be Philadelphia's ultimate challenge.

Also critical and, indeed, the ultimate test for whoever is managing the school system will be to build upon and continue Hornbeck's accomplishments in improving student achievement. This sine qua non of urban education reform will now likely have to be achieved under the conditions of a controversial state takeover that is still likely to feature a significant role for privatization and for-profit management. Can the state and Philadelphia in partnership find ways to productively combine the new governance arrangements associated with the takeover and privatization, despite the continuing opposition to privatization in Philadelphia?

About a less controversial set of strategies, Kirst and Bulkley observed that "A key issue is whether mayoral control can improve classroom instruction and the everyday lives of teachers and children." They noted that governance change usually has had little effect on classrooms, but that Chicago and Boston demonstrate that it can make a difference with the right leadership and policies.[65] Finding this combination of attributes, while operating under fiscal constraints in a state takeover likely to involve privatization, will be Philadelphia's ultimate challenge.

NOTES

1. School District of Philadelphia, *Children Achieving, Action Design* (Philadelphia: Author, 1995), p. i.

2. Interview with parent activist, May 2000. In the spring of 2001, the *Philadelphia Public School Notebook* 8(3) reported that press coverage of Philadelphia public schools in the *Philadelphia Daily News* and the *Philadelphia Inquirer* increased from 577 stories in 1993 to 717 stories in 2000.

3. C. Gewertz, "Unprecedented Change Eyed for Philadelphia Schools," *Education Week*, 7 November 2001, p. 3.

4. R. Johnston, "Settlement Averts School Shutdown in Philadelphia," *Education Week*, 7 June 2000, p. 3.

5. K. Reid, "Corporate-Style Team Sought to Take Charge of Philly District," *Education Week*, 6 September 2000, p. 11.

6. R. Johnston, "Legislature Signals Probable Takeover of Philadelphia Schools," *Education Week*, 31 October 2001, pp. 1, 16.

7. See S. Snyder's articles in the *Philadelphia Inquirer*: "District Abandons Its School Clusters," 1 May 2001; "Street Warns of District Takeover," 31 May 2001; and "Big Deficit, New Crisis for Philadelphia Schools," 1 June 2001.

8. B. J. Whiting, *Philadelphia: Prospects and Challenges at the End of the Decade*, Report to the Pew Charitable Trusts (May 1999).

9. Perhaps the city's and Rendell's greatest accomplishment, at least symbolically, was attracting the Republican National Convention—an irony given that by the time of the convention in August 2000, Rendell, no longer mayor, was the Democratic National Committee chair.

10. N. Lemann, "No Man's Town," *New Yorker*, 5 June 2000, 42–48.

11. Mensah Dean, "Proposal Is Unjust: PFT Files Claim of Unfair Bargaining," *Philadelphia Daily News*, 24 August 2000.

12. Philadelphia, unlike other cities discussed in this volume, had not completely uncoupled the relationship between the mayor and the school board during the progressive reforms of the mid-twentieth century.

13. "A District in Distress," *Philadelphia Inquirer*, 23 October 1994, pp. G1–G8.

14. Interview with business leader, October 2000.

15. C. E. Finn, Jr., and M. Kanstroroom, "Can Philanthropy Fix Our Schools? Appraising Walter Annenberg's $500 Million Gift to Public Education" (Washington, DC: Thomas B. Fordham Foundation, 2000), p. 20.

16. J. Christman, T. Corcoran, E. Foley, and T. Luhm, "Philadelphia's Children Achieving Initiative: The Promise and Challenge of Systemic Reform in an Urban School District," in *A Race against Time: Responses to the Crisis in Urban Schooling*, ed. J. Cibulka and W. L. Boyd (Westport, CT: Ablex/Greenwood, in press).

17. Consortium for Policy Research in Education, Research for Action, and OMG Center for Collaborative Learning, *A First-Year Evaluation Report of Children Achieving: Philadelphia's Education Reform*. (Philadelphia: Greater Philadelphia First, 1996). Superintendent Hornbeck accepted this description as an accurate statement of his theory of action.

18. E. Foley, *Contradictions and Control in Systemic Reform: The Ascendancy of the Central Office in Philadelphia Schools* (Philadelphia: Consortium for Policy Research in Education and Research for Action, 2001).

19. *Philadelphia Public School Notebook* 8(3).

20. Foley, *Contradictions*.

21. Ibid.

22. Although we have emphasized the high cost of Children Achieving, Michael Masch, a school board member and financial expert, argues that Hornbeck's plan was not so costly, that it made cuts and reallocated funds, but enrollments have grown, special education costs have soared, and charter schools have been a growing financial drain. Philadelphia Board of Education, "Why Does Philadelphia Have a $2 Million Deficit?" Summer 2001, n.p.

23. Christman et al., "Philadelphia's Children."

24. School District of Philadelphia, *Realities Converge, Revisited: School District*

Sees Gains on Test Scores and Management Efficiencies, But Fiscal Crisis Is at Hand (Philadelphia: author, 1998), p. 28.

25. School District of Philadelphia, *Realities Converge*, pp. 11, 29.

26. J. Century, *A Citizen's Guide to the Philadelphia School Budget* (Philadelphia: Greater Philadelphia First, 1998).

27. As quoted in the *Wall Street Journal*, 15 May 1998. The strong support for this bill reflected the legislature's negative view of Philadelphia as an insatiable and "bottomless pit," as well as their antipathy toward the unions and Philadelphia's school superintendent.

28. K. White, "Philadelphia Budget Passes, Easing Takeover Threat," *Education Week*, 10 June 1998, p. 6.

29. D. Mezzacappa and S. Snyder, "Candidates Agree: Mayor's Control of School Board Should Increase," *Philadelphia Inquirer*, 13 May 1993.

30. Interview with union leader, October 2000.

31. Interview with district administrator, February 2001.

32. Interview with advisor to Superintendent Hornbeck, February 2001.

33. Consortium for Policy Research in Education, Research for Action, and OMG Center for Collaborative Learning, *A First-Year Evaluation Report*.

34. N. Lemann, "No man's town," p. 48.

35. Interview with funder, October 2000.

36. Interview with business leader, August 2000.

37. Interview of GPF staff member, October 2000.

38. Interview with community leader, October 2000.

39. Interview with community leader, May 2000.

40. Interview with business leader, August 2000.

41. B. Useem, *Perspectives on Philadelphia's Teacher Shortage: Evidence from Five Studies of Prospective and New Teachers* (Philadelphia: Philadelphia Education Fund, 1999).

42. Teacher turnover is high in Philadelphia. From 1995 to 1999 in the average school in Philadelphia, nearly 40% of teachers were new to the school in which they were teaching. In some elementary and middle schools, turnover rates were as high as 60%. The district's analyses show that their teacher transfer policies (as spelled out in the collective bargaining agreement with the teachers' union) result in the least experienced faculties serving in schools with lowest achievement, highest poverty, and greatest proportions of African American and Latino students.

43. Susan Snyder, "Street Sets Contract Deadline," *Philadelphia Inquirer*, 28 September 2000, p. 1.

44. This study was part of the evaluation of the Children Achieving Challenge conducted by the Consortium for Policy Research in Education and Research for Action.

45. Susan Snyder, "Hard Times Doomed School Clusters," *Philadelphia Inquirer*, 6 May 2001; M. Stricherz, "Philadelphia to Scrap 'Cluster' Plan in Bid to Save Money," *Education Week*, 9 May 2001, p. 20.

46. Susan Snyder, "Big Deficit, New Crisis for Philadelphia Schools," *Philadelphia Inquirer*, 1 June 2001.

47. D. Kahn, testimony before the Senate Education Committee on the Charter School Law (Act 22 of 1997), Harrisburg, PA, 12 February 2001. A "Financial Update" of the School District of Philadelphia (March 2001, p. 13) reported that $25.6 million of the district's costs for charter schools was for children who were *not previously enrolled in public schools*.

48. S. Snyder, "Report: More Can Be Done to Ease Charter School Costs," *Philadelphia Inquirer*, 2 June 2001.

49. R. Johnston, "Edison to Study Woes of Philadelphia Schools," *Education Week*, 8 August 2001, p. 3; R. Johnston, "Legislature Signals"; C. Gewertz, "Unprecedented Change Eyed for Philadelphia Schools," *Education Week*, 7 November 2001, p. 3; C. Gewertz, "Philadelphia Takeover Deadline Marked by Protests," *Education Week*, 5 December 2001, p. 5.

50. An Internet archive of documents and newspaper articles on the takeover controversy is available at *http://www.researchforaction.org/edison.html*. See also *Education Week*'s archive at *http://www.edweek.org*

51. This Memorandum of Understanding is available at *http://saa.phila.k12.pa.us/communications/MOU.pdf*

52. D. Mezzacappa, S. Snyder, and O. Wiggens, "Pennsylvania Moves to Ease Its Takeover of Schools," *Philadelphia Inquirer*, 24 October 2001; R. Johnston, "Legislature Signals."

53. Gewertz, "Unprecedented Change", p. 3; the entire Edison report is available at *http://www.pde.psu.edu/philadelphia/philasdrpt.html*

54. S. Snyder, "Vowing Defiance, Street Opens Office in District Headquarters," *Philadelphia Inquirer*, 10 November 2001.

55. The Board of Education's statement is available at *http://www.researchforaction.org/edisonschoolboardletter.html*

56. M. Dean, "New Nonprofit Study Blasts Edison's Report," *Philadelphia Daily News*, 12 December 2001.

57. C. Gewertz, "Pennsylvania Governor Drops Privatization Plan for Philadelphia Schools," *Education Week*, 28 November 2001, p. 5.

58. C. Gewertz, "Philadelphia Takeover Deadline Marked by Protests," *Education Week*, 5 December 2001, p. 5; D. Mezzacappa, "Pennsylvania Threatens to Hold Up School Pay," *Philadelphia Inquirer*, 7 December 2001.

59. M. Dean and D. Davies, "Goldsmith Quits Amid Day of School Turmoil," *Philadelphia Daily News*, 14 December 2001.

60. K. Dilanian, "Secret Street Report Imperils School Talks," *Philadelphia Inquirer*, 14 December 2001; Dean and Davies, "Goldsmith Quits." Goldsmith's one-year interim appointment was to end on January 1 anyway, so his resignation was largely symbolic.

61. S. Snyder and M. Schogol, "Accord Reached on Philadephia's Schools,"

Philadelphia Inquirer, 21 December 2001; J. Steinberg, "In Largest Schools Take-over, State Will Run Philadelphia's," *New York Times*, 22 December 2001.

62. D. Mezzacappa, "Edison's Role in City Gets Murky," *Philadelphia Inquirer*, 24 December 2001.

63. D. Mezzacappa, "Political Tension Led to School Takeover," *Philadelphia Inquirer*, 23 December 2001, p. 1.

64. P. Hill, C. Campbell, and J. Harvey, *It Takes a City: Getting Serious about Urban School Reform* (Washington, DC: Brookings Institution, 2000).

65. M. W. Kirst and K. E. Bulkley, "Mayoral Takeover: The Different Directions Taken in Different Cities," in *A Race against Time*, ed. J. Cibulka and W. L. Boyd.

Chapter 6

THE CITY-STATE PARTNERSHIP TO REFORM BALTIMORE'S PUBLIC SCHOOLS

James G. Cibulka

As other case studies in this volume indicate, urban mayors are attempting to reassert influence and control over the public school systems in their jurisdictions. Baltimore provides a counter example to this trend. In 1997 Maryland state officials succeeded in largely reversing a long institutional history in which Baltimore's mayors had held authority and responsibility for the city's public school system. This dismantling of mayoral authority was accomplished in the name of improving educational opportunities and outcomes for the city's impoverished and largely African American schoolchildren. As an alternative to a state takeover of the Baltimore City schools, the city and state agreed to a "partnership." This partnership, whose features are explained below, basically involved three components: a new governance system, major reforms to the school system's management, and more state aid.

The city-state partnership was bitterly opposed not only by employees of the school system, whose resistance might be expected, but also by many segments of Baltimore's community, in an atmosphere characterized by racial conflict with civic leaders and state officials. Yet this realignment also was accomplished with the reluctant acquiescence of the city's African American mayor, Kurt Schmoke, whose election a decade earlier had been heralded as an opportunity to reform Baltimore's beleaguered and resource-poor public school system. While he had made education reform a top priority and used his considerable leadership talents and political resources in pursuit of that goal, in the end the mayor was seen as part of the problem rather than the solution to the steady decline of the Baltimore City Public School System (BCPSS). What Schmoke reluctantly settled for in the partnership was a Faustian bargain in which he gave up mayoral authority and historic autonomy of the city's public schools from state intrusion, in exchange for more money to support the cash-strapped school system.

The purpose of this chapter is to examine the political developments that led to this "counter case" of urban institutional reform.[1] The central problem I address here is how institutional reforms reflect shifting coalitions of political power. These coalitions, in turn, limit the willingness to examine the problem of institutional reform in all its dimensions, including raising academic achievement. I shall also discuss briefly what impact these reforms have had on school system performance. How have the institutional changes emerging from the 1997 partnership been implemented, and what are the emerging consequences for student achievement?

First, I begin with a description of the central features of the 1997 reforms. Then I explain two important factors which led to this political realignment: the perceived failure of mayoral leadership to reform BCPSS and the growing vulnerability of BCPSS to state oversight. In the concluding section I interpret the adequacy of the 1997 partnership, arguing that it has positive features but is an incomplete policy reform. The current reform, I shall argue, has succeeded in installing some valuable changes in governance, administrative structure, and organizational culture, which show promise toward improving conditions of teaching and learning throughout the school system. Yet the 1997 policy settlement glossed over some important problems and sharply underestimated the political consensus and leadership necessary to rebuild BCPSS.

THE MAJOR ELEMENTS OF THE 1997 AGREEMENT

The consent decree and subsequent legislative enactment, which were described as a city-state "partnership," provided for three basic improvements to the city school system: an overhaul of the governance structure, a dramatic restructuring of BCPSS's management, and additional state funds in exchange for continuing oversight by the state.[2]

Governance Reforms

A new nine-member board of school commissioners was appointed jointly by the mayor and governor, based on a nominating slate provided by the state board of education. The kinds of affiliations and expertise required for these members were enumerated: at least four had to possess a high level of expertise concerning a large business, nonprofit, or governmental entity; at least three would have a high level of knowledge and expertise in education; at least one member had to be a parent of a BCPSS student; and at least one member was required to possess knowledge and/or experience in the education of children with disabilities. Unlike the old board, which had been appointed by the mayor and which was controlled by him, the new board is vested with full authority and responsibility for running the school system. A 14-member parent and community advisory board also was created to solicit parental input and involvement.

Management Reforms

The new board hires a chief executive officer (CEO), who reports directly to it and whose contract specifies expectations of demonstrable and continuous improvement in the academic performance of students and sound management of BCPSS. The CEO, subject to board approval, appoints a chief academic officer, responsible for systemwide curriculum and instruction, and a chief financial officer. Both these officers also have contracts that are contingent upon effective performance of their duties.

Additional State Funds

The state agreed to provide $230 million in additional state aid over a 5-year period, beginning with $30 million in fiscal year 1998 and $50 million each year thereafter. These monies were to be targeted on improved educational performance for schools with high concentrations of children in poverty and on low-performing schools which had been placed under "local reconstitution" by the state (a designation that made them eligible for "state reconstitution" if they did not improve). In 2001, 82 schools in BCPSS were so designated (compared with only one school or a small number of schools in several other jurisdictions) at the elementary, middle, and high school levels. Beyond these schools there are a large number of other "marginal schools" which meet all or many of the characteristics of the reconstitution-eligible schools.

In addition, funds would go to other marginal schools, for raising teachers' salaries to close the gap between BCPSS salaries and those in nearby Baltimore County and other districts. The state also increased its contribution to BCPSS in the area of school construction. While the state continued to require a local contribution for construction funds coming from the state, it increased the state cost-share to 90% on the first $10 million of construction funds received, thus reducing the required local match.

In exchange for additional state funds, the new board was required to develop a transition plan and a master plan by specified dates. These plans have had to meet very detailed requirements regarding use of the new state dollars, implementation of reforms in the areas of curriculum, instruction, assessment, and so on. The master plan includes, among other things, a comprehensive plan for improvement of school management and accountability, including implementation of the Cresap Report, which had been commissioned by a member of the state legislature (discussed below). An independent consultant was retained by the state board of education to evaluate the progress of reform in BCPSS on an annual basis.

POLITICAL FACTORS CONTRIBUTING TO THE PARTNERSHIP

As other students of policy setting have observed,[3] often it is difficult to pinpoint the exact origins of a policy issue. Sometimes several strands of an issue occur before being joined together by some serendipitous combination of circumstances. This is true in the BCPSS case. One of its origins was a lawsuit (*Vaughn G. et al. v. Amprey et al.*) that had been brought against BCPSS in 1984 by a disability-rights organization, the Maryland Disability Law Center. The plaintiffs had argued that special education students were not receiving services to which they were entitled under state and federal laws. The federal court had ordered protections for special education children and removed operating authority for these programs from BCPSS, placing the programs under direct supervision of the court. The inability of the school system to develop an adequate management system, or to spend special education dollars effectively, proved to be a long-term problem and contributed to the perception that BCPSS was a dysfunctional bureaucracy.

There were, however, at least two other long-term political trends which help explain why events unfolded as they did in Baltimore and have a trajectory somewhat independent of developments in other American cities. To be sure, Baltimore shared essential traits with its urban counterparts. From the 1960s onward, it struggled with conflicts over race and desegregation, loss of a middle-class base, declining communities, growing entrenched poverty, and the panoply of related problems that have characterized urban education in recent decades. Moreover, the policy ideas about how to reform urban education, which circulated nationally, have played themselves out in Baltimore as well. Policy nostrums such as decentralization, privatization, and accountability, for example, each have been contested in Baltimore. However, these ideas have been filtered through specific institutional frameworks and political cultures unique to Baltimore and Maryland. The first of these is the historic role of the mayor in public education in Baltimore. The second is the strong role of the state board of education in Maryland and its early activism with respect to the development of accountability systems, which put it in a position to assert oversight of BCPSS by the mid-1990s. Each of these political factors is discussed below.

The Perceived Failure of Mayoral Leadership

Unlike many American cities, where early-twentieth-century Progressive reformers had succeeded in removing overt political control of the public schools from municipal governments, Baltimore's schools were historically a unit of city government, operated by a nine-member board of school commissioners appointed by the mayor. This institutional context is important, because it opened Baltimore's mayors both to the opportunities and perils associated with governance of schools. On the positive side, having schools be part of city government gave mayors direct access to one of the largest public institutions in the city, as mayors sought to balance competing demands of business and labor, sought to control tax rates and public expenditures, and sought to use access to jobs and contracts to reward allies and build support for their regimes. Such opportunities also had downsides, however, as many mayors in Baltimore and other cities learned. If they became too embroiled in public education, they opened themselves to inevitable criticism, because parents and communities feel strongly about their schools. Issues of school boundaries, hiring, budgets, racial and social-class composition, and a host of other thorny questions inevitably threaten to draw mayors into controversy and cause them to expend valuable political capital. Unlike expenditures on streets and sanitation, the benefits associated with increasing investments in public education can be elusive. Thus, through the 1950s and well into the 1980s, the conventional wisdom among mayors was to shun overt political control of the schools, because the political costs to mayors exceeded the benefits. In cities where Progressive reformers had succeeded in separating the two domains, this provided a convenient institutional wall legitimating mayoral indifference or passivity. In "unreformed" cities such as Baltimore, mayors found other ways of accommodating the risks.

By the late 1980s, however, a new breed of urban mayors was emerging, who saw the improvement of their city's school systems as inextricably linked to the fate of their cities, and ultimately, to their own success. In many cities these mayors struggled to regain some institutional control. In Baltimore, however, such a struggle was unnecessary.

Kurt L. Schmoke represented this new breed of urban mayors. He was elected in 1987 in a campaign that emphasized public education and downtown redevelopment. Schmoke had argued that the school system needed dramatic improvement. He had cited as evidence a 1986 report commissioned by the Morris Goldseker Foundation, *Baltimore 2000* by P. L. Szanton, which had issued a scathing indictment of BCPSS, warning that the city's future was imperiled by the poor quality of BCPSS. He promised a "renaissance in public education." Schmoke himself also seemed to represent a new generation of African American leadership, having been raised in the city yet a graduate of Yale University and Harvard Law School, as well as a Rhodes Scholar.

Initially, Schmoke's education reform agenda appeared to have wide political support and had helped him defeat the incumbent African American mayor, Clarence "Du" Burns. The new mayor's reform agenda resonated with renewed attention to school reform by the Greater Baltimore Committee, whose corporate leadership had focused mainly on downtown redevelopment since the 1950s. Schmoke's election encouraged local organizations to place a higher priority on school reform.[4] The Citizens Planning and Housing Association (CPHA), a nonprofit organization, began to organize parents and train community leaders on school issues in the 1980s. Baltimoreans United in Leadership Development (BUILD), a coalition of 55 black churches and labor organizations (including the Baltimore Teachers Union), had been active in antipoverty issues and in school reform since 1983. Schmoke had endorsed BUILD's agenda and embraced it as a close ally after he was elected.

Despite Schmoke's reputation as a reformer, it is important to bear in mind that he did not challenge, and in fact actively perpetuated, the patronage tradition in Baltimore City politics. The school system was a major source of patronage, which was used to build support for and reward loyalty to the mayor. For example, appointments to principalships were routinely used as a source of patronage. Schmoke's reliance on this traditional patronage system ran counter to his reformist goals when the latter challenged vested interests. This tension helps explain some of the difficulties and resistance he encountered when he wore the hat of an education reformer.

Despite much initial consensus on the need for school reform among key organizations that supported Schmoke, the new mayor became embroiled in controversy on a variety of education issues. The debate over site-based management beginning in 1988 was one example. Schmoke sided with a proposal drafted by BUILD that was heavily influenced and supported by the Baltimore Teachers Union, an important political ally. This plan would have provided for quite dramatic devolution of authority to local schools, compared to the centralized regime then in place; and it sought to give the community and teachers a voice in this new authority. However, the group only planned to try the reform in three schools, one each at the elementary, middle, and high school levels. This was in direct opposition to a plan which had been developed by the superintendent at the time, Alice Pinderhughes. That plan, developed by a widely representative task force, would have devolved the new decision-making authority to principals and their aides in a few areas, such as the right to decide what books and materials the school could use. At the same time, while it was much more modest in scope, this plan would have been applied across the school system. After Schmoke forced the retirement of Superintendent Pinderhughes, his handpicked replacement, Richard Hunter, rejected the site-based management plan of BUILD and the teachers union, which the mayor had endorsed. Thus the mayor found himself in an increasingly awkward position as political groups drew up sides in favor of or against the plan he supported.

In 1989 the mayor and superintendent differed openly on a proposal favored by Schmoke, to permit the Barclay School to adopt a curriculum used at the Calvert School, an exclusive, prestigious private school in the city.[5] Barclay is an elementary school located in a poor neighborhood north of the downtown area and not far from Johns Hopkins University. In the mid-1980s a steering committee of parents and staff at the school, led by a dynamic African American principal, Gertrude Williams, decided that the school's low performance was due to the watered-down curriculum in the BCPSS and the low expectations that it represented. By contrast, the Calvert School curriculum was highly structured, classical, and focused heavily on excellence in writing composition, with regular review of student work by staff and parents. The proposal was endorsed by the Abell Foundation. Its president, Robert C. Embry, Jr., a former school board president and one of the city's power brokers, was prepared to support the project with a grant. However, retiring superintendent Alice Pinderhughes sat on the proposal. After she retired, her replacement, Richard Hunter, also opposed the plan, calling the Calvert approach an outdated "rich man's curriculum." He also was concerned about Robert Embry's influence and sought to reassert his control over the school system and the curriculum. The Baltimore Teachers Union also opposed the plan, citing teacher workload issues. Parents actively protested, and the issue escalated into a citywide controversy. The mayor was forced to intervene and used his valuable political capital to eventually overrule Hunter. Despite Hunter's resistance, the experiment proved successful and was adopted at another school. On many other issues, Hunter became an object of controversy in the broader community, among school personnel, and the school board. Schmoke became so frustrated by the recalcitrance of Hunter that eventually he engineered the removal of his appointee.

Schmoke's choice to replace Hunter, Walter Amprey, however, proved just as controversial not only among local activists and civic leaders, but among key state legislators, who perceived him as unresponsive to decentralizing the school system's management. The impetus for this pressure came from state Delegate Pete Rawlings. An important factor in highlighting the issue of managerial incompetence was the leadership of Rawlings, who had pursued this issue relentlessly over a period of years in the Maryland General Assembly. Because of Baltimore's changing demography and its political culture that had a strong tradition of black leadership, the city sent to Annapolis a significant delegation of black Americans. Among them was Rawlings, a mathematician on the faculty of Baltimore City Community College, who represents a black district in the city. Rawlings described his bottom line as a growing concern over academic performance of children in BCPSS. As he became more active in school issues, he initially shared the view that the problem was one of a predominantly black school system being run by white administrators and a predominantly white school board. The belief system was that their children would do better if they had in control of the school system black role models who would be more apt to fight for their best interests, including better funding and a redesigned curriculum. However, by the late 1980s, once the system had a black superintendent, associate superintendents, and a black school board, black control was no longer an issue.

Yet the problems of BCPSS did not diminish. Rawlings, because of his role as a member, and later chair, of the House Appropriations Committee, as well as his role as cochair of the Baltimore City delegation in the House of Delegates, was able to obtain performance information he requested on BCPSS. (He formed a close alliance with State Superintendent Nancy Grasmick and the chair of the State Senate Budget and Taxation Committee, Barbara Hoffman.)

The picture that emerged was not reassuring to him. City officials told him that school officials were not completing reports, that money had to be returned because it was not spent, that city officials had to help BCPSS write funding proposals, and a host of other "horror stories." Further, Rawlings came to doubt the claim of advocates that BCPSS needed more money. Many counties that spent less than BCPSS were doing much better on state standards. Rawlings blamed the management culture of the school system that he believed preceded black control. It represented a "culture of complacency" oriented toward the status quo, and was protectionist, turf-oriented, and an environment in which people got jobs and held them based on friendship and loyalty rather than on merit and performance. He contrasted this culture with that in the private sector.

As a result, he decided to commission a management study of BCPSS. He arranged for the local organization Associated Black Charities to sponsor the study, not wishing for the school system to own and control the study. While the mayor and school officials acknowledged that there was a need for such a study, they claimed they had no money. Rawlings and his allies then turned to local foundations to obtain the $250,000 required. The general management–consulting firm of Towers Perrin/Cresap was retained. To validate the management study, an oversight team also was designated made up of BCPSS board members, a prominent state board member, Rawlings, and others.

The published report[6] was a scathing critique of the management of BCPSS—its organization, its culture, and in many cases the competence of individuals in the BCPSS bureaucracy. The Cresap Report, as it came to be known, reflected Rawlings' belief that BCPSS needed to operate more like a business, with stronger delegation and accountability, and more focus on a network of site-base-managed ("enterprise") schools. Over 100 recommendations and strategies accompanied the report. Shortly after the report was issued, BCPSS superintendent Walter Amprey endorsed all but six of the recommendations and appointed an implementation team and an enterprise school group to oversee implementation of the site-base management recommendations. The report had recommended an approach to school-site management that gave major authority to principals to design and implement educational programs, control staffing, and manage resources, in exchange for greater accountability for their school's performance.

The Cresap Report also had recommended the phase-in of enterprise schools. However, after no progress for 2 years following the report's release, Amprey eventually declared in the spring of 1994 that all city schools would heretofore be enterprise schools, with no time for planning or phase-in. Not surprisingly, his pronouncements were accompanied by little change, as documented by a study[7] commissioned by the legislature at Rawlings' behest. This controversy became one of the major political elements undergirding demands for reforming BCPSS governance. This protracted controversy with Rawlings and other members of the state legislature not only swirled around Amprey and the school system, but drew in the mayor as well.

Schmoke also had suffered a severe erosion of trust owing to the controversy between 1992 and 1994 over his endorsement of the Tesseract project in 15 elementary schools, a private management experiment by Educational Alternatives, Inc. (EAI). Amprey had endorsed the plan, but it encountered the bitter opposition of the BTU, deeply divided the city council and the African American community, and raised fears of loss of jobs and paranoia about white control (EAI was a white-run firm). The project terminated in 1996 because the city and EAI could not come to agreement on costs and because of alleged falsification of test scores by EAI. The controversy had become a major issue used by city council president Mary Pat Clarke in her unsuccessful primary campaign to unseat the mayor.

Thus, despite much promise and high expectations, Schmoke encountered one controversy and setback after another in his efforts to reform BCPSS. Of course, the mayor had some successes, such as creation of the Stadium School and the subsequent New Schools Initiative (NSI), but such cases involved much expenditure of political capital on his part. The Stadium School was a new school created in 1994 on the concept of an enterprise school, based on a proposal from parents and teachers. Amprey and the school system had resisted the idea in much the same fashion as Hunter had opposed the Barclay experiment. Schmoke's vocal support and intervention, amid protests from a resourceful and determined group of advocates, led Amprey and the board of school commissioners to reverse course. By 1998 under the NSI, ten nonprofit organizations operated public schools within BCPSS.

While Schmoke's education leadership was disappointing to many who had held high expectations for his ability to turn around Baltimore's troubled school system, the responsibility for many of the problems confronting BCPSS in the 1980s and 1990s could be traced to the policies of the city's former mayor, powerful, popular, and white William Donald Schaefer. Schaefer served from 1971 until his election as governor in 1986. Perhaps it was Schaefer's public controversy with the city's first black superintendent, Roland Patterson, that sensitized him to the political costs of becoming too engaged in school affairs. Patterson was an outsider appointed to his position just a few months before Schaefer become mayor in 1971. Patterson resisted Schaefer's use of school system jobs for patronage.[8]

In 1975 Schaefer's maneuvering to fire Patterson erupted into an intensely racial dispute between community activists and the majority-white school board. A teacher strike in 1974, in which Schaefer had taken a strong stand against teachers, also had become intensely racial. Thereafter, Schaefer allowed the school system's administrative, teaching, janitorial, secretarial, and paraprofessional jobs to shift to black control, even as he maintained white control over jobs at city hall. According to Marian Orr,[9] the mayor used the school system as a source of patronage. Appointing supporters allowed him to maintain control as mayor even as the city's population turned 59% black by 1980. (The school population had turned majority black in the 1960s.) Moreover, it was a strategy that removed race as a visible and volatile issue in school affairs. Schaefer focused instead on economic redevelopment of the city's downtown, paying little attention to public school issues. So evident was this that the *Baltimore 2000* report issued in 1986 criticized him and admonished future mayors to provide stronger leadership to reform BCPSS.[10]

Of course, it would be an overstatement to blame Schaefer totally for the larger demographic trends in Baltimore's population and the resulting problems this occasioned for BCPSS. Yet shifts in the racial makeup of the city were not in and of themselves problematic. Rather, it was the loss of middle-class residents, both white and black, which proved problematic. Under Schaefer's watch, BCPSS became overwhelmingly a school system of poor children, signaling the loss of a middle-class population and tax base in the city as residents fled to suburbs. Even those middle-class residents, both black and white, who remained in the city increasingly chose to send their children to private schools. Arguably, more assertive mayoral leadership might have stemmed these trends. However, as was stated earlier, mayors during Schaefer's era were not expected to assert strong leadership on school matters. By the time of Mayor Schmoke's campaign to create a renaissance in Baltimore's schools in the late 1980s and 1990s, the political and financial base supporting the Baltimore school system had narrowed, even as its educational problems mounted.

Growing Vulnerability to State Oversight

The second political factor explaining the 1997 partnership agreement was the growing role of the state of Maryland both as a political force critical of BCPSS and one upon which the city became dependent for resources. Here again, however, the institutional framework in Maryland differed from that of many states. Maryland invests its state board of education, whose 12 members are appointed to staggered terms by the governor, with the strongest regulatory authority of its kind in the nation, independent of legislative oversight. For many decades Maryland's state board of education had a reputation for competence and activism, although this increased sharply in the 1980s and 1990s with pressures for educational reforms in public education. At the same time, as the state increased its financial contributions to the state's 24 school districts, it argued for more accountability in the use of state dollars. Since the governor and state legislature have the power to tax and spend, this brought to play a wider range of state actors.

State leadership for school reform increased sharply in the late 1980s. In Schaefer's new role as governor, he reflected an interest in and activism toward public education that mirrored what governors were doing across the country. Ironically, his interest in education reform as governor was a departure from his earlier mayoral leadership. As governor he focused on state education issues; ultimately the education reforms he created shone an unflattering spotlight on BCPSS's performance.

In 1987 Schaefer appointed Baltimore business leader Walter Sondheim to chair the Commission on School Performance, also known as the Sondheim

Commission. The commission argued in its report[11] that there was little evidence of how well Maryland students were prepared by its public school system to function in the new economy, and made a series of sweeping recommendations for a more accountable and data-based system.

The adoption of many of these recommendations by Maryland's powerful state board of education, without the necessity of legislative action, made Maryland one of the first states to adopt high-stakes testing, accountability reporting, and a program of intervention in low-performing schools. The annual reporting of school scores in core subjects in Grades 3, 5, and 8 on the Maryland School Performance Assessment Program (MSPAP) began in 1992. Starting in 1994, the state declared low-performing schools "reconstitution-eligible" and set in place regulatory requirements to assure improvements.

Not surprisingly these state reforms were unpopular in Baltimore. While the idea of taking over failing schools had been endorsed in 1991 by the Greater Baltimore Committee, the state teachers union had seen it as a plot to privatize the schools, harkening to the ongoing controversy over EAI. Also, MSPAP was staunchly opposed by community, civic, and political leaders in Baltimore as likely to single out the city's poor children unfairly. The assessments were designed to be rigorous, criterion-referenced exams, linked to standards.

Whether MSPAP is unfair is a matter still being debated, but the fears of Baltimore leaders proved to be accurate. While performance on the new assessments was low statewide, a large percentage of BCPSS schools performed miserably. Indeed, the reconstitution program singled out Baltimore schools exclusively in 1994 and 1995, with only two schools named in other jurisdictions by 1997. (Subsequently, beginning in 1998, sixteen schools were added to the list from Prince George's County.)[12]

MSPAP thus provided a policy framework within which state officials could measure specific progress or regress both in the school system as a whole and in these low-performing, reconstitution-eligible schools in BCPSS. By 2001, out of 183 schools in the city 82 were under local reconstitution and 4 had been placed under state reconstitution. MSPAP also provided a rationale for arguing that the city's school performance deficiencies were not just a matter of providing more money, but were systemic problems. While the state provided extra resources to help these schools implement a required school-improvement plan, they left the responsibility for improvement with local districts, an approach which freed the state of accountability. The failure of any school in Baltimore to improve sufficiently to exit from the list also proved an embarrassment, although state criteria for exiting were not spelled out for a number of years. To exit from the local reconstitution-eligible status, a school must achieve the state average on the school performance index.[13]

The school system's growing dependence on the state for adequate resources to fund its schools only accentuated the tension between Baltimore and state officials in the 1990s. As the city's tax base declined in the face of deindustrialization and population loss in the 1970s and 1980s, it had less capacity to fund its public schools. At the same time, the declining size of the Baltimore system relative to growing school systems in surrounding jurisdictions and elsewhere in the state lessened its claim on state school dollars, aggravated by its loss of voting strength in the state legislature.

Baltimore officials lobbied the state legislature repeatedly for increased state funding. In 1979 Mayor Schaefer had initiated an unsuccessful lawsuit, arguing that the city suffered from overburdens caused by educational needs, costs, and municipal funding requirements. In 1986 BUILD had mounted an unsuccessful campaign for more funds from the state legislature. After his election in 1987 Schmoke threatened lawsuits and finally decided in 1992 to join the American Civil Liberties Union (ACLU) in a suit. However, he was dissuaded by a sympathetic Governor Schaefer, who hoped to provoke legislative action by appointing the Governor's Commission on School Funding, chaired by Donald Hutchinson, president of the Maryland Business Roundtable. The commission recommended an increase in state funding to school systems and individual schools with high percentages of student poverty, with $500 million or more going to Baltimore city over a 5-year period.[14]

The negative legislative response in 1994 set the stage for the city-state partnership agreement that would emerge 2 years later. Maryland was still in the throes of a recession. Besides, it was an election year, making a tax increase an unpopular proposal. Some jurisdictions such as Montgomery County and Prince George's County argued that they would lose money under the proposed changes. Much criticism was leveled at the commission's failure to include any accountability provisions in its school funding proposals.

When the legislature failed to take any actions, the ACLU filed the above-mentioned suit on behalf of parents and students in 12 BCPSS schools deemed at risk of school failure, charging that the state did not provide sufficient aid to deliver on its constitutional obligation to provide a "thorough and efficient" education (*Bradford v. Maryland State Board of Education*).

The city initially joined the suit, then withdrew under pressure from the new governor, Parris Glendening, who promised favorable legislative action. When the 1995 legislature again failed to act, the city filed its own suit in September 1995. Now it was arguing that the state failed to provide resources for an adequate education for BCPSS youngsters, and it sought to curtail the state's reconstitution provisions. This set up the argument for the state's countersuit arguing that BCPSS's difficulties stemmed from mismanagement.

Throughout this period Rawlings used his influence as a legislative leader to keep pressure on the school system. He had conducted a hearing in January 1993 and informed the entire legislature of the Cresap recommendations, thus introducing the question of managerial competence into annual discussions about state legislative appropriations for BCPSS funding. The House of Delegates, at Rawlings's urging, adopted a provision that would withhold 2% of the state share of BCPSS funding for current expenses until BCPSS agreed to enter into a 3-year agreement with the Maryland State Department of Education (MSDE) to monitor the implementation of the Cresap recommendations. The budget conferees later struck the financial penalty, but left intact the requirement for an agreement. In the summer following this legislative action in April 1993, State Superintendent Nancy Grasmick and BCPSS Superintendent Walter Amprey entered into an agreement. From the viewpoint of the Baltimore school system, the agreement contained a number of onerous provisions. BCPSS had to provide a written explanation of why it was not implementing any of the recommendations, it had to designate a contact person to work with the oversight team appointed by MSDE, and it had to agree to a third-party independent evaluation of the school system's progress in implementing the Cresap Report.[15]

While Amprey professed to support most of the recommendations, his ability or inclination to follow through on his promises proved very disappointing to Rawlings and Grasmick. For example, one of the key recommendations was for the development of a systemwide personnel evaluation system. Amprey was hardly in a position to implement this reform. Because BCPSS was a department of city government, it enjoyed no autonomy from political interference and, as mentioned earlier, was used as a source of patronage in filling jobs and letting contracts; and this had led to the demise of a predecessor who had challenged the mayor.

Hearings held before the legislature in 1994 indicated little progress in implementation. In September 1994, MGT of America, Inc., a Florida consulting firm, was retained by the state to evaluate BCPSS's adoption of the Cresap Report's recommendations. The following January, MGT issued its report indicating that 39 of 53 major Cresap recommendations had not been implemented. Its findings for why there was such a lack of progress were as scathing as the original Cresap report itself: no master plan, disbanding of oversight groups within BCPSS, high central office turnover, and so on. The report lent legitimacy to the criticisms made by Rawlings and Grasmick.[16]

In 1995 the legislature's confrontation with BCPSS escalated when $5.9 million of Baltimore City's state education aid appropriation was withheld, pending implementation of the systemwide personnel evaluation system alluded to above. BCPSS's total state aid appropriation was $423.6 million, so this amount was more symbolic than substantive in the scope of the penalty imposed. Nonetheless, BCPSS's reported $27 million deficit was blamed on the state legislature. This dispute was aired through the news media and press, particularly the *Baltimore Sun*.[17]

In September 1995 the city filed suit against the state, arguing that the city's share of state aid was inadequate. In early 1996 the state superintendent and state board stated publicly that BCPSS had not made substantial progress in meeting the Cresap recommendations. The legislature again withheld $5.9 million, this time specifying that administrators found responsible for failing to implement recommendations would have their salaries docked for the final quarter of the year. The legislature also attached strings to eventual release of the withheld money, insisting that it go directly to schools, be spent on school improvement teams, professional development, and instructional materials. If this had the air of micromanagement by the legislature, it is nonetheless indicative of how badly the dispute had escalated over its protracted life. In other legislative action that year, $12 million was withheld from the state-aid appropriation for Baltimore, $10 million for innovative programs, and $2 million for teacher salary parity.

Governor Paris Glendening, while generally supportive of the actions of the state legislature and state board of education, was under heavy pressure from Baltimore City to veto the above provisions in House Bill 608. Baltimore voters had been a key to his slim electoral victory in his first term, and for that reason alone had to be listened to carefully. In a masterful gesture of compromise (some would say waffling) he vetoed the bill, arguing that with 6 weeks left in the fiscal year, the bill would create a financial crisis for the school system. However, on the same day he informed Mayor Kurt Schmoke that unless a partnership with the state was forthcoming by 28 July 1996, he would withhold the $5.9 million. For the first time he also required that the agreement be incorporated in consent decrees for the two pending lawsuits.[18]

To the school system's embarrassment, newspaper exposés continued to document financial mismanagement, which had resulted in overpayment of state aid. Shortly after serving his ultimatum on the mayor, Glendening held out a carrot of $140 million in additional state aid during the forthcoming 4 years, targeted for teachers' salaries and improvements for low-performing schools, on these conditions: The city had to drop its lawsuit against the state and restructure its management.[19] The mayor responded by labeling the governor's offer as "insulting and paternalistic," and countered that nothing less than $100 million in additional aid per year would suffice.[20]

During the ensuing months of 1996 complicated negotiations occurred. The city proposed the outlines of a city-state education partnership agreement, which was lambasted by state legislators and the state board of education as lacking any accountability, particularly with respect to the contested management reforms. Rawlings proposed legislation dealing with both management and educational issues, which the state board endorsed. In the meantime, the governor and mayor worked out a "memorandum of understanding" that provided a conceptual framework for the proposed city-state partnership and included the consent decree component sought by the legislature. However, Mayor Schmoke balked at signing the proposed agreement. Glendening raised the ante by announcing not only the withholding of the $5.9 million in dispute but also another $24 million in fiscal year 1997. To protect himself against critics who claimed he was hurting Baltimore schoolchildren, the governor withheld the money from the city's school construction fund. Meanwhile, in October 1996 the legislature held hearings on proposed legislation for the forthcoming 1997 session.

With regard to the finance lawsuit brought by the ACLU, Baltimore City Circuit Court Judge Joseph Kaplan ruled in October 1996 that all children in

Maryland have a right to an adequate education as measured by contemporary educational standards and that the children in Baltimore City were not receiving a constitutionally adequate education. The focus of the case then shifted to whether the city or the state was to blame for this inadequacy. The circuit court judge and federal judge set the date for the consolidated trial for early November 1996, creating a deadline for the disputants. The judges announced a postponement to permit an agreement to be developed.

On 26 November 1996, a settlement was announced requiring major management and education reforms in BCPSS. The outlines of the agreement have been summarized above. In an emotional signing authority in one of the courtrooms, the mayor in a choked voice acknowledged that what he was doing was in the best interests of the city's schoolchildren.[21] The agreement provided that the state legislature in its forthcoming session must "substantially concur" with this consent decree if the revised trial date in May 1997 was to be avoided.

Accordingly, MSDE introduced the appropriate legislation that required passage before two separate committees in each chamber of the state legislature. After protracted debate and resistance from many jurisdictions, the state legislature enacted State Bill 795. The bill was similar to the consent decree, providing $230 million in state aid over a 5-year period in exchange for the management reforms, with the notable exception that the management restructuring of BCPSS was now permanent, not merely a 5-year provision as had been agreed to in the consent decree. Governor Glendening signed the bill into law. Following provisions of the new law, the governor and mayor appointed a new school board and an interim superintendent.

In sum, by the 1990s the city had become dependent on the state for additional resources to fund its public school system. This dependence, however, converged with another political development: the growing activism of the state in pressing an accountability agenda for BCPSS. Mayor Schmoke did not anticipate that this convergence would present him with a Hobson's choice: Either succumb to a state takeover or acquiesce to a state partnership that provided more state funding only in exchange for radical diminution of mayoral power and significant managerial reforms. Despite his vigorous resistance, which reflected widespread opposition within the black community and the school system, in the end he accepted the inevitable.

THE PARTNERSHIP FOUR YEARS LATER

Four years after the partnership began, most of the problems besetting Baltimore's troubled school system, with its student population of 106,000, remain. Arguably, however, both the low student performance and mismanagement have been ameliorated to a degree. Test scores at the elementary level began to rise, on both the Comprehensive Test of Basic Skills (CTBS) and the MSPAP.

MSPAP scores are also rising (though still last in the state). For years, MSPAP scores were stuck between 13 and 14% passing. In the last 2 years, they have crossed 20%. CTBS results showed a 3-year upward trend. In 1998, 29% of the city's first graders read at or above the national average for their grade on CTBS. By 2001, this had climbed to 56%. In math, the percentage of first graders at or above grade level had risen from 30% to 52%. About half of the city's elementary schools, 58 of 117, increased their first-grade reading scores, while 33 schools slipped and 26 stayed the same. A little more than two-thirds (79 schools) improved their first-grade math scores, while 35 slipped and 3 stayed the same. This improvement was mirrored to varying degrees in other elementary grades. Twenty-five schools scored above the national average in reading in at least three grades. In three elementary schools students scored above the national average in all grades in both reading and math.

Carmen V. Russo, the school system's chief executive officer, praised pupils' hard work; there is a "new, dynamic culture of 'can-do' taking hold," she exclaimed. School board president J. Tyson Tilden attributed the turnaround in part to the community's belief that the city's children could succeed academically. School board member Sam Stringfield, a nationally known expert on school effectiveness, read the test trends as evidence that the city-state partnership is paying off, but he cautioned that more of a state financial investment is needed.[22]

Despite this progress, BCPSS students at elementary, middle, and secondary levels continue to perform the poorest overall in the state. For example, in 2001 about 75% of sixth- and seventh-grade students scored below the national average on CTBS, and the scores rose only slightly over the previous year's. The school system is just now turning its attention to a set of new policies to improve student performance at the middle and high school levels. School officials announced that they will raise standards for all students in grades six through eight, increase the number of citywide magnet schools, expand remedial programs for students in the lowest performing middle schools, and improve the quality of instruction in middle schools, among other things. The $4 million cost of these improvements was to be funded in part through increased state aid from the partnership, although it was not clear how such improvements would be funded after the first year.[23]

The city-state partnership provided the framework and impetus for a series of local actions that have led to these improvements. In one major shift, the school system reversed the course set under its previous superintendent, Walter Amprey, who had been committed to decentralizing authority to individual schools. Whatever its merits, that policy had led to great inconsistency in the curriculum delivered from school to school. The absence of a citywide curriculum caused numerous problems, among them difficulty in providing effective instruction to the large percentage of pupils who move from school to school within the school year or from one year to another. In 1999, the restructured school board, responding to leadership from the new chief academic officer, Betty Morgan, set ambitious goals to boost student achievement for all students, elementary through high school, as measured by state and national standardized tests.[24] It discarded the first group of goals it had set earlier, because they were too complicated. Under the new rules, nearly half of the city's elementary schoolchildren were expected to pass statewide math and reading tests by 2002. While this goal still was short of the 70% goal of satisfactory performance set by the state for the MSPAP test, it was still criticized within Baltimore as unrealistic.

The criticism underscored another problem the interim school superintendent, Robert Schiller, who headed the school system in the first year of the partnership, and the new school board sought to overcome—a legacy of low expectations for the city's predominantly poor African American student body.[25] Schiller had declared the school system to be "academically bankrupt."[26] Beginning with his initiatives, all schools were required to make a 10% increase in test scores each year.

To achieve these ambitious goals, the school system at first focused its resources primarily on improvements at elementary schools. A citywide curriculum for elementary math and reading was established, although a limited number of schools still were permitted to use school reform models such as Achievement First and Success for All in 19 of the city's worst performing schools. The city expanded the kindergartners' school day from half-day to all day and has begun half-day pre-kindergarten programs for 4-year-olds in some schools. Class size was lowered, particularly in the primary grades; each principal was given three new teaching positions to fill. The school day was lengthened, reading and math specialists were hired, new reading and math textbooks were purchased, and teachers were retrained in math and reading, including use of phonics in teaching reading. A new systemwide discipline code was put in place to give principals additional authority. Yearly diagnostic tests were put in place for all students, after-school academies were begun, and summer school was added.[27]

The school system also committed itself to increase the percentage of certified teachers and the mainstreaming of special education students. These goals were part of the required master plan that had to be approved by the state board. Additional state aid made it possible to improve starting salaries for new teachers by 4% in 1999 and to provide financial support for housing. Bureaucratic reforms allowed graduating college seniors to be offered teaching contracts earlier than ever before. Efforts were made to recruit teachers and principals from outside the city. Although starting teachers' salaries were still below those in neighboring Baltimore County, these policy changes met with some success, reducing the number of unstaffed classrooms at the beginning of the school year. A monthlong summer support program was begun for new teachers, taught by veteran teachers.

Responding to a state requirement, teachers and principals were now held accountable through a new evaluation system that included information on how well their students learn. Some teachers were fired, and in the first year alone more than 50 principals were either fired or demoted.[28] In October 1999 the school board also set new passing standards for students in Grades 1 through 8, stating that it was seeking to raise expectations and achievement. The new policy also ended social promotion of students and planned to provide intensive math and reading courses for eighth graders who failed to meet the standards before moving on to high school.[29]

At the same time, it is important to place these improvements in perspective. The state has continued to add schools to its Local Reconstitution list (now totaling 82), and only one school improved dramatically enough to be eligible for removal from the list. In the meantime, the state placed three Baltimore schools that had shown no progress under State Reconstitution in spring 2000, and turned them over to private management. They declared a fourth school reconstituted in 2001, although it was agreed to give BCPSS greater discretion in how reconstitution was to be handled. The school system did create a special district for its lowest-performing schools, and required its reconstitution-eligible schools to adopt one of the comprehensive school reform models, such as Success for All. Thus improvements in student performance, while hopeful, remain tenuous and uneven. With 47% of the city's schools under state or local reconstitution, the hurdles still to be surmounted are daunting.[30]

Perhaps the greatest success in the partnership has been to recruit a school board that has functioned cohesively and been strongly committed to creating a change in the organizational culture toward improved student performance and accountability for results. Yet the recruitment of a new board that functions independently of mayoral oversight (and intrusion) has not automatically translated into managerial reforms. The board has had difficulty recruiting sufficient highly qualified teachers and central office administrators. For example, its first choice of a chief executive officer, Robert Booker, failed to prevent embarrassing scandals involving his chief financial officer and other business officials. The board has had difficulty gaining control of the personnel recruitment process, and it would appear that vestiges of a patronage or "friends and neighbors" appointment system continue to survive several years after ties with city hall have been severed.[31]

Moreover, arguments over resources continue to poison the working relationship between the state and BCPSS. From a political perspective, this may be the greatest challenge to the survival of the partnership. Since partnerships ordinarily occur among equals, the legal dependence of the city upon the state for its funding introduces a potential for endless friction between the partners and a reminder that they are not equals after all. Illustrative of this problem, the city took the state to court in June 2000, arguing that the state had failed to meet its obligation to provide additional necessary resources. The parties reached an out-of-court settlement, which provided less money than the city had asked for in its suit but which arguably was the best deal it could get in the bargaining. However, critics in Baltimore charged that city officials had sold out too cheaply, reopening arguments that had raged at the time the city-state partnership was created. In the meantime, a state Commission on Education Finance, Equity, and Excellence, created by the 1999 session of the General Assembly, after moving slowly, commissioned a financing "adequacy" study for schools statewide and issued recommendations to the General Assembly in 2001. However, given the emergence of a state revenue problem in 2001, created by recessionary trends and the aftermath of the September 11 terrorist attacks, a large infusion of new state education aid seemed unlikely.[32]

Thus the state has been in no position to argue that it has provided BCPSS pupils with resources sufficient to guarantee an adequate education. While this expectation was held out by Baltimoreans when the partnership agreement was signed, in fact the state promised only to provide more money, not to meet any legal or professional standard of "adequate" funding. This loose standard had left the door open for the inevitable disputes that have flowed from such an ambiguous compromise. A weather vane of the gap between expectations and actual progress is that even after the infusion of additional revenues, BCPSS still has the lowest starting teacher salaries in the area.

THE MAYORAL VACUUM

Kurt Schmoke left office shortly after the partnership agreement was implemented. His successor, Martin O'Malley, has proven a popular mayor, who has focused primarily on crime. No one doubts that violent crime has been one of the city's major problems. In 1997 only Detroit, New Orleans, and Washington, D.C., had a higher violent crime and murder rate.[33] More recently, O'Malley also has given attention to further economic development, particularly in the downtown area. In his reelection campaign the issue of education was not prominent.

Nominally, the mayor still has a role in public education, since he retains a voice in the appointment of board members along with the governor, working from a slate provided by the state board of education. Informally, it is reported that he has recruited some members to serve and made it known that he favored the choice of Carmen Russo as the new chief executive officer for BCPSS in 2000, rather than a local candidate Bonnie Copeland. However, O'Malley has limited his involvement in public education very sharply to providing occasional nominal support for the board's initiatives, such as its attempts to get more state aid, and sharing in credit for the modest improvements in student achievement seen in recent years. Unlike Schmoke, he has steered clear of any attempt to set out a specific course of reform. Not only did the partnership strip the mayor of formal authority, but also it implicitly reduced his legitimacy as a leader in this realm.

From an organizational reform perspective, this separation has a compelling logic. City hall's dominance of BCPSS in the past had politicized personnel and budgetary decisions to a high degree, initially under Schaefer in matters of patronage and later under Schmoke also as a means of achieving the mayor's reform objectives. Like the Progressive reforms in the early twentieth century, which were also strongly influenced by business principles, these reforms are intended to restore integrity and efficiency. But in contrast to Progressive reforms, the expectations for achieving productive student outcomes are much higher.

This raises the question of whether the partnership has created the political will necessary to reverse a pattern of organizational decline. Researchers argue that civic capacity is essential to renewal,[34] and this requires the concerted leadership of the mayor and civic and community leaders. Even with Schmoke's leadership, creation of this civic capacity proved elusive in Baltimore. However, the question remains whether structural reform in itself is sufficient if it lacks the political muscle in which the mayor must play a key role. A new power-sharing arrangement has reduced the formal authority of the mayor. While there now is more accountability for improved student performance, the current mayor no longer is as directly accountable for these student outcomes as were his predecessors. This raises an important question: Without a community-wide effort that includes the mayor as a major player in reform, will those dramatic improvements in student achievement be possible?

Equally important, without significant mayoral leadership will there be the political will at the state level to provide Baltimore City with the resources it needs? Student spending from state and local sources still is among the lowest in the state. When Maryland citizens were asked in a 2001 poll if they were willing to provide additional state funds to help Baltimore City schools, 52% said yes, but in a number of the regions of the state the number was well below 50%,[35] raising questions about whether legislative support for such an initiative could be garnered.

This aspect of the challenge to the future of BCPSS is inherently political owing to the city's economic dependence on state aid and its declining electoral and legislative strength. Despite the city's declining political power, the state has been willing to assume responsibility for funding a number of other public services to alleviate the local tax burden in Baltimore. However, the case for treating Baltimore schoolchildren is more complex than state funding of the zoo, the city jail, and city community college. It involves a profound moral question about the just treatment of poor children and constitutional claims concerning educational adequacy affecting the entire state. Unless the state is willing to confront these issues and deliver its half of the bargain in the city-state partnership, the current partnership is unlikely to succeed politically. Most important, the dramatic improvements in student achievement to which the partnership is committed are likely to remain unfulfilled.

NOTES

1. This paper is based on extensive documentary analysis of primary and secondary sources as well as interviews with approximately 40 government officials and civic and community leaders from the city, other local jurisdictions, and the state.

The research was conducted between 1996 and 2002. Many respondents were interviewed more than once as the partnership and policies surrounding it have evolved.

2. In addition, certain legal issues were resolved relating to the lawsuits. Court supervision of the special education programs of BCPSS was reduced. Continuation of the court monitor's function was left contingent on further negotiation, depending on school system progress. However, other provisions of the prior court orders in *Vaughn G.* remained intact.

3. J. Kingdon, *Agenda, Alternatives, and Public Policies*, 2nd ed. (New York: Harper-Collins, 1999).

4. M. Orr, *Black Social Capital: The Politics of School Reform in Baltimore, 1986–1998* (Lawrence: University of Kansas Press, 1999), p. 81.

5. For a more complete discussion of this issue, see Orr, *Black Social Capital*.

6. Associated Black Charities, *A Study of the Management of the Baltimore City Public Schools* (Baltimore: Author, 1992).

7. MGT of America, Inc., *A Report on the Monitoring and Evaluating Implementation of Management Study Recommendations in Baltimore City Public Schools* (Baltimore: Author, 12 January 1995).

8. Orr, *Black Social Capital*, 54–57.

9. Ibid., 58.

10. P. L. Szanton, *Baltimore 2000: A Choice of Futures* (Baltimore: Morris Goldseker Foundation, 1986).

11. Maryland State Department of Education, *The Report of the Governor's Commission on School Performance* (Annapolis, MD: Office of the Governor, August 1989).

12. Historical data on schools placed under local reconstitution and state reconstitution are available on the web site of the Maryland State Department of Education: *http://www.msde.state.md.us*

13. This is known as the Public School Standards Regulation, in the *Code of Maryland Regulations* (*COMAR*), 13A.01.04.07–08.

14. Maryland State Department of Education, *The Report of the Governor's Commission on School Funding* (Annapolis, MD: Office of the Governor, 1994).

15. Delegate Pete Rawlings, interview, 24 October 1997. Also see Orr, *Black Social Capital*, 177.

16. MGT of America, Inc., *Report on the Monitoring*.

17. K. Shatzkin and M. Bowter, "Maryland Fires a Salvo in School Dispute: Amprey Accused of Mismanagement; Reorganization Sought," *Baltimore Sun*, 21 October 1995, p. 1A.

18. P. Jensen, "City OK'd in Pay of City Schools Top Staff: Assembly Ties Funds from MD to Forfeiture," *Baltimore Sun*, 7 April 1996, p. 1C.

19. J. Thompson and T. W. Waldron, "Proposal for City School Aid Detailed: Glendening Offers to Add $140 Million over Four Years," *Baltimore Sun*, 20 June 1996, p. 1A.

20. J. Thompson, "Schmoke Says School Aid Falls Short: State's Demands Called 'Insulting,'" *Baltimore Sun*, 21 June 1996, p. 1A.

21. J. Thompson and E. Siegel, "City, State Sign Deal for Schools," *Baltimore Sun*, 27 November 1996, p. 1A.

22. L. Bowie and E. Niedowski, "Improving Test Scores Hailed as Turnaround," *Baltimore Sun*, 18 May 2001, pp. 1A, 8A.

23. L. Bowie, "Educators Extend Reforms to Middle Schools in the City," *Baltimore Sun*, 23 May 2001, pp. 1A, 13A.

24. L. Bowie, "Test Bar Set High for Schools," *Baltimore Sun*, 15 July 1999, p. 1B.

25. L. Bowie, "Booker Vows to Push Reform," *Baltimore Sun*, 6 July 1998, p. 1B.

26. L. Bowie and J. Daemmrich, "City School Chief to Quit: Low-Profile Booker Ready to 'Pass Baton' at End of Term in June," *Baltimore Sun*, 12 January 2000, p. 1A.

27. S. Henderson and J. Thompson, "School Board Maps Goals," *Baltimore Sun*, 7 August 1997, p. 1B. See also J. Thompson, "$30 Million Set for School Improvements," *Baltimore Sun*, 27 August 1997, p. 1B.

28. M. Maushard, "City Schools Blueprint Wins OK of State Panel," *Baltimore Sun*, 29 July 1998, p. 3B.

29. L. Bowie, "City Raises Standards for Pupil Performance," *Baltimore Sun*, 13 October 1999, p. 1B.

30. This was calculated using data in the BCPSS web site (*http://www.bcps.k12.md.us*) and Maryland State Department of Education web site (*http://www.msde.state.md.us*).

31. Interview with school board member, April 2001.

32. The commission's reports can be found at *http://mlis.state.md.us/other/education/index.htm*

33. K. Maguire and A. L. Pastor, *Source Book of Criminal Justice Studies, 1998* (Washington, DC: U.S. Government Printing Office, 1998), p. 281, Table 3.1222.

34. C. N. Stone, "Civic Capacity and Urban School Reform," in *Changing Urban Education*, ed. C. Stone (Lawrence: University of Kansas Press, 1999), pp. 266–67. See also J. Portz, L. Stein, and R. Jones, *City Schools and City Politics: Institutions and Leadership in Pittsburgh, Boston, and St. Louis* (Lawrence: University Press of Kansas, 1999).

35. The Maryland Poll as reported in the *Montgomery Gazette*, 12 January 2001.

Chapter 7

WHAT HAPPENED IN THE SIX CITIES?

Larry Cuban and Michael Usdan

"There is no better constructive publicity for a city than to be known over the entire country as a city of good schools," said a member of the Portland Board of Education in 1915. Connecting strong schools to a growing, family-friendly, culturally rich, and economically healthy city binds Progressive reformers from almost a century ago to their twenty-first-century counterparts who see better schools as a vehicle for creating better cities. Bumper stickers then and now could well read: Good schools = a vital city.[1]

In the early to mid-1990s, business, political, and educational leaders in the six cities profiled in this book sought to fix the problems crippling students' academic performance. They defined the problem as quarrelsome school boards; inept management that couldn't clean buildings, deliver supplies, or help teachers do their jobs; and little accountability for producing satisfactory academic outcomes among administrators and teachers. The problem was not located in society, the local neighborhood, or in insufficient funds; the problem was in the governance and management of schools. In city after city, these business and civic leaders urged district officials to restructure their control of schools and apply sound business principles in order to improve students' academic performance. They believed that higher achievement would produce smarter, independent, and reliable high school graduates who would function as suitable employees and dutiful citizens. How would this happen?

Business and civic leaders counted on governance reforms—that is, changes in political authority and supervision in tax-supported institutions—wedded to more effective district management, and individual school accountability to prod teachers to teach better and students to learn more. These reforms, in turn, would lead to improved student scores on standardized achievement tests and, ultimately, yield graduates with marketable skills and attitudes to perform satisfactorily in an information-based economy.[2]

Better urban schooling, then, would mean that mayors could attract companies (and increased tax revenues) to the city. Employers saw better schools in the city as an incentive to offer potential employees and their families. More companies locating in the city provide a deeper and broader tax base to fund a rich array of cultural, recreational, and social services that would reinvigorate urban economic and social health. Fix the schools' political problems of inept command-and-control authority and little accountability first, then educational performance will improve and cities will reap the benefits. Good schools = a vital city!

These beliefs, repeated to us again and again in an amazingly common refrain with can-do enthusiasm, became the dominant theory of action put into practice by mayors, business and civic leaders, school boards, and superintendents in these six cities during the 1990s. Less agreement, however, occurred over which political tools—mayoral control of education or appointing nontraditional educators, or both—were the best strategies. In Chicago, Philadelphia, San Diego, and Seattle nontraditional educators became CEOs. In Chicago, Boston, and Baltimore (until 1997), mayors directly appointed school boards and superintendents and controlled the school budgets.[3]

The snapshots we took in 2000–2002 of the governance reforms, managerial strategies to improve instruction and achieve desired outcomes in the six cities, capture nearly a decade of reform and make it difficult to generalize for all cities across time and to extract lessons for others to heed. Later in this chapter, we offer some reflections, informed by our knowledge of the past, which put these snapshots in a larger context. Before we analyze the governance and leadership changes that occurred in these cities, we summarize some basic facts about our six cities.

Table 7.1 shows the demographic profiles of the six cities. Given the historical connections between poverty and low academic achievement, Baltimore, Boston, Chicago, and Philadelphia had three-quarters or more of their students eligible for free or reduced lunch, a primary indicator of poverty. San Diego and Seattle had far lower percentages of impoverished children attending school. With these demographic figures in mind, we turn to the changes that civic and business leaders implemented in the six cities.

Table 7.2 lists seven aspects of political and governance reforms and their roles in each city. Business and civic leaders in five of the cities, strongly influenced by state legislation, designed and implemented districtwide changes from the top, that is, without much teacher or parent involvement. Also, school leaders who stayed 5 or more years—either having no experience in education or products of the traditional career path in schools—drew from the same sources in constructing their reform strategies.

Historically, superintendents performed three leadership roles simultaneously: managerial, instructional, and political. Often, a superintendent who was strong, say, in managing the district and dealing politically with community groups would appoint a deputy strong in instruction. In the 1990s, David Hornbeck, John Stanford, Joseph Olchefske, and Alan Bersin performed roles

TABLE 7.1. Demographic Profiles

	Baltimore	*Boston*	*Chicago*	*Philadelphia*	*San Diego*	*Seattle*
Total population[1]	651,154	589,141	2,896,016	1,517,550	1,223,400	563,374
School district population[2]	108,759	63,588	421,334	212,150	133,687	47,883
Dollar expenditure per pupil[3]	6,370	9, 545	7,827	7,669	5,328	6,723
Percent black and Latino	86	76	86	78	55	32
Percent poor	75	74	86	80	47	40
High school dropout rate[4]	10.4	8.3	15.5	11.8	14.4	13.4

[1]www.demographia.com/db-uscity98.htm
[2]Baltimore figures are for 1996–1997 in Gary Orfield and John Yun, *Resegregation in American Schools* (Cambridge, MA: Civil Rights Project, Harvard University, 1999), p. 9. Other figures come from each district's website for 2001.
[3]Figures for school district population, expenditures per pupil, and percent black and Latino come from National Center of Education Statistics, "Characteristics of the 100 Largest Elementary and Secondary School Districts in the United States: 1997–1998," Tables 9 and 10, July 1999. Other figures come from each district's website for 2001.
[4]Dropout rates come from websites for each district, 2000–2001.

that played to their respective strengths while delegating to key subordinates those roles in which they needed help. Tom Payzant, Paul Vallas, and a succession of Baltimore school chiefs focused on both the managerial and instructional while dealing politically with groups inside the system and letting their respective mayors handle overall negotiations and political responsibility for the district's performance.[4]

Table 7.3 shows which managerial and instructional strategies were implemented by the six cities. In almost every city, top school officials reorganized district staff; concentrated managerial and instructional authority in the superintendent's office; constantly searched for grants to fund reforms; aligned state and local standards, texts, and professional development; and installed rewards and sanctions for students, principals, and schools. Seeking to restructure a school system, corporate and civic leaders pressed school officials to use successful business practices in overhauling the district, including creating clear goals and tying those goals to high academic standards, frequent testing, and a brace of incen-

TABLE 7.2. Political and Governance Reforms

Action	Baltimore	Boston	Chicago	Philadelphia	San Diego	Seattle
Mayoral control of schools	Before 1997; state/district control since	1991	1995	1999; state/mayoral control since 2001	None	None
Noneducator superintendent	None	None	1995, 2001	1994, 2001	1998	1995, 1998
Superintendent tenure during reforms	Hunter 1987–1991 Amphrey 1991–1997 Booker 1997–2000 Russo 2000–	Payzant 1995–	Vallas 1995–2001 Duncan 2001–	Hornbeck 1994–2000 Goldsmith 2001–	Bersin 1998–	Stanford 1995–1998 Olchefske 1998–
Role of state in funding, setting standards, testing, and so on	Heavy	Moderate to heavy	Minor except for laws that authorize changes	Heavy	Moderate to heavy	Moderate
Union role in school reform	Episodically supports or opposes	Supports mayor	Supports mayor	Opposes	Opposes	Supports
Business elites' role in school reform	Episodic	Strong	Strong	Episodic and lessening	Strong	Strong
Parental involvement initiatives	Few	Few	Some	Some	Few	Few

TABLE 7.3. Implemented Managerial and Instructional Strategies

Strategy	Baltimore	Boston	Chicago	Philadelphia	San Diego	Seattle
Sought more funds from state, business, foundations	Yes	Yes	Yes	Yes	Yes	Yes
Consolidated district offices and administrative posts	Yes	Yes	Yes	Yes	Yes	No
Centralized/ Decentralized control of reform	Decentralized (1988–1997) Centralized (1997–)	Centralized (1995–)	Decentralized (1988–1995) Centralized (1995–)	Decentralized (1995–) Centralized (2001)	Decentralized (1980s–1998) Centralized (1998–)	Decentralized (1995–)
Aligned instructional support with higher academic achievement						
*principal role	Yes	Yes	No	No	Yes	Yes
* teacher professional development	Moderate to high	Moderate to high	Low	Moderate	High	Moderate
Aligned curriculum, texts, tests, professional development	Yes	Yes	Yes	Yes	Yes	No

151

tives and penalties to hold students, principals, and schools accountable for results.[5]

In the mid- to late 1990s, then, a national civic coalition of business leaders, public officials, and educators endorsed systemic reform, a phrase drawn from an academic article written by Marshall Smith and Jennifer O'Day. Since then, "systemic reform" has merged with the early to mid-1990s movement for creating curriculum, standards, performance standards for students and schools, expanded testing, and an array of accountability indicators aimed at prodding both students and adults to work harder in raising academic achievement as measured by tests. Part of this movement included state and district interventions into low-performing schools from reconstitution through state and district takeovers. Centralizing authority on school matters into the hands of district superintendents and aligning the different elements of school operations became a familiar recipe for improving district management and students' academic performance.[6]

What also became familiar in these districts were the difficulties in creating an instructional infrastructure and culture that supported principals and teachers to improve teaching and learning. Whether to centralize or decentralize instructional operations within a district was a question that the six districts answered throughout the 1980s and 1990s by switching from one to the other without much certainty over which was better and why. No research findings or expert advice could point with confidence to the most effective form of district organization.[7]

Uncertainty over district organization seldom spilled over educators in determining what to do about role of principals or professional development for teachers. In aligning district standards, curriculum, textbooks, and tests to make instruction both coherent and directed toward raising students' academic performance, at least three of the cities (Boston, San Diego, and Seattle) focused on converting principals from their historical role as managers to becoming instructional leaders. All of the cities reconceptualized (but implemented differentially) teacher professional development to concentrate on expanding practitioners' knowledge and skills in reading, math, and other subjects while building trust among teachers and principals and between them and their superintendents.[8]

Table 7.3 reveals such efforts were spotty. Whether as union members or as individuals, teachers played a minor role in designing reforms aimed at improving students' academic performance. Moreover, school board and superintendent efforts to amend teacher union contracts on issues of seniority and accountability in four of the six cities—an item placed on school officials' agenda by civic and business leaders in these cities—implicitly targets unions as part of the problem of low-performing students. School leaders' undisguised hostility toward unions in Philadelphia and San Diego, for whatever reasons, strongly tainted relationships between those superintendents and their teachers. Whether establishing such a coherent instructional guidance system, supported by new roles for principals, and a capacity-building infrastructure for both teachers and administrators actually produce improved students' outcomes is much too soon to judge. A few researchers, however, have claimed that governance reforms, particularly mayoral takeover of school districts have resulted in improved standardized achievement test scores in the lowest-performing elementary schools but have little to no effect on secondary schools.[9]

And what about outcomes in the six districts? Since states and districts have so often reduced students' academic performance to the results of standardized achievement tests, referring to "outcomes" has meant test scores. We want to include, however, other outcomes that civic coalitions in these cities sought from governance and leadership changes.

The implicit theory behind changing how urban school districts are governed and managed requires certain conditions to be in place either prior to or simultaneous with test score improvements. So, for example, tightly coupling district goals, curriculum, professional development, and tests in addition to accountability measures represents an important condition consistent with the internal logic of this reform. We determined whether the tight coupling materialized. Or to cite another example, in those districts where mayors have exerted control over schools, and business elites have actively endorsed the direction (e.g., Chicago, Boston), we would expect two outcomes to have occurred: first, increased coordination of city and school services since schools in those cities have largely become departments of the mayor's cabinet, and second, heightened political support for schools from mayors, business leaders, and major media outlets. We found only partial evidence of increased city and school coordination and, except in Baltimore and Philadelphia, moderate to strong political and media support.

We also know from the history of school reform in the United States that often there are unintended outcomes. For example, a stable corps of teachers and principals is critical for full implementation of desired changes in classroom practices to occur. Increased teacher and principal turnover in the six cities, then, would be unanticipated outcomes and might well threaten the long-term viability of the reform. Table 7.4 includes both intended and unintended outcomes.[10]

Table 7.4 shows a mixed bag of outcomes. By 2002, Boston, Seattle, and San Diego had moved ahead albeit unevenly toward aligning the various elements geared to supporting principals and teachers in helping their students improve academic performance. The other three cities were floundering or were just inching into the early phases of alignment. Although improved coordination of recreation, the arts, and medical and social services had seldom been a top item on the political agenda of civic coalitions stumping for mayorally controlled school districts, it is a reasonable expectation derived from superintendents becoming part of mayors' teams. In Baltimore (until 1997), there was no perceptible increase in coordinated services. Only in Boston were modest efforts made to tie city and school services together; in Chicago and Philadelphia efforts occurred but they could be only characterized as gestures.

Even with edgy criticism from parents and community groups over top-down decisions reducing their participation and hardly any service coordination be-

TABLE 7.4. Outcomes

Outcome	Baltimore	Boston	Chicago	Philadelphia	San Diego	Seattle
Aligned curriculum, professional development, tests, and rewards/penalties	Low	Moderate	Low	Low to moderate	High	Moderate
Political support of district reforms	Low	High	High	Low	High	High
Improved coordination of city and school services	None	Moderate	Low to moderate	Low	None	None
Increased turnover among:						
Teachers	Not available	Moderate	Moderate	High	Not available	Not available
Principals	Not available	High	High	High	Not available	Not available
Improved test scores:						
Elementary	Yes	Yes	Yes	Yes	Yes	Yes
Secondary	No	No	No	No	No	No
Reduced gap between white and minority scores	No	No	No	No	No	No

tween cities and schools, political support from business elites and city leaders remained strong in Chicago, Boston, San Diego, and Seattle. In those cities, school boards had extended their superintendents' contracts, and newspaper and television editorials praised the direction school leaders were taking. Paul Vallas worked hard for 5 years restoring the confidence of business and civic leaders. Although Mayor Daley in Chicago did remove Vallas, the CEO's earlier shoring up of political support paid dividends for his successor.[11]

And what about test scores? Table 7.4 displays our judgments about elementary and secondary school test scores and the stubborn discrepancy between white and minority scores. Except for slight to moderate improvements in elementary school students' test scores across the cities, little improvement emerges for secondary school students and the gap in achievement test scores remains largely as it was prior to initiatives undertaken by the urban school leaders since the mid-1990s.

Such test scores are neither a victorious trumpet call nor an epitaph for urban school governance reform. The theory of action behind changes in governance and leadership called for installing effective managers, aligning closely the key elements of a school system, and establishing individual school accountability. Systemic reform, advocates believed, would press principals, teachers, and students to work harder and produce better scores on standardized achievement tests. As the data from these six cities reveal—as do data from states that have engaged in standards-based systemic reform—the theory is shot through with ifs, ands, and buts. In a few cities, the theory is slowly and fully being implemented, but in other districts, much less so, or even abandoned.[12]

Moreover, in the early years of systemic reform both in cities and states, test scores are primitive measures and offer little proof of success or failure. Few noneducators, parents, and voters have come to realize or even appreciate the following points about standardized test scores about which informed policy makers, researchers, and seasoned practitioners are well aware:[13]

• *Different students get tested each year.* Because most urban districts administer their standardized achievement tests to a different group of students once a year, it is unclear whether the test score gains (or losses) seen in a year will be sustained or reversed in the subsequent year. Following a cohort of students year after year offers stronger evidence for the impact of changed instructional approaches. Few urban districts conduct such analyses, and when they do, few make them available to the public. Thus, attributing test score improvements in elementary schools to district governance reforms and new managerial and instructional strategies after 1 or 2 years is at best premature and at worst misleading.

• *Test preparation raises scores.* Gains in elementary schools across the six cities can come from determined (and ethically appropriate) efforts from teachers and principals to prepare all (not just selected) students for the test, tailoring of the curriculum to the test, extensive coaching of those students who can make the largest gains, and combinations of the foregoing. Thus, determining clearly why in a particular year elementary students score higher than previous groups is dicey without careful, detailed analysis of in-school and across-school practices.[14]

• *Test scores are poor predictors of future performance.* Few experts are willing to say with confidence that test score improvements in reading and math skills translate into students' applying those skills outside of school, displaying a greater desire to learn, or continuing their education.

• *Urban high school students do poorly on standardized tests.* Test scores for urban high schools enrolling high percentages of poor and minority students have been historically low and resistant to improvement. Accumulated reading and math deficits, repeated failure in earlier grades, substantial numbers of noncredentialed and inexperienced teachers, the large size of most high schools and the structure and organization of secondary schools—as compared to elementary schools—have worked against individual and group interventions to improve teaching and learning in these settings. Beyond calls for reconstituting failing schools, breaking high schools into smaller units, creating charter schools, and personalizing instruction, there is little research that points to credible formulas to improve academic achievement in secondary schools.[15]

• *Closing the test score gap has been elusive.* Reformers have proposed many solutions for reducing the test score gap between white and minority students. Proposals include increased racial integration of students, teaching that is responsive to cultural and ethnic differences, and extensive preschool and elementary school interventions. Research findings have yet to endorse these varied solutions.[16]

The previous points on testing argue for restraint in rushing to judgments about the linkages between test scores and reforms. Patience harnessed to a deeper understanding of how school districts work, the limits of applying business principles to schools and tests, especially how scores are evaluated, we believe, is sensible before leaping to conclusions about the success or failure of urban school governance reform. At least 5 to 7 years of full implementation of the theory of action and test scores will reveal clearly trends and patterns, especially if the performance of particular groups of students in and across schools are aggressively pursued for that period of time. The lust for quick results and the inexorable media rush to crank out a new story distorts what occurs in urban schools and prevents figuring out cause and effect.

What does all of this add up to? We conclude that civic coalitions in the 1990s seeking governance and organizational reforms—mayoral control or appointing noneducators as superintendents—may have established certain conditions for improved academic achievement, but have not yet led directly to improved classroom teaching and learning. The chain of command flowing from district decisions to classroom teaching and learning has many links; weak or nonexistent links can interrupt what occurs and break the chain. Even with shared views of what caused students' unacceptably low academic performance (e.g., poor district management, unresponsive bureaucracy) and common solutions (e.g., systemic school reform), one needs to look no further than Baltimore and Chicago to see that political effectiveness in launching governance changes and organizational success in implementing corporate-style management in the 1980s and 1990s have yet to reach the goal of sustained and widespread overall growth in educational effectiveness.

Another assumption driving the political logic of governance and managerial reforms leading to better teaching and learning is that in drawing leaders from noneducational organizations, more efficient and effective management practices anchored in business principles would be put into place. Bureaucratic obstacles would be reduced and students' academic performance would improve. San Diego becomes an attractive advertisement for the managerial part of this assumption in the 4 years that Bersin has been superintendent. Yet, even here, test score gains plateaued in 2000 and varied greatly between elementary and secondary schools. Attributing gains to effective management and systemic reform, for the reasons offered above, still remains premature. Although Chicago offers an instance of a CEO decisively acting in determining budgets, waiving rules, and slicing through bureaucratic layers, the accumulated evidence for the city counters civic and business leaders' deep wish to connect governance changes and better management to improved student outcomes.[17]

Finally, reformers believed that school leaders who were wired into existing city political and economic structures (including business elites) would increase chances of improving and sustaining students' academic achievement. While promoters of these reforms could nicely point to Boston in support of this assumption, skeptics could just as easily point to counter examples of Baltimore, where two-term mayor Karl Schmoke had his appointees running the schools with paltry results, and Chicago, where the mayor dumped the superintendent and school board president when elementary school test scores leveled off.[18]

EXPLAINING MIXED OUTCOMES

Why have the highly motivated reformers' political, organizational, and educational theory of action and assumptions shown such mixed results in these six cities? One reason may stem from how we did this study.

Basically, we collected documents covering events over the past decade in each city and interviewed key players in the reforms. Thus we have a snapshot of large school districts undergoing change, taken at one point in time. Snapshots are very helpful in describing events but less helpful in figuring out patterns. It may well be that the picture we have laid out for readers is part of an evolving process of change within a school district that would yield very different conclusions had we had an album of photos, much like an in-depth history of the district. Had we taken the longer view, we could see more clearly whether the events we recorded and the outcomes we documented were singular or patterned. Perhaps in time the reforms would have matured and the desired results would have emerged. So much (but not all) of the recent literature on urban school districts consists of snapshots rather than albums, resulting in a curious set of pictures frozen in time. Thus the mixed bag of outcomes may be a result of our methodology.[19]

Variation in outcomes may also result from a history of decentralized decision making within a federal system of divided powers. In 2001 there are 50 state school systems with nearly 15,000 school districts housing almost 90,000 public schools. Such a decentralized system of school governance means that variation in districts—urban, rural, and suburban—is a constant. Thus the mix of outcomes may have occurred because of different urban contexts.

Although reformers in the six cities held common political conceptions of what caused the problem of low academic performance in schools (e.g., too much district bureaucracy, poor management, and so on) and what political solutions should be applied (e.g., mayoral control, standards-based curriculum, testing, and accountability), each district's demography, history, and past leadership inside and outside the schools influenced what occurred.

To understand Boston, for example, one must know the ethnic and racial school politics that colored the district since World War II, the explosive growth of largely white suburbs prior to, and accelerated by, the conflict-filled court-ordered desegregation battles of the mid-1970s, the growth of the parochial school population, the concentration of poor minorities in the city schools, and the elected school committee's loss of political respectability. The struggle to eliminate the elected school committee took many years and is a unique story unlike Seattle, San Diego, or Baltimore. Thus mixed outcomes may well result from the simple fact of historical and demographic differences among these districts.[20]

If context matters in shaping the direction and texture of reform in a city, as we believe it does, so does concerted city, business, and district political leadership. Seattle's business community joining with the teachers' union to endorse and support John Stanford, a former U.S. Army general, and then his trusted lieutenant, Joseph Olchefske, after Stanford's death speaks to the importance of not only initiating political changes but a continuity in civic and business leadership that extends beyond one term of a superintendent. Similarly, stability in political leadership has led to Tom Payzant's contract being extended to 2005, as have contracts for Alan Bersin and Anthony Alvarado in San Diego.

Hard as it is to find leaders to initiate reforms aimed at improving teaching and learning, it is doubly hard to keep leaders (or replace them with like-minded successors) who sustain the reforms over time. Consider that the decentralized organization and major reform initiatives that Philadelphia's David Hornbeck promoted in Children Achieving for 5 years were thoroughly dismantled a few months after he left.[21]

Reforms tailored to unique city contexts and political coalitions supporting school leaders are far from a recipe for improving urban districts. The fevered search among reformers for just the right formula of urban school improvement to apply to each and every city—what policy makers call "going to scale"—given the experiences of these six cities in the 1980s and 1990s, is a fool's errand. That has been the sorry record of urban school reform for the past quarter-century and represents the major challenge to these six cities. Establishing the right conditions for district reform matched to the unique features of a city is painstakingly crafted work that often puts off impatient advocates but is necessary, based on the evidence of these six cities. And that is why we have entitled this book *Powerful Reforms with Shallow Roots.*

Of the six cities, three stand out now as examples of powerful reforms uniquely fitted to their settings: Boston, San Diego, and Seattle. We also believe that the roots that these cities have thus far sent down into their soil are shallow. Why powerful? And why shallow?

Why powerful? Boston and San Diego are very different districts in size, history, cultural diversity, and socioeconomic composition. For example, Boston has 74% of its children receiving free and reduced price lunches while San Diego has 47%; Boston has 76% minority school enrollment, mostly black and Latino students, compared to 55% for San Diego, mostly Latino and black. Even with these demographic differences the business-driven civic coalitions that placed Payzant and Bersin into the superintendencies are still active, have continued to give full support to their school leaders, and insured that their contracts are extended (see Tables 7.1 and 7.2).

Bersin has had no experience as an educator although he did appoint a veteran school administrator from New York City as second-in-command. Bersin has had few contacts with the mayor, city manager, and council in San Diego and remains at loggerheads with the school board and teachers union. Payzant—former school chief in San Diego—sits in Mayor Tom Menino's cabinet and has congenial relations with the teachers union. Both superintendents, with very different personal styles and working at very different paces, have leveraged private funds and state legislation to design and put into action an instructional infrastructure sharply focused on teaching and learning. Budgets are built around the mission of improved academic achievement in literacy and math so that teacher-coaches assigned to schools, professional development, and principals acting as instructional leaders are increasingly aligned to both performance benchmarks and state and local tests. Both school chiefs are trying to implement the theory of action by creating district and school cultures that support teaching and learning. In effect, a powerful machine fueled by top-down decision making and geared to helping teachers teach better and students achieve has been built piece by piece, amid errors and fumbling, in each city.

Why shallow roots? Shallow roots is a metaphor for unstable political support among civic and business leaders for school reform, and intense, unrelenting conflict between and among the school board, administration, and teachers over the direction and logistics of the reform agenda. The phrase suggests the overall fragility of top-down, centralized reform.

Based on our study of the six cities, the reforms are "shallow" in three senses. First, these reforms are heavily dependent on the visible presence and continuity of school leaders. The history of urban school leadership since the 1960s has seen civic coalitions championing a reform and losing interest in it after a few years. No surprise then that some of our city coalitions lost steam and abbreviated school board and superintendent tenures resulted.[22]

Second, constructing an inviting instructional infrastructure for principals and teachers is tough organizational work. Sustained and rich professional development accompanied by accountability measures that translate into a district and school culture leading to improved classroom teaching and learning is logistically demanding and requires school-based professionals to remain in their jobs. Building this infrastructure and creating a culture that concentrates on classroom teaching and learning requires school leaders' strong commitment, extensive time, access to specialists, and much money.

Third, because the aim of top-down systemic reform is to impact classroom teaching and learning, securing teachers' endorsement and parents' support for changes are essential. Evidence of substantial parent and teacher approval and shifts in classroom practice has yet to emerge. Based on the history of classroom innovations, without parent endorsement and active teacher cooperation in putting the changes into practice, urban school reformers again will be disappointed.[23]

In 2002, for Philadelphia, Chicago, and Baltimore, "shallow roots" in the three senses that we have used applies all too clearly. Deep changes have occurred in the three cities' reform coalitions. There have been leadership mishaps, intense conflicts between powerful constituencies, tortuous difficulties in establishing instructional infrastructures and cultures, and the absence of teacher enthusiasm for converting reforms into classrooms practices.

For San Diego, Boston, and Seattle where the conditions for sustained powerful reform have been put in place, "shallow roots" also applies. Their civic coalitions, demography, leadership, and determined actions, however, offer more promise for sinking deeper into soil than the other three cities.

In San Diego, shallow roots refers to the ongoing struggle between the teachers union and Bersin and the slim 3–2 majority the superintendent carries into each school board meeting. Subsequent school board and union elections may change the school board configuration and union leadership. The possibility of continued hostility of the teachers union leadership may seep into the rank and file to the point of teachers ignoring and undermining school and classroom re-forms. Few urban district leaders have altered classroom practices without the cooperation of teachers and, ultimately, the endorsement of their union.

Moreover, although the superintendent has pointed out 2 years of gains in test scores—always acknowledging that more has to be done—the gap in minor-ity and white test scores remain substantial and unchanged thus far. San Diego reformers have tackled the bottom tier of lowest-performing schools where cul-tures of failure have persisted for years and whose students are largely poor, mi-nority, often nonnative language speakers, and disproportionately assigned to special education. In such schools, small victories come at great cost to both adults and children and take much time.

Finally, both Bersin and Alvarado, even with extended contracts and con-tinued support from business elites, may still throw in the towel and say "enough." Reform fatigue from armor-piercing criticism takes it toll; it is a common ail-ment among school leaders.

For Boston, shallow roots refers to the slow improvement in test scores in elementary and secondary schools, the low-level of those improvements (e.g., going from the 15th to 20th percentiles), and the high percentages of secondary students failing the state test. Impatient reformers deeply concerned over the undiminished gaps in test scores between white, Latino, and black students com-bined with flagging support from business leaders and community activists de-prived of access to an elected school board may take its toll on Mayor Menino by increasing political pressure on him to find a more aggressive superintendent who will produce the desired results faster.

Seattle is a different story. Powerful changes have been underway since 1995, and while questions remain about how deep the reforms' roots are, chances of sustaining the reforms appear to be the strongest of the districts we studied.

Of the six cities, Seattle has the smallest enrollment (under 50,000 students) and has the lowest number of children in poverty (40%). Demographically, then, the scale of the city and its population is seemingly more manageable than, say, Baltimore, which is double the size of Seattle and far poorer.

In addition, with higher test scores than the other cities, a decade-long friendly union-board relationship, and a business-led civic coalition wanting improvements but hardly a takeover of the district, as in Chicago, San Diego, Boston, and Baltimore, conditions in the Seattle schools were favorable for any superintendent seeking to increase public confidence in the schools. What deeply troubled business and civic leaders were the differences in black and white achieve-ment on standardized tests and the seeming inability of the school staffs to ag-gressively attack these discrepancies.[24]

General John Stanford in his brief tenure focused on academic achievement through new funding formulas for schools, site-based decision making, school assignment choices for parents, a new labor contract, and reshaping the princi-pal into a school-site CEO. He convinced key constituencies that these strategies would yield higher academic achievement and that teachers and principals would be focused on teaching and learning. He connected the community to the schools in his persistent trumpeting of a can-do attitude in raising students' achievement. He worked smoothly with the business and civic elites, community activists, parents, and students. Even when disagreements arose, Stanford listened and responded openly to critics, often enlisting their help in improving schools.

In effect, Stanford helped restore confidence of key political constituencies that schools can succeed in crafting better teaching and learning. This is a major achievement in itself when one considers the open hostility of groups critical of school district leaders in Baltimore, Philadelphia, and San Diego.

After Stanford's death in 1998, the school board appointed Olchefske as permanent superintendent. Since then, he has basically forged ahead with initiatives begun under Stanford, particularly translating a standards-based curriculum into every Seattle classroom. The school board's decision to appoint Olchefske and his actions since taking on the superintendency reflect public confidence in the public schools and a basic continuity in district direction. Whether the civic coalition and union support will continue, and whether sufficient funds will be available in the years to come to sustain the building of the instructional infrastructure and create school-based cultures that, indeed, will alter classrooms practices and reduce the gaps in achievement between white and minority students is too early to say.

Of the cities with powerful reforms and shallow roots, Seattle's history, demography, district leadership, and broad civic coalition that has provided continuous political support offers the most promise of sustaining changes begun in 1995 through the first decade of the twenty-first century.

REFLECTIONS ON URBAN DISTRICT REFORM

For readers who appreciate irony, contrast the actions of school reformers a century apart. At the beginning of the twentieth century, Progressive coalitions fought to eliminate political influence from schools. Progressive reformers transformed big city school districts with unwieldy school boards, often appointed by mayors and political bosses who dispensed school jobs and contracts, into smaller corporate-looking copies composed of elected business and professional men and women who hired university-prepared superintendents to run districts in an efficient business-like manner.

In these decades, reform-minded superintendents, working closely with their boards, expanded the role of the school to take in the health, social, recreational, and economic needs of the child. Administrators used scientific management to develop policies and procedures and new specialized positions. They expanded layers of district bureaucracy to implement policies in schools and classrooms aimed at achieving broader social and economic goals. In divorcing education from partisan politics and hiring professionally trained superintendents to manage their schools efficiently, boards of education reaffirmed beliefs that good schools alone could make children into fine citizens and workers.[25]

That was then. Reform slogans of getting politics out of schools and having professionally-trained managers run schools have been forgotten and since the 1970s have been replaced by charges that big city schools had become bloated, mismanaged, and unresponsive bureaucracies.

Late-twentieth-century reformers have latched onto solutions for dysfunctional urban schools by making them more political, business-like, and responsive to market competition. For current civic and business leaders, urban districts should become another department in a mayor's city government, or noneducators should be appointed to reverse the district's failures. With educators and noneducators using managerial practices based on business principles, bureaucracies would become responsive and monies would be found to fund an instructionally coherent system that helps principals and teachers do a better job of teaching. Moreover, establishing clear lines of responsibility and holding students, teachers, and principals accountable for results would breathe vigor into a lethargic organization. Solutions such as these, reformers believe, will make districts into lean, efficient machines that will increase academic achievement, reduce the differences in test scores between white and minority students, and prepare good citizens and workers.

A combined corporate/political model of urban district governance has—in 2002—become the prevailing wisdom among political reformers, media pundits, and educational experts. Even with increasing mayoral influence, centralized control in urban districts, and obvious losses in public participation in education, few voices call for a return to the older reform model of separating politics from schools, sticking with superintendents who rise through the ranks, or establishing closer ties between communities and their schools.

Common to reformers in the late nineteenth and late twentieth centuries, then, is an unalloyed enthusiasm for corporate language, organization, managerial principles, and the deep-seated belief that a district system's application of effective business practices will improve both teaching and learning and the futures of poor minority children.

The irony we describe, of course, gets compounded when Progressive governance reforms of the past century had become by the 1970s the very problems a later generation of reformers claimed had blocked urban school improvements, locking poor minority students into lifetimes of despair. Current solutions for these problems are to import political authority (a mayor, a governor, a president) back into school governance.

By the early twenty-first century, reformers had embraced a political solution of tying urban districts directly or indirectly to city governance and concentrating on improving classroom teaching and learning. Then and now, both

Progressives and current reformers look solely to the school in overcoming poverty and social inequities while largely ignoring issues of race and class. This "schools-alone" strategy shows promise in a few cities but hardly constitutes a recipe for sustaining urban school reform over a decade given the obvious variation among cities and their resources, much less the critical institutional conditions that need to be in place prior to and during the changes.

In making the schools-alone assumption, reformers then and now excluded other explanations (and thereby, other solutions) for students' unsatisfactory academic performance. The core assumption is that once largely poor urban schools have new principals and hardworking teachers, they can overcome by themselves the grim effects of poverty, racism, and community neglect.

Certainly there is some basis for the strategy. Much has been written about urban principals and teachers holding low expectations for poor and minority students' academic performance. Studies have shown again and again how children in large schools easily get lost in the impersonal throng and overlooked by overworked, underpaid staffs. Other studies reveal that low-performing schools suffer few consequences. This research gives credibility to the belief that hard work, high standards, and accountability will translate into improved student academic achievement.[26]

What weakens the assumption, however, is other evidence that civic and business leaders neglect. When the economy is expanding and jobs are plentiful, employers plead for more and better-trained workers. But when an economic downturn occurs and unemployment rises, the unforgiving spotlight on high school and college graduates' skills dims because of labor surpluses. Stay in school becomes the mantra civic and business leaders repeat. Employers and policy makers care less about what students know and can do than that they are occupied; more schooling is a better alternative than unemployability no matter the skills learned.[27]

Other evidence is also unnoted. Anyone who has visited an urban school for at least one week (not a drive-by visit) to sit in classes, listen to teachers and students, observe lunchrooms, playgrounds, corridors, and offices would begin to appreciate a simple but inescapable truth: An urban school is deeply influenced by the neighborhood and families from which it draws its students.

Also of importance is that tax-supported public schools in a democracy are more than training grounds for future employees. Schools are expected to instill in students civic and social attitudes and skills that shape how graduates lead their adult lives in communities. Schools are expected to build respect for differences in ideas and cultures. These are historic civic aims of public schools that have been largely neglected in the rush to direct urban schools to be engines for the local and global economy.

Yet the present agenda for urban school reform, narrowly concentrating on all students taking the same academic curriculum, raising test scores, going to college or getting jobs, largely ignores the pervasive influence upon the school of the community's particular racial, ethnic, and social-class strengths and limitations. In middle-class and wealthy neighborhoods, focusing only on what the school can do is reasonable since these families have the money and networks to provide help for their children should there be academic, health, economic, and emotional problems.

That is not the case in poor, often racially or ethnically isolated, communities. Families lack the personal and institutional resources middle-class communities take for granted. They put their hopes on their children's shoulders and depend upon the local school and other public agencies. In short, in cities with impoverished neighborhoods, schools can't do it alone.

Thus the theories of action at the heart of urban reform then and now flip-flopped over the relationship between politics and schools, yet both rested upon the same assumption: Schools alone can solve severe social inequities while producing fine citizens and workers. Note that of the six cities we studied, only one—Boston—had made some effort at building closer ties between the city's medical and social services, recreation and arts, and daily activities in schools. The assumption still casts a long shadow.

Treating schools as isolated institutions is unwise in the post–World War II social geography of the city that finds urban neighborhoods divided by class, race, and ethnicity. Extensive walking in most big cities establishes this basic social fact of residentially segregated neighborhoods. In the contemporary passion for governance-driven reforms few elected public officials care to tackle elite and popular commitments to maintaining homogenously separate communities that characterize so many American cities today.[28]

Depending upon changes in governance anchored in an assumption that schools can do it alone is both rational and politically strategic to federal, state, and local policy makers. It is rational because past and contemporary reforms assume a command-and-control connection between superintendents, principals, teachers, and students. Yet what appears rational has not been what occurs daily in school systems, past or present.

The reforms are politically strategic to policy makers at all levels in restricting the reform agenda to governance, organization, curriculum, and instruction. Avoided are mentions of race and poverty in dealing with issues of housing and access to jobs as they relate to schooling. To include families, neighborhoods, and city agencies in the reform agenda would entail major expenditures by officials such as reconceptualizing schools as youth-serving agencies rather than places where the single most important job is to produce higher test scores. It would mean reorganizing existing city cultural, civic, medical, housing, employment, and social services. Contemporary urban school reformers stammer when faced with the scale of such changes.

Of course, broadening the urban agenda to encompass a community-based strategy to school improvement does not mean that students, teachers, and principals should be held less responsible for working hard to achieve their goals. Nor does this recognition of a racially, ethnically, or class-segregated school being nested in the larger community suggest that there should be different standards for those who are well off and those who are poor. The obvious fact that schools are entangled in their communities and in the larger economy only sharpens the tasks that face urban school reformers. They need to mobilize civic and corporate elites and educate these opinion setters to the plain fact that raising academic achievement in big city schools involves far more than designing merit pay plans, paying cash bonuses to schools that raise test scores, threatening teachers and principals, or withholding diplomas from students who failed a graduation test.

Nowhere is this fundamental fact more evident than in the inability of the leaders in six cities to improve academic performance in urban high schools with high percentages of low-income minorities. High school size, departmental organization, curricular choices, teachers' subject matter specialization, and the societal demand that graduates be prepared for the workforce, military, or continued education is too often mismatched to urban youth. Many have either experienced failure in earlier grades, found school next to useless in improving their daily lives, or want to do well in school but face unqualified teachers, dumbed-down programs, and inhospitable surroundings. High school becomes a salvage operation skimming off the highly motivated students whose resilience has carried them through the ninth grade and trying to keep the rest from being harmed.

Punitive measures to fire a school's staff and start anew or create a charter school out of the ruins of a failing high school comprise one strategy. Another approach is to develop community-based high schools, establish youth-serving agencies that work closely with small groups of teachers and students, cultivate small high schools and personalized instruction, and enlist employers to hire high school students as interns while attending school to connect neighborhoods, work, and going to college. These initiatives show at least as much promise as threatening to fire staff of underperforming schools or maintaining the prevailing approach of focusing on all students taking the same curriculum and taking out large chunks of instructional time to prepare students for tests that determine whether diplomas are awarded.[29]

Our reflections, if anything, suggest that schools in our six cities require more than a one-size-fits-all strategy, particularly one that rests on century-old theories of school reform that assume governance and managerial changes will produce higher student achievement. District leaders need to reframe the problem of urban school reform to take into account the varying contexts of their cities and schools, the multiple goals of tax-supported public education, and the social geography that sustains segregated neighborhoods.

If schools are as vital to the future of cities as reformers say—and we concur—then a broad vision not a politically clever strategy, fortitude not impatience, and courage not caution become virtues in the struggle for fairness, equity, and better schools.

NOTES

1. *Portland Oregonian*, 1 January 1917, cited in David Gamson, "District by Design: Progressive Educational Reform in Four Western Cities, 1900–1940" (Ph.D. diss., Stanford University, 2001), p. 2.

2. Dorothy Shipps, "Regime Change: Mayoral Takeover of the Chicago Public Schools" in *Reforming Urban School Governance: Responses to the Crisis of Performance*, ed. J. Cibulka and W. Boyd (Westport CT: Greenwood Press, in press).

3. The phrase "mayoral control" applies to those places where mayors have, indeed, taken over school operations in Boston, Chicago, Cleveland, Baltimore (until 1997), and New York City. But there are cities where mayors are involved but have not taken over full control of the schools such as Philadelphia, Los Angeles, and Oakland. In addition, there are cities where hybrids of influence and control exist. We thank Mike Kirst for helping us see this continuum of mayoral control to mayoral influence. These tables represent snapshots at one point in time and our interpretations of the evidence we gathered in the six cities. Our judgments of level of effort and success, of course, are limited by the time period in which we collected our data, what our informants told us, and the familiar human frailties that researchers bring to bear on the data they collected.

4. Larry Cuban, *The Managerial Imperative* (Albany: State University of New York Press, 1988).

5. Ibid. See also Susan Moore Johnson, *Leading to Change: The Challenge of the New Superintendency* (San Francisco: Jossey-Bass, 1996); Arthur Blumberg, *The School Superintendent: Living with Conflict* (New York: Teachers College Press, 1985).

6. Marshall Smith and Jennifer O'Day, "Systemic School Reform," *Politics of Education Association Yearbook, 1990* (1991): 233–267. See also M. Knapp, "Between Systemic Reforms and the Mathematics and Science Classrooms: The Dynamics of Innovation, Implementation, and Professional Learning," *Review of Educational Research*, 67 (2): 227–266 (1997). Also Ken Wong and Francis Shen, "Does School District Takeover Work? Assessing the Effectiveness of City and State Takeover as a School Reform Strategy" (paper presented at the annual meeting of the American Political Science Association, San Francisco, 2001).

7. Allan Ornstein, "Centralization and Decentralization of Large Public School Districts," *Urban Education*, 24 (1989): 233–245. See also David Tyack, "Restructuring in Historical Perspective: Tinkering toward Utopia," *Teachers College Record*, 92 (2): 170–191 (1990).

8. Tying policy changes to pedagogy, that is, policy makers guiding classroom teaching and learning, was a direction administrative Progressives in the early decades of the twentieth century pursued with great confidence. See David Tyack, *One Best System* (Cambridge, MA: Harvard University Press, 1974). In the past 2 decades, the work of David Cohen, Richard Elmore, and others have inspired policy makers and school administrators committed to systemic reform to tightly connect policy to classroom instruction. See David Cohen and James Spillane, "Policy and Practice: The

Relations between Governance and Instruction," *Review of Research in Education*, 18 (1992): 3–9; David Cohen and Carol Barnes, "Pedagogy and Policy" in *Teaching for Understanding*, ed. David Cohen, Milbrey McLaughlin, and Joan Talbert (San Francisco: Jossey-Bass, 1993), pp. 204–239. Richard Elmore and colleagues have studied District #2 in New York City since the early 1990s where Anthony Alvarado put into practice many of these ideas. See Richard Elmore and Diane Burney, *The Challenge of School Variability: Improving Instruction in New York City's Community District #2* (New York: National Commission on Teaching and America's Future: Consortium for Policy Research in Education, 1998).

9. K. Wong and F. Shen, "Does School District Takeover Work?"

10. See David B. Tyack and Larry Cuban, *Tinkering toward Utopia* (Cambridge, MA: Harvard University Press, 1995).

11. Karla Reid, "Chicago Chief Named amid Urban Turnover," *Education Week*, 11 July 2001, p. 3.

12. For conclusions that can be drawn from test score data and other outcomes of standards-based reform in states, see Susan Fuhrman, ed. *From the Capitol to the Classroom: Standards-Based Reform in the States* (Chicago: National Society for the Study of Education, 2001), Part 2, pp. 5–8.

13. Robert Linn, "Educational Assessment: Expanded Expectations and Challenges," *Educational Evaluation and Policy Analysis*, 15 (1): 1–16 (1993); Lorrie Shepard, *Measuring Achievement: What Does It Mean to Test for Robust Understanding?* Third Annual William Angoff Memorial Lecture (Princeton: Educational Testing Service, 1996); Craig Bolon, "School-Based Standard Testing," *Education Policy Analysis Archives*, 8 (23): *http://129.219.89.99/epaa/v8n23* (2000).

14. Nicolas Lemann, *The Big Test* (New York: Farrar, Straus, and Giroux, 1999), pp. 227–229, 273.

15. See Michael Klonsky, "Small Schools: The Numbers Tell a Story," paper at Small Schools Workshop, University of Illinois at Chicago, 1996; Deborah Meier, *The Power of Their Ideas: Lessons for America from a Small School in Harlem* (Boston: Beacon Press, 1995); Bruce Fuller, ed., *Inside Charter Schools: The Paradox of Radical Decentralization* (Cambridge, MA: Harvard University Press, 2000).

16. Christopher Jencks and Meredith Phillips, eds., *The Black-White Test Score Gap* (Washington, DC: Brookings Institution, 1998).

17. Dorothy Shipps, Joseph Kahne, and Mark Smylie, "The Politics of Urban School Reform: Legitimacy, City Growth, and School Improvement in Chicago," *Educational Policy*, 13 (4): 518–545 (1999).

18. For Baltimore, see Marion Orr, "The Challenge of School Reform in Baltimore: Race, Jobs, and Politics" in *Changing Urban Education*, ed. C. Stone (Lawrence: University Press of Kansas, 1998), pp. 93–117. See also James Cibulka, "The City-State Partnership to Reform Baltimore's Public Schools" in this volume.

19. Researchers have shied away from archival or even contemporary histories of school districts, urban or suburban. Exceptions are Jeff Mirel, *The Rise and Fall of an Urban School System: Detroit, 1907–1981* (Ann Arbor: University of Michigan

Press, 1993); Louis Smith, David Dwyer, John Prunty, and Paul Kleine, *Innovation and Change in Schooling: History, Politics, and Agency* (New York: Falmer Press, 1988); Diane Ravitch, *The Great School Wars, New York City, 1805–1973* (New York: Basic Books, 1974).

20. For Boston, see Peter Schrag, *Village School Downtown* (Boston: Beacon Press, 1967); J. Anthony Lukas, *Common Ground: A Turbulent Decade in the Lives of Three American Families* (New York: Alfred Knopf, 1986); John Portz, Lana Stein, and Robin Jones, *City Schools and City Politics* (Lawrence: University Press of Kansas, 1999).

21. Mark Strichez, "Philadelphia to Scrap 'Cluster' Plan in Bid to Save Money," *Education Week*, 20 (9 May 2001), p. 10. In Memphis, after 8 years of getting each school in the district to choose a whole-school reform that each staff would implement and after test scores in elementary schools had improved, Superintendent Gerri House resigned. Within 3 months, House's successor had suspended these efforts and moved the system away from mandatory whole-school reform. Aimee Edmondson and Michael Erskine, "School Reform Put to Test, Now to Rest," *The Commercial Appeal*, http://www.gomemphis.com/newca/o62001/20reform.htm (2001). Positional leaders often dismantle programs of their predecessors in corporations, churches, hospitals, and so on.

22. Gary Yee and Larry Cuban, "When Is Tenure Long Enough? A Historical Analysis of Superintendent Turnover and Tenure in Urban School Districts," *Educational Administration Quarterly*, 32 (Supplement): 615–641 (1996).

23. Richard Elmore and Milbrey McLaughlin, *Steady Work* (Santa Monica, CA: Rand, 1988); L. Cuban, *How Teachers Taught* (New York: Teachers College Press, 1993); James Spillane, "Challenging Instruction for 'All Students': Policy, Practitioners, and Practice" in *From the Capitol to the Classroom: Standards-Based Reform in the States*, ed. S. Fuhrman (Chicago: National Society for the Study of Education, 2001), Part 2, 217–241; Frederick M. Hess, *Spinning Wheels: The Politics of Urban School Reform* (Washington, DC: Brookings Institution, 1999).

24. The gap in achievement scores between whites and blacks has been a persistent issue. In September 2001, when results from the state test again revealed a large discrepancy between minority and white scores, the local NAACP threatened to sue the district on grounds that black students have been denied equal protection under the 14th amendment. Keith Ervin, "NAACP May Sue Seattle Schools," *Seattle Times*, 28 September 2001 (*http://seattletimes.nwsource.com/html/localnews/134347108_naacp28m0.html*).

25. Lawrence Cremin, *The Transformation of the School* (New York: Vintage, 1961); David Tyack and Elisabeth Hansot, *Managers of Virtue* (New York: Basic Books, 1982); Paul Peterson, *The Politics of School Reform, 1870–1940* (Chicago: University of Chicago Press, 1985); Ira Katznelson and Margaret Weir, *Schooling for All* (New York: Basic Books, 1985).

26. See Ray Rist, *The Urban School: A Factory for Failure* (Cambridge, MA: MIT Press, 1973). Ray McDermott, "Achieving School Failure" in *Education and the Culture Process*, ed. G. Spindler (New York: Holt, Rinehart, and Winston, 1974).

27. See, for example, David Tyack, Robert Lowe, and Elisabeth Hansot, *Public Schools in Hard Times: The Great Depression and Recent Years* (Cambridge, MA: Harvard University Press, 1984).

28. Katznelson and Weir, *Schooling for All*, pp. 210–222.

29. For different views on reforming high schools, see Evans Clinchy, *Creating New Schools* (New York: Teachers College Press, 2000); Milbrey McLaughlin and Joan Talbert, *Professional Communities and the Work of High School Teaching* (Chicago: University of Chicago Press, 2001); Michelle Fine, ed., *Chartering Urban School Reform: Reflections on Public Schools in the Midst of Change* (New York: Teachers College Press, 1994).

About the Contributors

William Lowe Boyd is Batschelet Chair Professor of Educational Administration and Professor-in-Charge of Graduate Programs in Educational Administration at Pennsylvania State University. Specializing in education policy and politics, he has published over 120 articles and coedited twelve books. He has been a visiting scholar at seven universities abroad and has served as president of the Politics of Education Association and as an officer of the American Educational Research Association.

Jolley Bruce Christman is a founder and the principal at Research for Action in Philadelphia. She has extensive experience in conducting qualitative research in urban settings and received the Ethnographic Evaluation Award for excellence in the scholarly application of ethnographic procedures to policy decision making from the American Anthropological Association. Dr. Christman writes in areas of urban school reform, students' perspectives on their schools, evaluation methodology, and feminist theory and research methods. She recently concluded work on a 5-year evaluation of Philadelphia's systemic reform effort. Dr. Christman is an associate faculty member at the University of Pennsylvania Graduate School of Education where she earned a Ph.D. in Educational Administration.

James G. Cibulka is a professor in the Department of Administration and Supervision and the Department of Educational Policy Studies and Evaluation at the University of Kentucky, where he is also the dean of the College of Education. He received his Ph.D. from the Department of Education of the University of Chicago and his A.B. in Government from Harvard University. Dr. Cibulka has worked in the public school systems of Chicago, Illinois, and Duluth, Minnesota. He has published widely on the politics of education and education policy, including issues of urban education governance and state education accountability programs.

Larry Cuban has spent 25 years as a teacher and administrator in urban schools and 20 years as a researcher. He is Professor Emeritus of Education at Stanford University.

Barbara McCloud serves as Senior Associate in Leadership Programs at the Institute for Educational Leadership (IEL) in Washington, D.C. In that capacity she works on a variety of IEL leadership initiatives and programs. At IEL, Dr. McCloud also serves as the director of "Superintendents Prepared," a yearlong leadership development program for persons aspiring to the superintendency. Previously she has served as the director of the education program for the D.C.-based Joint Center for Political and Economic Studies, as the special assistant, in the office of the first United States Secretary of Education, and as the special assistant to the deputy director of the National Institute of Education (now the Office of Education Research and Improvement in the U.S. Department of Education). She has served as a teacher and as a board of education member, and received an award as the nation's youngest school board president.

Dorothy Shipps is an assistant professor of Education at Teachers College, Columbia University. She is co-editor with Larry Cuban of *Reconstructing the Common Good in Public Education: Coping with Intractable American Dilemmas* (Stanford University Press, 2000) and author of several articles, chapters, and reports on school reform in Chicago. She was a Carnegie Scholar for 2000–01, an award that supports the research and writing of *School Reform, Corporate Style: The Nexus of Politics, Business and Education Change in Twentieth Century Chicago*. Her research interests include business involvement in education and the governance of urban schools.

Michael Usdan is currently a senior fellow at the Institute for Educational Leadership in Washington, D.C., after serving as the organization's president for 20 years. He formerly was Connecticut's Commissioner of Higher Education and president of the Merrill Palmer Institute in Detroit, and has taught in a number of universities and public schools. He was a member and president of the school board in New Rochelle, New York. He is the author of numerous articles and books on the politics of education and related topics.

Gary Yee is Chair of the Education Department at Holy Names College in Oakland, Calif. He was the director of the Oakland Education Cabinet, a community collaborative of local leaders that meets monthly to discuss ways to improve schools in Oakland. A former teacher and principal, he was recently elected to the Oakland Board of Education.

INDEX